Readers are invited to review and download the
supplementary Instructor's Manual for *Designing and
Planning Programs for Nonprofit and Government Organizations*.
Its many highlights include a syllabus, reading lists, writing
assignments, small-group exercises, and a simulation.

The Instructor's Manual is available FREE on-line.

If you would like to download and print out an
electronic copy of the Instructor's Manual, please visit
www.josseybass.com/go/pawlakvinter

Thank you,

Edward J. Pawlak
Robert D. Vinter

DESIGNING AND PLANNING PROGRAMS FOR NONPROFIT AND GOVERNMENT ORGANIZATIONS

DESIGNING AND PLANNING PROGRAMS FOR NONPROFIT AND GOVERNMENT ORGANIZATIONS

Edward J. Pawlak

Robert D. Vinter

JOSSEY-BASS
A Wiley Imprint
www.josseybass.com

Published by Jossey-Bass
A Wiley Imprint
989 Market Street, San Francisco, CA 94103-1741   www.josseybass.com

Jossey-Bass books and products are available through most bookstores. To contact Jossey-Bass directly call our Customer Care Department within the U.S. at 800-956-7739, outside the U.S. at 317-572-3993, or fax 317-572-4002.

Jossey-Bass also publishes its books in a variety of electronic formats. Some content that appears in print may not be available in electronic books.

Readers should be aware that Internet Web sites listed in this work may have changed or disappeared between when this work was written and when it is read.

Credits are on page 270.

Library of Congress Cataloging-in-Publication Data
Pawlak, Edward J., date.
  Designing and planning programs for nonprofit and government organizations / Edward J. Pawlak, Robert D. Vinter.—1st ed.
     p. cm.
  Includes bibliographical references and index.
  ISBN: 978-0-470-52977-5
  1. Human services—Planning. 2. Social planning. 3. Nonprofit organizations. I. Vinter, Robert D. II. Title.
  HV40.P325 2004
  361.2′5—dc22

                                                          2004012065

CONTENTS

TABLES, FIGURES, AND EXHIBITS

Tables

Figures

Exhibits

PREFACE

Both nonprofit and governmental organizations help people meet their interests and needs by sponsoring all kinds of human service programs (for example, disaster relief, adult and child day care, juvenile and adult corrections, recreation, counseling, job training). The ideas for these programs can come from a variety of prime movers: elected and appointed officials, influential citizens, advocacy groups, individuals and groups affected by particular problems or conditions, organizations, and staff and volunteers. These ideas are championed in the public arena or in political back rooms, or both. When these ideas receive sufficient legitimacy or acceptance—or when someone or some group with clout can impose preferences—a handoff is arranged to officials in a nonprofit organization or a government agency, whose job it becomes to initiate a rational planning process to bring the service program into being (it is political to be rational). The officials then form and charge a planning team of staff, and often some volunteers, consultants, and representatives of prospective recipients, to design the service program to address the interests, needs, or conditions of concern. This book was written to help these individuals carry out planning ventures effectively and to help students who aspire to work in service programs to learn how to engage in service planning.

This book offers essential knowledge about the *process of planning* new or significantly changed service programs in nonprofit and governmental human service organizations. Our emphases are the *stages*, *tasks*, and *issues* intrinsic to carrying out planning projects. Planning is presented as an extended, goal-directed activity carried out in stages with tasks that should be undertaken in an orderly, progressive manner. However, our approach is developmental rather than linear, because planning is a back-and-forth process: work at later stages leads to enhancement or revision of work completed earlier. Our narrative guides practitioners through the initiation and completion of planning projects as they unfold and are carried out.

We limit ourselves mainly to organizations that provide services in the *public (governmental)* and *private nonprofit* sectors. Some for-profit organizations also plan and implement service programs for employees and family members (for example, on-site day care, wellness and fitness programs, and recreational services). Other well-known for-profit organizations, such as health maintenance organizations (HMOs) and trade schools, offer services to particular categories of persons. Though aspects of planning in this book (for example, program design) may have relevance for the development of service programs in the for-profit sector, we have largely excluded for-profit organizations from our discussion.

Our book builds on the contributions of others and addresses several aspects of the planning process that have not been adequately developed earlier. Chapter Two, Determining Work Group Participants, Leadership, and Relationships, discusses the composition and role of work groups in planning projects, points out some factors to consider in selecting team leaders and members, and explores some aspects of group relations. Chapter Three, Initiating a Planning Project, addresses the preparations for the planning project. These include the analysis and understanding of the planning group's charge, how the condition of concern came to the attention of officials, who the stakeholders are, what the external mandates are that are relevant to the planning venture, and what the reporting requirements are that have been set by officials. The development of work plans is another preparatory task of this planning stage. Chapters Six and Seven pertain to the design stage of planning. They detail approaches to program design decisions, the essential components of service programs, and how they can be developed. Our discussion of the approaches to program design offers a practical framework for systematically constructing new programs or changes in existing ones. Planning ventures should end with a written work product that is submitted to the organizational officials who authorized the planning effort. Chapter Eight, Documenting the Completed Program Plan, sets forth the typical requisites established by officials and funders for detailing the results of a planning group's work.

Our book is not an all-inclusive volume. We decided early on to establish some content boundaries pertaining to budgeting, human resource issues, program evaluation, and grant writing. For example, content on proposed program resources and estimation of program costs is included, but extensive content on budgeting is excluded. Content on task analysis and position descriptions is included, but extensive content on human resource management is excluded. Budgetary and human resource matters are complex (for example, compensation packages, salary structure, collective-bargaining agreements, civil service regulations, personnel classifications). In government agencies and large nonprofit organizations, these matters are managed by specialists, such as budget officers and human resource managers. In small organizations, the executive manages these matters. In our experience and the experience of others, the leader and one or more members of the planning team inform and work with these officials or specialized staff on budgetary and staff needs. These persons then develop the budget and the staffing plan.

Our discussion of documentation requirements will be useful to those who write proposals seeking support from external funders, as well as to those who must produce a written program plan for internal implementation in the organization. Practitioners whose work product must result in an application for program funds will find our book useful, because it addresses what must be done before or concurrent with the application writing process, but we do not address the many other aspects of preparing these applications. We take a comprehensive approach that recognizes that officials, grantors, and funders have variable informational and documentation requirements.

We also decided to exclude program evaluation as a major topic. But we do bring up program evaluation in the course of our discussion of problem analysis and program goals and objectives in Chapters Four and Five, respectively. We also briefly address evaluation in Chapter Eight, Documenting the Completed Program Plan, in the section Procedures for Monitoring Program Processes and Assessing Results. In our experience, and as we checked with others, when a substantial evaluation component is required by officials or funders, an in-house specialist or a consultant typically assists the planning team, or a different team is formed to develop the evaluation component, especially if it focuses on outcomes or effectiveness. Readers who want information on these four matters—budgeting, human resource management, program evaluation or grant application writing—can consult the ample specialized books, manuals, and Web sites that deal with these subjects in detail.

The references cited in this book include early writings on theories and models of planning, technical writings on aspects of the planning process, and research reports on service recipients and aspects of program design. We carefully searched the journals of some professional groups for articles pertaining to aspects of program planning. The yield was fruitful, but not abundant. We did not engage in a systematic review of the many specialized journals that focus on particular problems, programs, or service populations (for example, poverty, delinquency, HIV and AIDS, addictions, adoptions, ethnic and cultural diversity, immigrants and refugees, adolescents, and elders). In a cursory review of some of these journals, we found some articles that planners would find useful in understanding the characteristics and needs of particular service recipients. We also found some program descriptions and reports on program evaluations that planners would find helpful as they design new programs or changes in existing ones.

The book is organized in two parts. Part One has two chapters. Chapter One introduces readers to the essential features of human service programs and to the human service organizations in the nonprofit and governmental sectors that sponsor them. We also discuss the nature of program planning and explain the differences between planning and implementation. We introduce readers to the stages of program planning and how we approach our discussion of the tasks within stages. We close the chapter with a discussion of how the book's contents are organized and presented. Chapter Two covers some common issues that must be addressed by organizational officials and planning team leaders as they form planning groups. Part Two is the core of the book. The introduction to Part Two explains what we mean by planning program changes and new programs and provides readers with an overview of the stages of planning. Chapters Three through Eight focus on the five stages of program planning and detail the tasks within each stage. The conclusion of the book looks back at the planning venture, discusses the aftermath of a planning project, and looks ahead to implementation.

Acknowledgments

The following individuals are thanked for their permission to use or adapt material for this text: Jean Modrzynski Skalski for sharing her proposal on pet adoption programs for elders, which was used to develop the case example in the chapters on program design and documentation; and Janet Ferguson and Sally Lindsay for sharing their manual on parents' respite cooperatives, which was used to develop the case example on program goals and objectives. Sharon Roepke and Colleen Gallagher served as consultants on the child sexual assault case example.

John Flynn and Dan Thompson, professors at Western Michigan University, and Rhea Kish, professor at the University of Michigan, made helpful comments on early versions of the manuscript. A number of assistants and support staff helped in the writing project or the preparation of the manuscript. Michele McGowen, a former graduate assistant, read the manuscript from a student's perspective and searched the literature on planning. Deana Loar Strudwick, also a former graduate assistant, searched the Internet and compiled a list of durable sites useful to planners. Shannon Penny prepared the charts and provided other secretarial assistance. We would also like to express appreciation for the suggestions of four anonymous reviewers. We are grateful for the assistance received from Johanna Vondeling, Allison Brunner, and Xenia Lisanevich, our editors at Jossey-Bass. Special thanks are owed to Marcy Marsh for her masterful editing of the manuscript.

Our book draws on our instructional experiences in graduate courses and workshops on program planning in both nonprofit and governmental organizations. We are indebted to our students and trainees, whose experiences with our case examples, simulations, and exercises enabled us to improve them. We are grateful to all the officials from a broad variety of nonprofit and governmental organizations who provided us with opportunities to serve on and lead planning teams and engage in program evaluation. Many aspects of those experiences found their way into the book. The first author was able to pursue the writing of this book in earnest thanks to a sabbatical leave awarded by Western Michigan University.

Finally, the first author is profoundly grateful to his wife, Maureen, for serving as a sounding board, and for her patience, encouragement, and unfailing support throughout the writing project.

June 2004

Edward J. Pawlak
Kalamazoo, Michigan

Robert D. Vinter
Ann Arbor, Michigan

THE AUTHORS

Edward J. Pawlak earned his doctorate from the University of Michigan and his master of social work from Wayne State University. He is Professor Emeritus at Western Michigan University, School of Social Work.

Pawlak was a faculty member in the Policy, Planning, and Administration Concentration for twenty-two years. He taught a graduate course in program planning in the school and in the university's multidisciplinary Nonprofit Leadership and Management Program. His understanding of program design and planning is anchored in eleven years of experience in service programs, either as a provider of services or a program manager. Early in his career, he worked with nonprofit organizations that provided services to inner-city families, juvenile offenders, and troubled youth in schools. As a faculty member, he engaged in community service as a leader or member of program planning teams in local United Way organizations and departments of county government. He has served as a consultant in nonprofit and government organizations at the local and state levels.

His community service and consultation projects have focused on needs assessments, priority studies, vocational rehabilitation, services for sexually abused children, program objectives, and organizational and program change. He is the author of twenty publications, including articles and book chapters on various aspects of human service organizations and programs.

Robert D. Vinter earned his doctorate and his master of social work from Columbia University. He is Dunham Professor Emeritus at the University of Michigan, School of Social Work.

Vinter taught in the School of Social Work's group treatment, administration, and doctoral programs, where he also served as associate dean and acting dean. Since his retirement, he has remained professionally active in community and university service, consultation, and writing projects. His areas of interest are funding, budgeting, fiscal management, agency administration, program design and management, juvenile and criminal justice, and organization studies. He was awarded several federal research grants and has an illustrious record in juvenile corrections research. He is the author of forty-three publications, including seven books in which he served as senior author, coauthor, or editor; seven articles in professional journals; thirteen book chapters; and several monographs and research reports. In addition to his substantial experience as a consultant in juvenile corrections on the international, national, and state levels, he also has a record of contributions as a consultant and volunteer in community service to local governments and nonprofit organizations in various aspects of policy, planning, and administration.

DESIGNING AND PLANNING PROGRAMS FOR NONPROFIT AND GOVERNMENT ORGANIZATIONS

PART ONE

PROGRAM PLANNING FUNDAMENTALS

Part One provides a fundamental introduction to program planning and the organizational and group contexts in which planning is carried out. Chapter One examines the basic features and structures of human service programs and the organizations in the nonprofit and governmental sectors that sponsor these programs. The discussion also differentiates service programs from planning projects. Considerable attention is given to the nature of program planning, the differences between planning and implementation, and the stages of program planning. Chapter Two covers some fundamental issues that must be addressed by organizational officials and planning team leaders as they form planning groups: their composition, factors to consider in selecting the planning team, and group leadership. The chapter concludes with a discussion of the patterns of social relations that work groups must manage.

CHAPTER ONE

EXPLORING THE NATURE OF PROGRAM PLANNING

This chapter begins by discussing the features and structure of human service programs and differentiating these programs and planning projects. Then the chapter examines the organizations that conduct human service programs. These sections provide the context for the subsequent discussion of the nature of program planning and how it differs from program implementation. The chapter ends with a clarification of terms and a discussion of how the book's contents are organized and presented.

Human Service Programs

This book analyzes the planning of *human service programs*. (The terms *service program* and *program* are often used as substitutes for human service programs throughout the book.) The service programs at the core of attention are those intended to provide direct benefits for persons rather than for other organizations (as do corporate law firms, for example). Programs are the main vehicles in modern society through which all kinds of formal services are provided to people: adult education programs; vocational training programs; consumer education or protection programs; parks and recreational programs; libraries; museums; symphony orchestras and civic theaters; services designed to address employment, housing, marital, health, mental health, substance abuse, or legal problems; assistance offered by religious organizations; membership services of professional associations; and so on.

Many distinctive features are shared by these programs and the organizations that conduct them. They are held to a variety of legal and civic standards and are expected (or required) to adhere to these standards in their treatment of the persons served. Two examples are a patient's right to confidentiality, privacy, and participation in decisions about health care, and the regulations governing the treatment of juvenile and adult offenders. The primary targets, or intended recipients, of human service programs are vested with special moral value—that is, as human beings, they must be served with methods that are acceptable. Examples of this include tolerance and respect for diversity and differences in ability and values, selection of the least-restrictive placement for frail elders who cannot live independently, and the provision of housing that optimizes opportunities for independent living for persons with physical or developmental disabilities. The choices and behaviors of service recipients are not easily predictable, and they respond (or refuse to respond) in unique ways to services offered to them. Their views and reactions usually have consequences for the organizations responsible for the delivery of services (Hasenfeld, 1983, pp. 7–11; Hasenfeld, 2000). All of these critical factors are discussed.

These programs and services come into being in response to the demands or the presumed needs of some persons for particular services, and they continue to exist because attention is given to their management, support, and degrees of achievement. The diversity of programs should not mislead us into thinking that they lack fundamental similarities. Because they possess common features, they constitute a class of enterprises, they can be compared in important respects, and we can learn how to analyze, design, and implement—or improve—them.

Although each human service program is unique to a given locale, organization, mission, and recipient population, for purposes of this book, a human service program is characterized by the following features:

- It is designed to provide specific benefits of some kind to particular persons who are believed to have distinctive needs or problems.
- It is administered by a private nonprofit or a government organization through designated program personnel who engage in services that include direct interactions with persons receiving the service, within a particular locale, and under certain conditions.

Structure of Human Service Programs

There is no uniform or standard way that one type of service or another must be structured in order to constitute a single, identifiable program. In one organization, services such as first-aid training and water safety instruction may be combined in the same program. But services that appear related and compatible to one organization may not appear similarly interrelated in another context. So it is not at all uncommon for a program to offer only a single service such as first-aid training or water safety instruction.

A *service* can be conceived as a set of concrete activities performed for recipients and with recipients, and a program can be conceived as a composite of linked services that constitute an integrated enterprise. Two or more closely related services may be joined to become one program because all or many of the intended recipients are known to need both services, and the services are compatible. So combining them for service delivery purposes makes sense. For example, one can understand why occupational testing or training services could be linked to employment and career counseling, and perhaps both can be linked with job placement services. Persons seeking employment for the first time (or perhaps change of employment due to a factory closing, for example) could proceed from one service unit to another in the same location, which is more convenient than being successively referred to another organization in a different part of town. Of course, not every person who uses one of these services would need to use the other services.

In addition to compatibility and convenience, reasons for integrating two or more services into a larger entity—which itself may be a single program or a composite of programs—usually have to do with the host organization's policies, funding, resources, and overall structure. Some local government and nonprofit organizations are required, as a condition for receiving state or federal funds, to provide specific related services that are imposed by enabling statutes, policies of the funding source, or regulatory standards. For example, community mental health programs in one state must provide outpatient child and adult services, substance abuse services, crisis counseling, and other services, as a condition of receiving state funds. All of these examples illustrate that there are variations among organizations as they develop service programs and go about structuring (and reorganizing) their constituent parts into endlessly diverse administrative patterns. On a related note, programs, as such, should not be confused with organizational units, such as departments.

Distinction Between Service Programs and Projects

As used in this discussion, there is a distinction between the terms *service programs* and *projects*. Service programs have the character of *cycles* in that their operations are composed of a series of activities that are repeated over particular periods. The most obvious example of a cycle is represented by K–12 school programs. The teaching of each grade is repeated for the next group of advancing pupils during the following school year. The cycles of some programs are far shorter, perhaps lasting only as long as a few interviews or just a few minutes or hours. The cycles of some programs are bound by particular periods, such as school years. Others are known as *constant flow* in the sense that they are continuously repeated according to the needs evidenced, such as hospital emergency rooms. Each program cycle may be almost identical to the one before it but different in minor details. A given program cycle may also become significantly different when changes are deliberately introduced according to some plan.

Service programs are almost continuously being modified, cut back, or started up in response to changing conditions and opportunities. These activities are undertaken in every organization, with some persons becoming responsible for their planning. This process is conceived as a *project* because it has the character of being conducted one time only, unlike the cycles of service programs. A planning project is not repeated in the same way for the same purpose in the same organization (or elsewhere). Planning projects also have time-limited durations for accomplishing their aims. Each is distinctive to a time, place, participants, and intended results. New or changed service programs are the deliberate products of these projects.

This book covers only the process of planning by which significant changes, or new programs, are designed—that is, those endeavors that necessitate carefully planned projects to improve or initiate a program or adjust to critical events and trends in the organization or environment. Much of even deliberate program change is actually just tinkering, coping, or adjusting and does not involve making major changes. Programs are always in a state of flux, but much of it is unintended, often unacknowledged, perhaps even unnoticed. These kinds of deliberate and unintended changes are not central to this discussion.

Projects involving planned change in an existing program are far more common than those initiating new service programs. Starting up a new service often seems more interesting and more exciting than modifying an ongoing program, but this is often mainly in the eyes of the participants. It's like building a new home versus making major renovations in one's existing home. Some remodeling, especially of valuable older houses, is as creative, ambitious, and taxing as building a modest home using conventional plans.

Organizations That Conduct Human Service Programs

This book applies to the kinds of service programs that are almost always located within formal organizations. They are corporate entities that host or sponsor programs in the sense that they have administrative structures through which services are supported, coordinated, and managed. The organizations are often referred to as *agencies* because they are regarded as agents of governments at all levels. For private nonprofits, they are regarded as representing community interests. Some programs are also conducted by various neighborhood, communal, and self-help groups and by other associations that are neither corporate bodies nor chartered by state government.

Formal organizations are chartered or otherwise authorized to operate as enterprises under state laws and by the Internal Revenue Service (Lampkin, Romeo, and Finnin, 2001). All formal organizations have some kind of governance structure that defines their purposes, determines their policies and service priorities, and assumes responsibility for funding, space, personnel, operations, and other necessities. Different phrases are employed to convey the governance, legal, administrative, and fiduciary responsibilities an organization assumes for its programs: "sponsorship," "under the aegis of," "under the auspices of," and sometimes simply "administer" or "operate." Thus the organization sponsors the service program, while the program conducts the activities that provide services for persons and is directly accountable to officials in the sponsoring organization.

Human service programs are conducted by governmental organizations at all levels—municipal, county, state, and federal—and are frequently called *departments,* as in the case of city consumer affairs departments or county departments of public health. Some state government agencies offer certain local-level services to citizens through district offices, even while performing many other, different public sector functions. Departments of public health, mental health, social services, education, labor, and corrections are found in every state, but they differ in size, structure, and the particular duties and functions they are assigned. At the federal level, of course, departments are huge bodies headed by cabinet-level secretaries, which do many things, including regulating or funding service programs that are conducted by other organizations, as well as many of their own. Many of these governmental units allocate funds to support services administered by other organizations in both the profit and nonprofit sectors and also support numerous programs offered by lower levels of government (Austin, 2003; Young, 2000).

Service programs are also conducted by a bewildering array of *private nonprofit* enterprises (Grønbjerg, 2001). They are also known as *voluntary organizations,* members of the *voluntary* or *private sector,* or *nongovernmental organizations.* Some of these organizations are faith based or sectarian organizations that are governed and operated by a particular church or religious denomination (Chaves and Tsitsos, 2001; Farnsely, 2001). Others are nonsectarian, that is, not affiliated with a religious denomination. Some nonprofit organizations are national, some regional, and others statewide in scope, but most are found within local communities. These organizations are so numerous and so varied that there is no single listing of them, but local telephone and community service directories list most of them. These enterprises can be thought of in categories according to the kinds of services or benefits they provide or to some other distinguishing aspect. For example, private, nonprofit medical hospitals comprise a universe of organizations that provide specialized health services in their locales. Another set of organizations offers arts and cultural services, such as art programs for children, annual festivals, museum and other artistic exhibitions, theatrical classes and performances, and so on.

Another way of looking at organizations is to focus on the persons being served by the program. For example, there are shelters, hot meals, and emergency food programs for the homeless and for disaster victims. A well-known set of national and local organizations are concerned with services for children and youth, including the Girl Scouts and Boy Scouts, 4-H Clubs, and Big Brothers Big Sisters. And these have their counterparts at the other end of the age range in programs for the elderly. Nonhospital health service, education, and advocacy programs are offered by diverse organizations for persons with almost every major illness and disability, as well as many less common problems. An entire class of organizations—membership associations—sponsor particular programs to serve their members; perhaps best known are the professional associations; and many are aimed at other interests that bring people together, such as religious congregations, Little League, historical societies, and collectors' clubs.

Regardless of their other activities and reasons for being, the organizations focused on here are those through which particular human service programs are hosted and conducted and that are in the governmental or private nonprofit sectors. Within these contexts, persons design, start, change, and conduct service programs.

Regardless of the differing cycles among programs and how they are structured within organizations, many are designed and conducted to connect—more or less directly—with services offered by other agencies. The recipients of service in one program are frequently referred to a program in another organization. These *serial* service linkages are most apparent among local *service centers* or *bureaus* that are explicitly designed to help route persons to appropriate service providers elsewhere in the community. These include such services as Travelers Aid stations and similar information and assistance centers in major airports, local area agencies on aging, and referral agencies for troubled youth.

The following case illustrates these *service delivery* interrelations between human services and the organizations that conduct them. Each of the units that provides distinctive but closely linked services is italicized in this example.

◆ ◆ ◆

A person walking through a shopping center suddenly experiences an acute attack of some unfamiliar kind. Luckily, a *passerby* has received special home medical emergency training as a *Red Cross volunteer.* She seats the ill person on a nearby bench, checks him over, asks a few questions, suspects a stroke, commandeers another shopper to stand by, rushes to the nearest telephone, and calls 9-1-1. In this location, the 9-1-1 *emergency communications center* is operated as a central areawide unit jointly funded under county-city agreements, with immediate computerized access to every fire, police, sheriff, ambulance, hospital, and related emergency organization. The 9-1-1 operator assures the Good Samaritan that an ambulance staffed by paramedics will arrive at the site within five minutes, dispatched by that locale's *Metro Ambulance Service* under contract with the city, local hospitals, and third-party insurers. After its prompt arrival and pickup, the ambulance races to deliver the ill person to the *ER* at *Community Medical Center,* owned and operated by an area public-private consortium, where appropriate diagnosis and treatment is immediately given (and information obtained for later billing to the patient's *health plan insurer*). The patient is soon transferred to the center's intensive care unit and shortly thereafter to a semi-private hospital room (with more billing to follow). Before the patient's release from the hospital, arrangements are made through the patient's *private physician* with *Home Health Care, Inc.* (a unit of a regional for-profit corporation, with more billing to third-party insurers, including *Medicare*) to obtain assistance so the patient can return to his home. Because the patient lives alone, Home Health Care will provide in-home basic care for as long as his physician determines is necessary, until he can care for himself and resume his activities.

◆ ◆ ◆

Note how many service providers there were in this extended chain. Critical assistance was initially given by a passerby using knowledge gained through training by the Red Cross, a multiprogram nonprofit organization. Except for the passerby, all services were then administered in tandem by highly specialized personnel employed by a variety of governmental, nonprofit, and for-profit organizations. The central community service routing facility in this and many comparable situations was the 9-1-1 police and emergency call-in phone line. This service is explicitly designed to distinguish among the needs of callers—often including non-emergency problem circumstances and injuries—and route them accordingly through their special switchboards.

In this example, most services were provided in serial order, as discussed earlier in this chapter in regard to the job training and placement programs and progressive class grades in K–12 school districts. Alternatively, interorganizational service relationships may be centered on providing *concurrent* services to the same persons. For example, programs for the homeless typically forge linkages with other local agencies to cope with the multiple problems of shelter residents. Occasionally, a single program is jointly conducted by two organizations who pool their resources. All of these collaborative associations depend on interorganizational agreements and arrangements, which are required by some funders as a condition for receiving funds.

Service Program Planning

Planning a service program is a systematic future-oriented endeavor that involves analysis of problems or needs, determination of goals and objectives, exploration of alternative service designs, and development of the chosen design. The scope and complexity of the program at issue, especially if the planning effort is focused on change in an ongoing service, determines which of these elements must be addressed in a particular project. The product of a planning project is a written program plan that must be forwarded to organizational officials for their approval. It might also have to be submitted for early review by relevant funding or oversight bodies. Once approved, the completed plan will serve as a concrete guide or blueprint for those who will implement it, typically with additional directives. The implementers may or may not include some of the planners.

Although the process of planning is the focus of this book, it is important to differentiate it from program implementation and program operations. *Program implementation* is the decision and action process aimed at actually introducing a new service program or modifying an existing service program according to the approved plan, not at serving persons directly. *Program operations* follow implementation and refer to the activities required to provide services to recipients. Planning and implementation have some common features, but they are separable processes. Planning and implementation projects are carried out sequentially, but they have linkages.

Implementation is also a systematic future-oriented endeavor, but it denotes all of the decisions and steps that must be taken to bring a plan from the drawing board to operational reality. Many things must be done to "open the doors" and begin service to people. Space has to be found and properly equipped, personnel have to be trained or recruited, prospective service recipients must be notified, the phones have to be installed, equipment and supplies have to be purchased, and appropriate forms must be ready to be filled out. All of these things—and more—must be planned, arranged, and done before program operations can begin. Planning and implementation endeavors take place for both new programs and those to be significantly changed.

The organizing framework of the book rests on the belief that planning should precede implementing a significant change in an ongoing program, and certainly before launching a new program. Because introducing program changes or launching new services both follow prior planning to some degree, these two major processes can be viewed as an extended continuum, as closely intertwined phases of a single larger process. There are important connections and overlaps between them. Some of the individuals who work on the first process, planning, may also be active in the second process, implementation. Similarly, there are continuities between these two processes and program operations, which follow on and are greatly influenced by planning and implementation.

It's important to underscore a desirable set of relationships among these processes. Many different kinds of resources and critical arrangements must be assembled and melded to bring into being a service program—from personnel through space to public information—that can survive and therefore deliver benefits for its recipients. Failure to provide a program's essential wherewithal obviously hampers its conduct or makes it wholly impossible. To ensure that all of these provisions are in place when the program is brought into actual operation, prior preparations must be completed. Program implementation is the composite of these prior steps, whether applied to a new service program or a significant change in an ongoing program. But these preparations must be guided by some blueprint that specifies what is needed, what is to be done, and what resources will be used to do it. The activities that produce this blueprint are the program planning. In short, the probable achievements at each point in this chain of processes are greatly influenced by the work that has preceded it.

Rational, Cumulative, and Back-and-Forth Process

Service program planning is essentially a *rational* decision and an activity process carried out in successive stages of work. Planning is rational in that it is a means-ends driven process. Planning is also purposeful, just as the program-to-be is intended as a purposeful system of activities. The *means* are the creative, analytical, and technical tasks that are carried out in an orderly manner. These tasks are instrumental activities intended to reach a designated *end*—a plan for a new or changed service program that fulfills the assigned *charge* (the authorization to engage in the project). That is why the directions issued by officials to the planners should be considered first (and last). These charges authoritatively empower the conduct of the planning project and define the ends to be attained, as well as the directives and provisions for carrying out the assigned tasks. Rational pursuit of these stated purposes necessitates planning the new program or planning the changes to the existing program *before* their introduction through implementation.

Planning involves numerous interdependent decisions and actions, which proceed in *back-and-forth* and *cumulative* ways as work moves forward. Teams frequently have to retrace some prior steps, often several times. Sometimes retrospection enlightens current efforts. Sometimes earlier efforts need to be reconsidered in light of emerging formulations and then require adjustments. For example, as a new service program is being designed, planners may realize that they had set standards of performance for program outcome objectives too low, and they must now be redefined. As participants complete tasks and stages, their decisions and actions must be accumulated and brought forward in order to connect them to the ongoing work at hand, so that progress builds on prior thinking and results. This is the main reason why work teams should continuously document their thinking and decisions, extending cumulatively toward their end products.

The logical order suggested here does not mean that there is only one right way to do planning. Participants may have to follow different pathways that are adapted to the particulars of place and persons, the discoveries made as the process unfolds, and the complexities of the issues. Generally speaking, however, there is a general and efficacious way to go about program planning, and that way is fundamentally rationalistic.

From the perspective of participants as decision makers, planning takes place in a context of bounded rationality and limited discretion. This is because participants are unable to comprehend and examine all planning alternatives, weigh the usefulness of each, and then decide on the best alternative (York, 1982, pp. 29–30, 45–47; Simon, 1976). The complexity would be overwhelming. As a result, work groups make decisions that "satisfice," meaning that they are good enough (Simon, 1976). Planners' decisions are also bounded by directives and constraints on the substance and procedures of their projects. These directives and constraints are directly or indirectly stated in the planning charge, external mandates, and the organization's mission, policies, and commitments to and investments in particular programs, service delivery designs, or staff competencies. (See Chapter Three for a detailed discussion of these issues.)

It is important to note that there is a fundamental source of disjunction between the products of planning and the products of implementing, and it is so even when there are no changes in either plans or personnel. It is an inescapable fact that no endeavor can fully anticipate, predict, and control—through any kind of planning—the future, the unexpected, and the changing circumstances of life. The products of these two processes include both desired and undesired, anticipated and unanticipated, developments. These developments must be managed, as they unfold over time, by members of the planning work group, and subsequently by those who undertake to provide the program services. As a result, whatever changed program or new program is finally initiated will be different from the plans on which it was based, for better or for worse. But none of this justifies minimizing the crucial importance of preparing good plans and implementing them effectively (Pressman and Wildavsky, 1974). It is necessary to anticipate as fully as possible in both processes.

It's important to acknowledge the reality and the importance of what can be thought of as the *social and political dynamics* of the planning process. Case studies and reports of experienced planners have identified these dynamics and have clarified potential flash points and risks (University of Kansas, 2004; McClendon and Catanese, 1996; Schorr, 1988, 1997; Lauffer, 1978, pp. 6–29; Delbecq and Van de Ven, 1977). The direction often taken by those using the social-political approach has been to identify the conditions under which one or another mode of planning or acting seems to succeed, fail, or just get by. In attempting to generate guidelines for deliberate endeavors, this approach has helped alert practitioners to relationships and circumstances that can either hamper or facilitate change and to actions that offer greater potentials for success. For example, some officials believe that the best decision is to appoint influentials to the planning team and have them make the "right" decisions, whereas others believe that prospective recipients or outside consultants should also be on the team so as to lend credibility to its decisions (Lauffer, 1978, p. 7).

Some social and political dynamics facilitate the planning process. Others are irrational intrusions or exercises of power, or both. For example, an influential volunteer accepted an appointment to a priority study committee because she wanted to have a say in how youth-serving agencies were responding to reports of increases in juvenile street crime in a particular neighborhood. An analysis of recent crime statistics revealed a low incidence of such crimes. The volunteer later revealed that a close relative was mugged by a purse snatcher in her neighborhood. No amount of data could convince her about the randomness of the offense and that crime on the streets in that community did not merit a high-priority rating. In another planning project, an influential member of the community declared that he did not want any money allocated to programs that "incited people in those neighborhoods to march on city hall." Yet that very same week, some residents of his neighborhood lodged a protest at city hall in an adjoining community. When he was gently confronted with his contradiction, he said, "It's not the same." Community empowerment programs were assigned a low priority. Sometimes planners are motivated by what they perceive as enlightened self-interest—personal, departmental, organizational, or professional. For example, one participant in a planning project admitted that "he joined up to get as much of the pie as possible." In another situation, a participant confided that he agreed to serve on the planning committee to make certain that planners did not interfere with his programs. In still another situation, the chair of the planning committee stacked it with members of her own profession when senior officials asked her to develop a plan to restructure services that would require redistribution of staff to other units. All of these examples are indicative of some social and political dynamics that occur in the course of rational planning. Other examples of these dynamics will occasionally be introduced in the discussion of different stages of planning, but the rational model of planning is the primary focus of this book.

The social-political dimension of planning deserves much more study before valid, systematic guidelines for action can be formulated. Regardless of what this knowledge reveals, it must then be synthesized with the substantive and methodological matters presented in this book. The practical tools for planning must still be acquired and employed if effective service programs are to come into being.

Planning and Value Preferences

Although a rational model of planning is promoted in this book, planning is also inevitably value driven. Human service organizations and their officials, staff, supporters, and recipients all have their own set of ideals, including altruism, empowerment, justice, civic pride, assimilation, tolerance, community harmony, and protection of the vulnerable.

Planners bring their values to planning projects, and it is hard to imagine that their values would not influence their participation and decision making. Planners are not required to declare their values when they are appointed to a planning team, and there is no suggestion that officials or the team leader should seek such declarations. Sometimes planners announce their value orientations or reveal them through their patterns of decision making.

Shared values can serve as the source of cooperation, and value differences can serve as the source of conflict in planning teams (for example, charity versus justice, rehabilitation versus punishment, a strengths approach versus a problem-and-deficits approach, doing for versus doing with). Consequently, the team leader and the other members must be attuned to value preferences and how these preferences can be reconciled in the interest of moving the planning project forward. Sometimes team members have some value differences, but they have some values in common, or they may recognize a hierarchy of values that can surmount impasses. For example, in one planning project focused on services for abused children, one group supported independent disclosure interviews of victims by different law enforcement agencies and service providers, whereas another group supported joint interviews. After several rounds, a team member invoked the "best interests of the children" and reminded the team about a recent "worst case" in which a victim was subjected to ten interviews. The team eventually worked out a compromise by agreeing to videotape interviews or to engage in joint interviews in particular cases to reduce the number of times victims would have to disclose the details of their abuse.

Stages of Planning

Planning service programs proceeds over time and involves various participants in successive stages of work: the *initiation stage,* the *analysis stage,* the *goals and objectives stage,* the *design stage,* and the *documentation stage.* Issues and problems arise at each of the stages and should be identified and addressed by the responsible participants. These issues and problems, in turn, pose challenges and requirements that define the tasks that need to be performed and that are common to planning all programs, although every project presents unique demands. For each stage of planning projects, the series of tasks to be accomplished has to do with obtaining information, making choices, seeking alternatives, and drafting summaries and reports. Other tasks have to do with resolving dilemmas, producing materials, locating resources, and starting some activity.

This book examines the issues and decisions faced in planning and describes the successive tasks and steps in this process. Tasks are clustered into progressive stages based on the logic of rational decision making and action, the interrelatedness of the tasks, the authors' relevant experiences, and their judgment about whether a particular boundary-spanning task belongs in this or that stage. This five-stage planning model provides a structure that readers should be able to apply to their own circumstances, even though it is clear that there is no one arbitrary, lock-step approach to planning projects.

Within any particular planning stage, some tasks must be addressed concurrently or interactively with other tasks. Some tasks within a particular stage must be carried out while anticipating certain tasks of one or more subsequent stages. For example, in the analysis stage, planners must decide which of the factors that are believed to have contributed to the problem should be explored. Some factors may be so intractable that it would be infeasible for an organization to devise approaches to deal with them, and there is no point in exploring these factors. Planners must also look ahead to the implementation stage. For example, planners of a new admission program might pose this question: "What are the information technology and staff requirements of the admission system that we have designed so far?" Similarly, implementers must return periodically to the program plan to refresh their recollection of what it intends, or they must revise their forward steps in light of actual organization resources and capabilities.

In actual situations, boundaries between stages are not clearly marked. They typically flow together. Tasks of some stages have their origins in prior stages, and the activities of early stages extend into subsequent efforts. Movements from one to another may be incremental and disjointed due to the circumstances of particular ventures. It is advisable for participants to take stock of where they are in the process and to manage their movement through each stage. This entails taking into account which tasks are currently preoccupying most of the team, which ones are stragglers from an earlier stage, and which ones are moving the team into the next stage. During some periods, some team members may be "picking up loose ends" or completing activities from a previous stage, and other members may be easing into the activities of the next stage. These transitions are commonplace in planning ventures. Work should be managed to keep the team moving toward fulfillment of its charge to complete a program plan.

Planning projects are usually more demanding and difficult than expected. They frequently extend over a longer period of time than was intended at the outset, especially when the program is new for those working on it or for the organization.

Use of Terms

A number of terms are used throughout this book. The most important are the key words that denote critical concepts (for example, *service program* and *projects*, as discussed earlier in the chapter). They are italicized initially and are defined at that point or soon after. To minimize monotony, synonyms (for example, the *planning effort, endeavor,* or *venture*) are sometimes substituted for *project* or *planning project*.

Planners, participants, work group, team, members, and *committee* refer to the individuals who become directly engaged in the actual work of planning. *Coordinator* and *leader* refer to the individuals who provide guidance to participants, coordinate their activities, and report directly to officials. (The critical roles and features of these work groups are examined more fully in the next chapter.)

Decision makers, officials, and *policymakers* refer to the executives, administrators, and board members of voluntary human service organizations, as well as the elected and appointed officials of government agencies who have the authority to initiate planning and to whom the planners are directly accountable for the process and the products of their work.

Host organization or *sponsoring organization* refers to the nonprofit or government organization that authorizes the planning effort and under whose auspices it is carried out.

The official impetus to undertake program planning is referred to as a *charge*—an authorization to a work group to engage in a project. The charge informs the work group about what is to be achieved and provides guidelines that direct or constrain project work. At the outset of planning efforts, work groups must review and interpret the charge with the officials who issued it, especially its concrete elements, to determine its focus and whether it is complete and clear enough to begin project activities.

Recipients is the generic term for the primary persons to whom program services are given. It refers to a variety of designations given to these persons by human service organizations, including beneficiaries, clients, patients, members, patrons, offenders, residents, and students.

Planners must develop, monitor, and revise *work plans* to guide their efforts. These plans are formulations developed by participants that provide a shared understanding of what needs to be done, who will be doing it, when it will be done, and how it will be done. *Documentation* is the general term for all forms of reporting and communicating the progress and results of the planners' work. Both work plans and documentation will be addressed in more detail in the next chapter in the discussion on work groups and some of their tasks.

Program plan document is a general term that refers to the final written work product of the planning team. Sometimes the terms *proposal* or *report* are used in the book to denote that document. Many planning projects in nonprofit and government organizations do not result in a grant application. For the purposes of this book, *grant application* refers to a document prepared for submission to a funding organization.

How This Book's Contents Are Organized and Presented

This book spans a range of basic topics, from the beginning to the end of the planning process, rather than concentrating on a few specialized methods or features. The emphasis here is on the process of program planning so as to avoid the risks of looking at specific methods out of the larger context in which they can be applied. But this book is not another general "theory of planning," nor is it an eclectic framework that attempts to synthesize major approaches to be applicable to all sorts of enterprises.

This book presents the means by which the planning process should be advanced in a logical order. In Part Two, the chapters address planning according to its successive stages of work. For example, determining the objectives of a service program are dealt with before deciding its operational features (the lowest level of the ends-means chain). The major tasks that should characterize planning projects during each stage are laid out, from the initiation of the activity through its completion with the production of final program plan materials. Various subsidiary steps and procedures are described for many of these tasks. This does not render the processes linear, however, such that at each point there is only one next step to be taken. Substantive matters are addressed within a distinctly methodological approach. There is practical procedural guidance for application in the real situations where people engage in these tasks. Special planning problems and important variations are discussed here as well.

A wide array of practitioners have responsibility for planning new programs and planning changes to existing ones. Many nonprofit organizations and governmental departments do not have staff in specialized roles who are responsible just for planning or program development. Nevertheless these staff members have to plan program modifications and new programs that are responsive to the changing conditions in their communities and to funding opportunities. Even in large-scale organizations with specialized staff, middle managers and frontline staff serve as leaders and members of planning teams. The materials in this book are relevant to both specialized and nonspecialized staff, regardless of their roles or positions.

The book is intended for both classroom and job-related studies. In several kinds of courses, it can serve as either a main or a supplementary text to help students gain the knowledge and competence to carry out a planning project. It can also provide additional knowledge and competence to persons—in all kinds of organizations that sponsor human service programs—who are concerned with improving their abilities to undertake planning duties.

Different readers will, of course, proceed through the book in different ways. Generally speaking, those with less experience should work through the book chapter by chapter. Those with considerable experience will probably prefer to select particular chapters or parts of chapters that are relevant to them. It would be useful, however, for them to scan the other chapters for information that is new to them.

Types of Examples Presented

The book uses several types of examples, from brief parenthetical inserts, to short sketches, to extended case examples. Practical, real-world examples from a range of organizations are included in every chapter to illustrate how planners can approach planning tasks and to amplify the text, including illustrating some approaches that are less than desirable. These same examples are revisited several times, so the reader can follow the progress of a work group as analysis and prescriptive text unfold. This approach provides for continuity and follow-through.

The extended case examples focus on local governmental settings and nonprofit organizations, and they include several occupational and professional groups. The extended case examples may be challenging, but readers will be able to engage intuitively or through their life experiences. None of the case examples requires complex technical knowledge. Many will likely have a ring of familiarity.

Exercises for Readers

At several points, readers are invited to engage in an exercise in order to develop insight into the methods proposed in the book and then assess their work in light of these guidelines. These exercises also involve the reader in working through a concrete problem in order to become familiar with all of its aspects. Readers are urged to try these exercises and see whether they fully understand what is expected, regardless of the degree of their prior experience or their familiarity with the matter at hand.

The Book's Prescriptive Approach

Planning is discussed from an action framework—that is, as an exposition of all of its stages and tasks. Guidance and operational recommendations are offered for persons who have responsibility for planning projects or who want to learn how to plan. From this view, the book is not *about* planning, but about how *to do* collaborative planning. It is not a theory book (though it agrees with such valid theory as exists). These guides are derived in considerable part from the authors' own real-world experiences working on a variety of community and organizational projects as consultants, program evaluators, and volunteer members and leaders of nonprofit and governmental agency planning committees. At many points in the text, the authors assume the voice of a coach, as if sitting at the elbow of the planner, reflecting on a particular task, cautioning about this and that, and reminding practitioners about what lies ahead.

◆ ◆ ◆

The next chapter examines some common issues that must be addressed by participants in planning projects: the composition of work groups, the essential competencies required by its members, leadership, and the patterns of social relations experienced by work groups.

CHAPTER TWO

DETERMINING WORK GROUP PARTICIPANTS, LEADERSHIP, AND RELATIONSHIPS

Because planning is conducted by work groups, this chapter addresses such issues as their composition, factors to consider in selecting the planning team, and group leadership. The chapter concludes with a discussion of the patterns of social relations in which work groups are often engaged.

Participants: Insiders, Outsiders, and Others

The planning of new or changed programs is sufficiently complex and demanding that the efforts, abilities, and perspectives of diverse persons are needed. Almost anyone in—or closely affiliated with—a human service organization may sooner or later assist in these projects: managers, supervisors, line staff, board members, service recipients or their spokespersons, policymakers, volunteers, representatives of other organizations, and consultants. Most will probably be employees holding positions at various levels within service organizations, from administrators down through the ranks of all paid staff. Participants may be assigned from within because of their current duties, experience, and training. Other times, they are assigned because they have a certain level of responsibility and are considered able to guide a staff team effort or merely because they seem to be creative, to have initiative, or not to be already overloaded. For all of these reasons, individuals with creditable performance records who are already working in organizations are typically considered to be competent to engage in program planning, whether or not they have had any preparation in the required skills.

Large service organizations are most likely to have specialized planning staff members. Some have formal education and training in planning and management. Others have had some years of on-the-job experience and have been reassigned from other positions within the same organization but may have little formal training or preparation for planning tasks. Regardless of these considerations, such personnel are typically designated to lead or assist program planning endeavors.

Organization personnel who play important roles in planning projects are located at every level of authority, and at almost any formal position. Policymakers—for example, organization board members or senior executives—usually define the charge that empowers and steers planning efforts, and some may continue to be involved. Administrators then authorize, assign, and direct the planning of staff personnel. Those who carry out administrative responsibilities, including middle managers and supervisors, typically guide and coordinate the team activities of line staff, who participate when the effort involves their own service areas or requires their particular skills.

Many organizations depend on the active participation of their governing board members in some aspects of planning new or changed programs. Community service organizations—including governmental agencies—also call on citizen volunteers to join in these activities, such as school boards and their associated citizen advisory and parent groups. However, after plan proposals have been submitted, the work of implementation in such organizations is typically transferred to employed staff. Membership organizations of all kinds, and especially professional associations, routinely call upon the expertise and efforts of their primary members to contribute in planning projects. And when parents or other relatives become involved (or when service recipients are invited to represent their peers in considering new or improved services), identity distinctions as insiders or outsiders become even more blurred.

Organizations may also engage outside experts (consultants) to play key roles in planning projects, because the endeavor requires specialized technical or professional knowledge or particular familiarity with the program under consideration. In addition, officials may wish to balance "inside" views with the views of persons having broader, perhaps more disinterested, perspectives, or they may just need to augment the workforce in order to get the job done on time. Consultants are usually brought in to work in collaboration with insiders, but they are occasionally engaged to develop the whole plan (under guidance from organization leaders) for submission and review in completed form. The optimum arrangement is to join insiders and outsiders in collaborative planning processes. This should entail suitable forms of cooperative work, allowing for specialization of tasks and encouraging the interplay of differing perspectives. Persons in every category and at all levels are likely to become involved in aspects of program planning and usually while they continue with many of their daily tasks.

There are others who have major influence on planning processes but who seldom participate directly. This category includes funders, whose resources are needed for program support, and perhaps even for support of the planning process; officials of regulatory agencies and similar authorities; and legislators whose enactments affect organizations and their services. Officials of these entities exercise influence on the process in numerous ways, both direct and indirect. In general, the closer they are to the organization, the more immediate their influence, the more specific its intent, and the greater the desirability of engaging their constructive involvement.

Factors to Consider in the Selection of Planning Teams

The first column of Table 2.1 is a list of the key factors to consider in selecting members for planning work groups. It is an illustration of an organized way to track decisions in the course of selecting members for the planning team. At the end of the chapter, there is an exercise you can do, using Table 2.1 as a guide.

Required Participants

Although officials must consider "what does it take and who has what it takes?" in order to carry out a successful planning effort, they may not be entirely free to assign whomever they wish to the work group. Participation may be controlled, in whole or in part, by legislation, requirements of funding, licensing or accrediting agencies, or the organization's own policies. Such requirements constrain or direct the appointment of individuals with particular characteristics, the number and types of representatives from particular groups, and the procedures for their nomination and appointment. For example, one mental health recipients' rights committee must include at least three former patients; some county health-planning committees must have equal numbers of providers, consumers, and payers; and city human relations commissions are required to have members who reflect the minority composition of the community.

Required Expertise

In determining the composition of work groups, officials also have to address the functions or tasks to be carried out and the requisites of success for each plan-

TABLE 2.1. FACTORS IN SELECTING MEMBERS FOR AND ASSESSING THE COMPOSITION OF PLANNING WORK GROUPS.

Factors	Leader	Nominees to the Work Group				
		Nominee #1	Nominee #2	Nominee #3	Nominee #4	Nominee #5
Required representation	DOES	NOT	APPLY	DOES	NOT	APPLY
Planning skills and experience	X				X	
Active engagement in the group process and the group's work	Meets expectations	Meets expectations	Meets expectations	Engages when called upon	On funding and governance issues	Medical matters
Relationship skills in groups	Meets expectations	Meets expectations	Meets expectations	Low	Meets expectations	Meets expectations
Knowledge of the problem, condition, needs		X	X	X		Medical matters
Experience with the problem, condition, needs		X	X	X		Medical matters
Knowledge of service programs	General	Related to the project	Related to the project		General	Medical
Experience with service programs	General	Related to the project	Related to the project	Former recipient		Medical
Knowledge and experience with current or prospective recipients			X	Former recipient		Medical issues
Leadership skills	X	X			X	Unknown
Diversity	Male	Female	Female	Female	Male	Hispanic female
Stakeholder—Inside or outside		Inside	Inside	Outside	Outside	
Credibility with stakeholders		X	New staff member	Highly respected	X	
Current or prospective recipient, or a representative						
Influential with officials who will approve proposal	X	X			X	Medical matters
Staff member		X	X			
Volunteer	X			X		
Representative from collaborating organization					X	X

ning venture. A person must be selected who has the leadership qualities for a particular project and a particular set of team members. The leader must also have credibility with the officials who authorized the planning project and with the members of the planning team. In the best of all possible worlds, a team should have at least one member who has technical knowledge and skill and also has experience in nonprofit or public service planning. Some participants should have knowledge about the target population, its problems, and its needs.

Some minimum number of members must be able to develop concept papers, search files and documents, carry out studies, access resources, and write working notes and reports, but all members should be expected to prepare for team meetings. Work groups also need members with the ability to formulate a series of activities within a detailed step-by-step framework and to conceive, state, and organize them coherently. These essential tasks in preparing procedural guides involve a mode of thinking that not everyone shares. Even experienced service personnel may have difficulty describing, in an orderly way, exactly what they do in the course of their daily work. They can, however, provide this information when questioned in a systematic manner by persons who are attentive to the patterned progression of decisions, activities, and contingencies. Again, anyone demonstrating these abilities should become a valued participant in the work group.

At least one member should be selected (or be available) who possesses a clear understanding of the perspectives and value orientations of key members of the "audience" who will receive and make decisions about the proposal. This knowledge can be extremely helpful in sensitizing planners to how the final materials will be received and to the concerns and issues that need to be addressed in their work and in their materials. With some exceptions, there are advantages in having one or more prospective implementers of the plan on the team or having staff representation from the units likely to be affected by the plan.

Expertise with Work Plans

Another skill needed by work groups is the ability to develop work plans. As discussed in the previous chapter, work plans are needed to provide shared understandings of what needs to be done, as well as who will do it, when it will be done, and how it will be done. Teams develop work plans by listing, clustering, and sequentially ordering the substantive, procedural, and housekeeping matters that are identified and that must then be addressed by the team. All concrete details included in the charge that authorize the team to begin the planning process automatically serve as elements in the work plan (for example, definition of the problem, kind of service to be planned or changed, and due dates).

Work plans are almost invariably formulated in a progressive manner and amplified while work is under way, but almost never completely detailed. They cannot be highly detailed until participants have immersed themselves in the project and are able to identify numerous elements necessary to its achievement. Participants should reference their work plans at every meeting and should remain open to change, extension, and adaptation as experience develops, more matters are determined, and the unexpected is encountered. The degree of detail or specification appropriate for a work plan should be sufficient to provide clear directions for work and coordination, to ensure optimum use of participants' time and skills, and to assess progress toward project goals.

Work plans are among the key topics in the initiation stages of planning. These plans are intrinsically dependent on the nature and scope of the particular project, on the context within which the work is carried forward, and on the persons who compose the team.

Expertise in Documentation of Work Group Progress and Products

In planning projects, at least some work group members must be responsible for documenting the team's progress and its work products. For the planners, this includes the identification of persons and problems to be served, program goals, and the program design. Funders usually present detailed documentation requirements that should be reviewed and followed from the outset of project work. Work groups must also address many other requirements imposed on them within their charges.

When someone on the team demonstrates the ability to write in a well-organized, clear, and concise manner, that person should be promptly engaged in preparing these text materials. Ordinary narrative text is, of course, the most common form of documentation, but what is sometimes known as *technical writing* must take precedence over simple exposition. Task analyses and resource inventories are critical parts of the documentation and differ from ordinary descriptive text. Manuals that specify standard operating and monitoring procedures are increasingly necessary. All of these follow rigorous formats. Diagrams and charts of several kinds are widely used to convey particular aspects of entire plans. Some of these are explained and illustrated in our case examples. In each chapter, the reader will see the essential documentation requirements of that particular stage of planning.

Throughout the book, there is an emphasis on the importance of producing textual documentation (work sheets, note taking, write-ups, working drafts) as project tasks are advanced. Continuous recording helps work groups bring their accomplishments forward and build on work that is completed or under way. Because planning is a cumulative developmental process, documentation helps the group unify and link planning stages, link planning with implementation, and link implementation with operations. For the planners, ongoing documentation will ease the preparation of the final program plan document, which eventually must be submitted for approval to the officials who issued the charge to plan. These materials will also serve as a set of blueprints that can be followed by the implementers, who will then build, or install, the new or changed program.

Recipient Participation

Current or prospective recipients, or their representatives, have knowledge about the problems, conditions, and needs of the target population, and their perspectives and participation are essential, particularly during the problem analysis and program design stages of planning. Furthermore, in contemporary society, providing recipients with opportunities to participate is expected, and participation has to be meaningful if it is to be viewed as legitimate by the constituencies it represents. Sometimes staff have reservations about such participation and are careful about how much influence nonstaff members are allowed to have. To reduce the likelihood of marginalization, some planning teams instruct current or prospective recipients in group participation, appoint more than one recipient to the team, ensure the right to vote for all team members, and appoint a recipient as cochair of the team. Other persons who may be knowledgeable about the target population include those who have work experience with its members, those who have similar attributes or background, and those who have familiarity with the locale where the service will be provided.

Required and Desired Perspectives

When considering program changes, possible new services, or the implementation of these services, it is important to seek the perspectives and knowledge of the individuals who are already working in the program. However, overreliance on these persons may compromise the planning process and its results. Their conceptions and definitions of the problem or their views on what needs improvement are necessarily colored by their positions in the organization, their training, and their experiences—just as they may perceive the viewpoints of management personnel as often slanted toward budgetary, productivity, or efficiency concerns. Consideration should also be given to service recipients, their relatives, persons in the target population who are not receiving services, women, minorities, appropriate representatives of organizational units, and members of organizations whose collaboration is essential to the new or changed program. All of these representatives may have quite different but equally definite conceptions of the problem and what needs improvement, based on their interests and experiences (Raskoff and Sundeen, 2001).

Dilemmas

In some projects that depend on employed personnel, officials face dilemmas as they select staff to serve on the planning project. Staff ideas about solutions to program problems may be focused mainly on their own concerns and perspectives. Some staff may have valid questions about the program change or the new program and may be understandably skeptical or resistant. Officials may be ambivalent about assigning them to the work group. Yet lack of staff involvement in planning may lead to problems in implementation down the line. Then again, staff may perceive the request for their involvement as a ploy to "rubber-stamp" a decision that has been "wired." Top-down decision making deprives teams of any significant freedom of choices in their assigned work and deprives officials of the benefits of frontline staff experience. The restriction of staff engagement to basically trivial aspects of the planning endeavor, along with false claims that such involvement represents participatory decision making in the workplace, is likely to backfire. The principles of quality management and other approaches that genuinely rely on mutual learning and problem solving with officials and staff may be effective in resolving staff concerns (Martin, 1993). Judicious balancing of staff perspectives with those of other participants, including current or prospective recipients, is necessary to overcome these risks to the projects.

Leadership

Throughout this book, there is an emphasis on the critical role of project leadership, primarily by outlining effective methods for the designated group leader (however titled) to use. The extended case examples portray the actions of the group leader and other group members who serve in leadership roles. This approach allows for stepping back somewhat and adopting a broader perspective. To maintain desirable work group relations, leadership functions can and should be as broadly shared as feasible among work group members. This means that all participants should be able to contribute to guiding the group process based on their individual experiences, skills, and motivations. Needless to say, the varying amounts of work time that individuals can devote to project activities must be taken into account in determining concrete task assignments.

Prior to the initiation of the planning project, the leader should confer with officials to find out whether the staff who have been assigned to the project have workloads that will enable them to carry out the charge. If team leaders perceive imbalanced workloads, they have the responsibility to champion reductions and inform officials about the consequences of their decision on the planning project. Difficulties can be anticipated when workloads are not adjusted to accommodate the planning project, resulting in overtime that may be neither desired nor reimbursed or in work group tasks that are piled willy-nilly on top of ongoing service responsibilities. Such workload pressures frequently result in disadvantages to both sets of responsibilities.

Everyone possesses some distinctive attributes or abilities that can be profitably applied in team endeavors, and those attributes should be drawn upon to the fullest. As previously observed, some persons serving on teams are chosen because they have special knowledge of the kind of program to be changed or instituted, others may offer insightful advice in defining activity steps and durations, and so on. Appointed team leaders bear a special responsibility to work out a division of labor that will enable participants to make contributions.

An example of reliance on particular group members for special roles involves assignments to handle selected interactions with host organization peers whose assistance is needed for project work. Similarly, some team members might provide useful service when ongoing collaboration with personnel in another service organization is necessary in developing some program plans. These kinds of tasks are often difficult to fulfill for a team leader—even one who is drawn from an organization's management cadre—who is already carrying onerous duties in guiding a complicated project.

In some projects, none or few participants are fully under the authority or supervision of the project coordinator for their regular duties—that is, by definition, they are only temporarily and partly answerable to the project team. Presumably, most have other concurrent duties under their regular supervisors, or they are merely on loan to the team—which lessens their accountability to the coordinator. Consequently, their consent and active participation are essential to the solution of many of the difficulties that beset projects.

One of the coordinator's important duties is to serve as the primary intermediary between the project team and the oversight officials within the organization. The coordinator needs to become thoroughly familiar with what officials expect to be achieved and should assess the adequacy of the team's composition in this light.

One of the most critical competencies required for program planning projects is the ability to coordinate diverse persons with varying abilities in effective patterns of collaborative work during the several stages of the planning process.

Middle managers in many organizations carry comparable duties in guiding the performance of the staff assigned to their usual work units. In these situations, however, the work to be done—and the results to be achieved—are already more or less known, often in very determinate terms of reference. But program planning begins with a problem and ends with a written plan, and the best feasible solutions are not known or knowable in advance—they must be borrowed, discovered, or created.

Guiding, enabling, scheduling, assigning, and particularly envisioning future operations are project leadership tasks that necessitate managerial skills. This is why middle (and sometimes upper) managers are so frequently chosen to lead projects. However, they usually find this a very different kind of task, and the team itself is a different kind of work unit. Participants must be able to make contributions that are often not solely or even directly derived from their regular duties. And they must be aided in working together in new ways, seeking new approaches to problems that are often not well understood.

At the outset of the planning project, the leader should guide the work group in a discussion of its role in relation to the charge and other directives issued by officials. Planning work groups study, formulate, and recommend program changes and new programs, but officials review and then reject or approve them, sometimes with modifications. This division of authority and labor is important for all members to understand, especially when current or prospective recipients, or their representatives, are included in the work group. Project leaders, as enablers, should encourage work group members to contribute information, perspectives, evaluations, projections, and advice. These contributions are likely to be made if leaders promote a climate of openness and collaboration and if they avoid imposing their own views and solutions on team members in ways that may be customary for them in their usual areas of work. (For practical tools in group leadership, see "Part E. Leadership, Management, and Group Facilitation," Chapters Thirteen to Sixteen, University of Kansas, 2004.)

Patterns of Social Relations

The chapters ahead pertain mostly to the procedural or technical aspects of planning projects. There are also some social relations to address in the execution of these projects: work group relations, intraorganizational relations, and interorganizational relations. These will be referred to at appropriate points in some chapters.

Work group relations refer to relations among participants who are directly engaged in the conduct of projects. Of concern here are the degrees of cooperation among participants, the coordination and leadership demonstrated among them, their motivation and availability for the task at hand, the timeliness of their efforts, their adjusted workloads, and their relevant skills.

Intraorganizational relations refer to interactions between members of the project team and other personnel within the host organization. Of particular importance are the interactions that involve the organizational officials who authorize these projects; who assign their participants, tasks, and resources; and to whom the work groups are directly accountable. The scope of these relations also includes the team's interactions with (and assistance from) other units (for example, support staff, human resources, accounting, custodial services) and sometimes includes relations with board members, service recipients, or consultants. Of concern here are the resources, information, and assistance provided for work groups to accomplish their tasks, such as access to files or reports, personnel or budget expertise, and especially the project's empowerment within the organization.

Interorganizational relations refer to the work group's or the host organization's relations with external entities (for example, funders, licensing and regulatory agencies, other service providers, community associations, and the news media). These relations may pertain to compliance with professional and governmental standards and regulations, funders' preferences for components of the service program, cooperative arrangements with other service providers, and endorsements of former or prospective recipients or their representatives.

Reflection on the patterns of relations within each of these categories may reveal their significance for the work and accomplishment of planning. What kinds of influences and consequences do each of these sets of social relations imply for the project? Some statements made by work group members provide insight into these matters: "We shouldn't do that, because it will look like we're trying an end run around them." "They have to take ownership of the problem." "Let's make sure we confirm that with the personnel people." "They don't want any surprises." "Better to be safe than sorry." "Before we move ahead, we should check it out with . . . "

It's helpful to outline these relations in an ordered way, proceeding from "close" relations among members of the team, to those that are "allied," and then to those that are customarily more "distant." Under most circumstances, relations among work group members are close due to the frequency and intensity of meetings and the degrees of interdependence required to accomplish their work. Under many circumstances, relations between the work group and other staff or units within the host organization are allied, episodic, and focused on functionally specific purposes (for example, budget estimation) or administrative or legal approvals. Interorganizational relations are typically distant in that representatives of external organizations seldom participate directly in ongoing projects, and contacts are likely to be consultative on an as-needed basis.

Social relations among participants within these three categories may enhance or bode ill for almost any project. What if there were ineffectual leadership or inadequate coordination of work group activities, continuing dissension among participants, or other work obligations that conflict with time required for project activities? From an intraorganizational perspective, what if support staff were frequently tardy in retrieving information or records, or what if personnel from another unit perceive exclusion from decisions affecting their legitimate interests? But suppose that officials' enthusiasm about a project's progress report was widely disseminated. Would that not tend to increase the degree of needed cooperation and assistance from others within the organization? And from an interorganizational perspective, what if a funder wanted to closely monitor governmentally required program revisions as they were worked on by project teams, or what if an advocacy agency wanted the right to review the proposal for a new program at a public meeting? Sometimes this "closeness" is viewed as intrusive by the host organization, stemming from the norm that interorganizational relations are ordinarily distant.

These patterns of relations are both dynamic and interdependent—that is, sets of them are typically in flux, and strains or reassurances stemming from one set often have ramifications for another. For example, a work group's high level of timely accomplishment typically wins the support of other units within the organization and assures funders and other external bodies that have a stake in the program. In contrast, a team's inability to accomplish its charge is likely to cause difficulties across a range of relationships: organizational officials, other staff, affiliated agencies, and funders. Critical opposition from outside groups, especially with news media support, is likely to press upon officials, who, in turn, may try to deflect these influences, but if they're not successful, they might redirect or terminate a project unless it is highly valued.

Such concerns emphasize the need for vigilant attention to patterns of social relations and their effects on planning projects. Neither the team nor its coordinator can reasonably be expected on its own to sustain or even know about the entire network of these relationships or to anticipate all contingencies: many are the direct responsibilities of other staff, senior administrators, and an organization's governing officials. It is impossible to alert readers to the variations in social relations that might be encountered or the degrees of social connection that might be desirable or necessary. However, it is necessary to stress the importance of continual attention to these social relations, including both the supportive and challenging aspects that might influence planning processes. Anticipation management is preferred over damage control.

Exercise

Now that you've had a chance to read and think about all of the factors to consider when determining work group participants, go back to Table 2.1. The first column lists the factors that are often considered, as officials, perhaps with the help of the work group leader, think about the appropriate composition of the group. They have to think about "what does it take and who has what it takes to carry out the planning project?" Depending on the nature of the planning project, some factors in the list may not apply (for example, the first and last factors). Depending on the requirements of the particular planning project, officials and the leader can reconstruct the chart and substitute specifications of particular factors (for example, replace Diversity with Representative from Latino Community). Factors can also be reframed, added or deleted.

The second row of the table is used to list the nominees to the work group. (For the purposes of this example, nominees have been limited to six members.) As officials and the leader consider the nominees and the factors pertaining to their selection, an X can be placed in the appropriate cells when the factors apply. Notations can also be inserted.

As an illustration of how the table can be used, the cells have been filled in based on an adaptation of one of the author's experience with a planning team. Note the array of factors among the nominees and the array of nominees within a factor. Even though you do not know the charge to the group represented in the table, what are your observations and conclusions? As an exercise, use or adapt the table to assess the composition of a planning group in which you were a member.

◆ ◆ ◆

The introduction to Part Two will provide the reader with an overview of the stages and tasks of planning projects. Then Chapter Three will discuss the initiation stage, during which planners interpret the charge, put together an initial work plan, review the requisites for the program plan document, and develop an overall work plan for the entire planning venture.

PART TWO

THE STAGES OF PROGRAM PLANNING

Part Two focuses on the stages and tasks required for planning new service programs and for planning changes in existing programs. Here is a brief explanation of the differences between these two kinds of service planning and the distinction between program changes and organizational changes. Then there is an overview of the five stages of planning and their respective tasks.

New Programs and Program Changes

New programs are original, novel for a particular organization, or adaptations of former or existing programs produced by others, but not currently offered by the organization. These new service programs might be directed toward long-prevailing conditions and problems or new and emerging ones. *Program changes* refer to significant program-related modifications that are likely to be consequential for the target or service population and for the outcomes that recipients want or that are intended for them. Examples include changes in program performance standards, funding, eligibility or admission requirements, the way services should be delivered, the number of persons to be served, and other program features.

Part Two does not focus on organizational changes, such as the introduction of computer technology or modifications in administrative structure or personnel policies. It is not assumed, however, that organizational changes have no particular bearing on service programs and their recipients. Such changes may well have significant effects on both the service program and its recipients. For example, the introduction of flextime sometimes results in inadequate staffing and service inaccessibility or in untimely provision of services. Changes in managerial roles in correctional facilities have led to oversights in responsibility for secure custody of offenders. Officials need to explore the likely effects of organizational changes on the service program and its recipients. They should investigate these and other spillover effects after the organizational changes have been implemented.

The Stages and Tasks of Planning

The initiation stage of planning is discussed in Chapter Three (Initiating a Planning Project). It focuses on the planning work group's initial set of tasks. At the outset, participants must review and interpret the charge and other directives issued by the officials who authorized the planning project. Mandates of other organizations (for example, funders, regulatory agencies) that pertain to the project may also have to be reviewed. After gaining an understanding of what officials expect to be accomplished, the work group must develop an initial work plan, review officials' documentation requirements, and develop a preliminary work plan for the whole planning venture.

In examining the charge during the initiation stage, planners ascertain the problems or conditions of concern to officials. Often planners conclude that they must learn more about these problems or conditions in order to plan or improve a service program. At this point, they engage in problem analysis and needs assessment, which are the subjects of the analysis stage of planning, discussed in Chapter Four (Analyzing Problems and Assessing Needs). Some of the tasks included in the analysis stage are these: find out what planners already know about the nature of the problem and needs; plan the approaches to needs assessment; decide on the methods for carrying out the problem analysis and the needs assessment; collect and analyze data; determine priorities; and write the preliminary draft of the problem statement.

The problem analysis and needs assessment typically uncover complexities and more needs than programs are capable of serving. As a result, planners target services to selected aspects of problems and needs, and this is accomplished through the process of goal and objective setting.

The goals and objectives stage of planning, covered in Chapter Five (Setting Goals and Objectives), focuses on the tasks involved in setting program goals and objectives: review the boundaries and guidelines for setting program goals and objectives; translate needs into program outcome goals; specify the program goals as concrete program outcome objectives for service recipients; formulate process and output objectives; and document, organize, and check all program goals and objectives.

The design stage of planning, discussed in Chapters Six and Seven (Laying the Foundation for a Successful Design and Developing the Essential Program Components), addresses the development of the new or changed service program to be directed toward the program goals and objectives that pertain to specified recipients with a particular condition and needs. The developmental tasks of this stage include these: review the boundaries and guidelines for selecting and designing program changes or a new service program; select the services or decide the changes in the existing program; develop the essential components of the program changes or new service program; organize staff activities into service roles; decide the linkages of the service program with the host organization and other organizations; and identify resource requirements.

Finally, the documentation stage of planning, covered in Chapter Eight (Documenting the Completed Program Plan), focuses on the use of the Requisites for a Program Plan Document and the original charge to guide the preparation of the final written plan detailing either the program changes or the new program. The chapter also examines the collaborative work that one or more members of the work group must still complete with administrative personnel or officials of the host organization. Such work includes development and documentation of the staffing plan, units of service, and the program budget.

Must Planners Go Through All Stages and Tasks?

As a general rule, in planning projects that are focused on a new program or on a new problem and a new set of needs, planners should consider all tasks within these stages and then decide whether all must be carried out. However, in some projects that are focused on new programs, the analysis stage and the program goals and objectives stage, or the tasks within them, are bypassed. Sometimes this occurs when one organization duplicates the program model of an organization in another locality, because the latter is perceived to have recipients with similar problems and needs as the former. Bypassing also happens when there are recurring, common needs among members of a service or target population, and these needs are transformed into standardized program goals and objectives for all prospective recipients (for example, prospective first-time parents, prospective retirees, children who don't know how to swim, all Girl Scouts). Bypassing might also occur when a program is goal or value driven (for example, a civic organization may believe that everyone should experience the performing arts, and it sponsors an encounters-with-the-arts program for inner-city school children). The programs developed for these types of recipients are sometimes known as off-the-shelf, "canned," or model programs. They are developed by the program services offices of national organizations for their local affiliates, by central planning departments of state agencies for their branch offices, by membership and professional associations, and by entrepreneurs. The documentation for these programs is distributed through program notes, manuals, CDs and cassettes, and at conferences. For readers who want examples, just leaf through the announcements and advertisements in newsletters of professional and membership associations.

Planners should not take a model program off the shelf and just plunk it into an organization or community. Planners first have to assess whether the model fits local conditions and capabilities. For example, a model program of weeklong competitive activities developed by the national office of a youth-serving agency might be carried out without incident in a stable community, but not in one with gang rivalries. Often model programs must be customized to the *particular* problems, needs, and characteristics of *particular* persons in a *particular* location. For this reason, it may be wise to go through the stages and tasks and then omit those that are unnecessary, rather than bypassing them right away.

In planning a change in a current program, the team must decide whether some tasks can be omitted and how much or how little effort must be invested in each. For example, the team may not have to assess the needs of the target population, because that was done when the program was established, or only part of the original study might have to be updated in recognition of some changes in the community or the program's recipients.

The point of departure for the planning effort may be program change, but it may have unintended effects on recipients and the outcomes they and others want to achieve. The planning team must be vigilant about these effects, preserve the positive ones, and try to modify or eliminate the negative ones. Neither program changes nor new programs can be followed from their intent to all of their consequences, and some may not be seen until implementation or program operation. However, vigilance can be fostered if recipients are kept uppermost in the minds of the planners as the relevance of each task to the planning effort is considered. Bypassing tasks is explored further in the discussion of the stages of planning.

CHAPTER THREE

INITIATING A PLANNING PROJECT

The initiation stage of program planning refers to the time when officials of service organizations decide to undertake planning, formulate and issue a charge, and invite or assign individuals to the planning group. It is also when the group conducts initial meetings. This chapter focuses on the major tasks of the planning group during the initiation stage:

- Review and interpret the planning charge.
- Develop an initial work plan.
- Review the requisites for the completed program plan document.
- Develop an overall work plan for the whole planning venture.

As individuals are asked to serve on a team, they are likely to have some questions about the planning endeavor. What are we supposed to accomplish, and how are we supposed to do it? Why are they (officials) launching this effort? How much leeway do we have? Why did I get picked for this job? When does it have to get done? These questions point to some of the issues that have to be addressed by the team during the initiation stage of planning.

The acceptable ways of addressing these questions and commencing planning are too numerous to cover here; however, to illustrate the point, here are a few common practices: some officials brief the designated leader of the planning team prior to its first meeting and delegate the issuance of the charge and the orientation of the other planners to this person. Other officials attend the initial meetings of the team to make introductions, help define the charge, provide background information, and explain the role of the leader (for example, organizes and guides the planning endeavor, facilitates communication and problem solving, coordinates the activities of team members, mediates differences and conflicts, and schedules and chairs meetings). Some leaders of a planning effort do the preparatory leg work, such as gathering and organizing pertinent documents during the interim between the decision to go forward with the planning and the first meeting of the planning team, whereas others distribute the workload among team members. In this way, some matters may be addressed before or at the first set of meetings (and during other stages of planning) by officials, the leader, and the other members of the planning group. Organizational practices, the role of the leader of the planning team, styles, the team's composition (for example, staff members, board members, program recipients), and the complexity of the planning venture all influence how planners are prepared to initiate the planning process. There are acceptable variations in the initiation of planning. The following guidelines constitute good practices but do not address when they should be carried out and other details pertinent to a particular planning situation. The primary focus in this chapter is on the major tasks of the planning team during its initial meetings. For simplicity, key players are referred to as either *officials* or *planners* (though there are individuals in all capacities that can serve in these roles). The first major task of the first meeting of any planning team is to review and interpret the planning charge.

Review and Interpret the Planning Charge

Planning processes are undertaken by organizations that almost invariably have formal policies and procedures that direct (and facilitate or curtail) most deliberate activities within organizational boundaries, including planning changes in existing programs or initiating new programs. Persons are authorized to engage in such planning, and time and other resources are allocated to this work. Both the planning effort and the desired results are guided by established methods of oversight and accountability.

The official impetus to undertake program planning is the *charge*—the authorization to act given to representatives. A charge is a directive to engage in planning in order to produce a plan document that can be reviewed, modified, and finally approved and modified (or rejected). The charge sets forth who will do the work to prepare a plan for a new program or to change an existing program; in the latter case, it states what elements of the program will be changed. In the case of a new program elements of the new program may not be specified in the charge. The charge to commence planning can contain authoritative pronouncements, expectations, guidelines, boundaries, agreements, or perspectives that direct or constrain planning decisions. At the outset, it is essential to review and interpret the charge with the officials who issued it, especially its concrete elements, to determine its focus and if it is complete enough and reasonably clear enough to commence planning. Sometimes the charge is not written, or if it is written, it is not well thought out. Planners should press officials for a clear written charge, because failure to do so could lead to the undoing of the planning project. However, planners may fear that questioning the charge will be interpreted as noncooperation. Officials often need some help in thinking through what they want or in anticipating outcomes that they may not have considered. (This will be discussed further later in the chapter.)

Charges set forth as injunctions to the staff members who are employed in a service organization should have several key features that guide and affect planning: substance or aims, scope or limits, source of authority, and determinateness. The review and interpretation of the charge may begin by disassembling it according to the key features.

The Substance and the Aims of the Charge

Every charge has some substance or some aims that distinguish it from others and identify the problem or the need to be addressed, the goals that must be achieved, or the matters that require attention. The substance or the aims of a charge typically focus on social problems, social goals, or perceived problems of effectiveness or efficiency. *Social problems* (homelessness, child abuse) include those problems that have been in existence but have received inadequate or no community attention; those problems with new features (the homeless now include families); and those problems that are new, emergent, or critical (sexual abuse of children by members of the clergy, children with AIDS, natural or manmade disasters, such as tornadoes or toxic waste dumps). *Social goals* embody community values, or concerns about the quality of life, or conditions that are not problematic but are likely to become so unless something is done about them (for example, the promotion of community cohesion or ethnic group relations through block clubs, festivals, exhibitions, or sporting or entertainment events; solid waste management; park improvements; the use of leisure time and continuing education among retirees). *Perceived problems of effectiveness and efficiency* pertain to conditions in an existing program (for example, failure to improve a targeted condition, inequalities in the use of services among recipients, long waiting lists, and concerns about eligibility criteria to qualify for services). One or more of these issues typically constitute the substance of a charge. At the outset, planners should explore the charge with officials to obtain first impressions about its substance—the condition that officials want the planners to address.

The Scope and the Limits of the Charge

Every charge sets some scope or limits on what is to be achieved. It may specify or delimit the characteristics of the target population, or it may predetermine the scale of the planning or program effort to be undertaken, such as numbers of persons to be served or dollars to be allocated. The charge may circumscribe the areas within which the problems or conditions are to be addressed according to agency, municipal, county, regional, or other boundaries.

Organizational Mission. The scope or limits of a charge are inherently bounded by the mission of the service organization. Most often, officials take for granted that the planning effort must relate to the purposes of the organization or to the societal or community functions it performs. However, sometimes planners do not take that for granted and initiate planning that is not consistent with their organization's mission. It is important that planners be mindful of the mission as they review and interpret the charge. The mission statement often contains one or more of the following elements:

- The problems that the agency intends to resolve (for example, substance abuse, developmental disabilities)
- The target population (for example, military families, minorities, library patrons)
- The geographical or political boundaries of agency activities (for example, a governmental jurisdiction, a community, a district, or a neighborhood, depending on the auspice and domain of the agency)
- The principles that guide the organization's development and decision making (for example, services must be directed toward prevention)

The mission is often set forth in legal documents at the service organization's founding, through legislation or administrative regulations for government agencies, through charters or articles of incorporation for nonprofit organizations, and through injunctions by other authoritative external bodies. In the unlikely event that officials issue a charge whose substance is not consistent with the mission statement, planners should check with officials to confirm that the organization is making a fundamental shift in its character. Perhaps the mission needs to be reconsidered to better legitimate attention to problems that have become important to beneficiaries or influentials. If officials do not want to reconsider the mission, they may have to reconsider the charge.

Organizational Policies and Commitments. The mission statement is sometimes out-of-date and tends to give only a general sense of what the domain of organizational responsibility might be. Officials (including administrative staff and board members) develop additional interpretations and descriptions of the mission in the form of policies that direct the contemporary affairs of the organization and that inevitably limit the scope of the charge (for example, shelters that provide temporary housing for homeless families exclude substance abusers; recipients of public assistance have high priority for admission into some adult literacy classes). Such policies can be found in organizational handbooks or manuals, annual reports, minutes, memoranda, and public relations materials. As organizations evolve or develop, they take on commitments (to a target population, problems, services, and staff competencies) that reflect allocations of resources among activities, which in turn commit organizations to do some things at the cost of others. Investments in the current operations of an organization are among the most powerful reasons for electing not to do other, different, or new things that it might like to do but cannot, given its finite resources. For example, school counselors who have helped students improve their functioning in school often want to extend the counseling relationship to help them with their troublesome family relationships. However, the policies of the special services department limit assistance solely to students' problems that are strictly related to their school performance. A mental health worker who discovers that community misunderstanding and anxiety are barriers to the integration of former patients into a downtown business-residential community may want to offer training programs for frontline employees in businesses patronized by former patients. However, his organization's policies restrict the provision of services to former patients of the psychiatric hospital.

Proper attention to the mission, policies, and commitments of an organization prevents it from drifting too far away from obligations, domains, and boundaries; gives a holistic grasp of agency ends and activities; and facilitates planning of service programs that are responsive to the primary purposes of the organization. Even the most experienced of planners, those who know the organization and its programs, sometimes stray off course. That is why, regardless of the planner's expertise, tenure, and experience, it is advisable to collectively address these matters at an early meeting so that everyone starts out with a shared understanding of what is to be done and within what boundaries.

The Source of Authority

Another key feature of a charge is the source of authority that issues the charge to the planners. For service organizations under governmental auspices, sources of authority might include legislative bodies, such as a county commission or a policymaking board, or they may be administrators of departments or bureaus. For nonprofit organizations, sources of authority might include the board of directors, the executive director, or an interagency consortium. Whatever the auspice, the charge must come from or be passed through the organization's own policymakers and administrators, who, in approving the charge, impose the terms for planning.

The charge—in whole or in part—may be embedded in the minutes of organizational meetings, memoranda, policies, records, or files. Officials do not always transmit these documents to planners, usually due to an oversight, lack of recognition of their relevance, or assumptions that planners know about them and will retrieve them. Consequently, one of the first responsibilities of the planners is to determine whether there is a higher-level policy declaration containing the formal, written charge, its key elements, or information pertinent to the charge and planning task.

The source of authority for a charge might also be outside the service organization. The term *mandates* applies to external orders or requirements that compel the organization to commence planning and to take one direction or another. There are a host of directives (thou shalt do this) and constraints (thou shalt not do that) that planners are obliged to follow. Planning mandates may govern virtually any aspect of the planning process and program design. The discussion here focuses on how mandates condition an organization's freedom, readiness, and the decision to undertake planning.

Sometimes mandates are identified in the planning charge. However, the charge and the mandates are distinct in several key respects. The authorization to spend work time on a plan is set forth in the organization's official charge, and that serves as the point of departure for what is to be planned, but it often does not cite directives and constraints that come from an external source. The external sources of mandates include the following: (1) statutes (for example, state statutes require county public health departments to strive to control infectious disease, so they must engage in health planning concerning AIDS; normalization and mainstreaming legislation require school districts to integrate students with developmental disabilities into conventional classes and school programs); (2) funders (for example, a community mental health agency required its funding recipients to plan its services for people with serious impairments in social functioning rather than for the worried well); (3) standards set by accreditation, regulatory, or professional organizations (for example, programs that are out of compliance with medication management protocols, clinical record-keeping practices, personnel qualifications, or staff-patient ratios are required to take corrective action); (4) judicial decisions (for example, judges have ordered the development of plans to reduce the size of inmate populations in overcrowded prisons); and (5) the preferences and demands of service recipients or powerful special-interest groups (for example, advocacy groups promote the principle of least-restrictive alternative to influence the planning of facilities and programs that enable the elderly to live as independently as their health permits and to avoid costly nursing home placements; advocates exhort library officials to develop specialized programs for mental health patients who live in the community and to stop expelling them from the library when they "hang out").

The Determinate Aspects of the Charge

Each charge has its own degree of determinateness with respect to the focus (substance, aims, scope) of the planning effort, the planning process, and the desired product or results. *Determinate* refers to the defined limits or aspects of the charge. For example, when changes in an existing program are sought, they may be specified in very concrete terms that provide detailed guidance for the planners. For example, complaints about waiting lists and waiting periods or about line-staff belligerence may have reached organizational decision makers and stimulated calls for remedies in present modes of operation. In each of these situations, particular features of a program, not all of its aspects, are the targets of change, and plans must address these elements at a minimum if they are to be acceptable. Determinateness may govern deadlines for completion of the planning effort and submission of the plan document, the composition of the planning work group (for example, health care providers and patients), and the specifications of the plan document (its format, the kinds of detail, and supporting evidence). Some charges require incremental planning with successive reviews as decision making proceeds from preliminary through final drafting to completed plans—all perhaps according to firm deadlines. But some of these or still other elements in the charge may be only vaguely stated, thus giving the planners both limits and degrees of freedom in their work.

To illustrate the discussion about the initiation stage of planning, the following case example examines a city administrator's formation of a planning committee and his issuance of its charge. Notice how the committee reviews its charge and begins its work at the first meeting.

◆ ◆ ◆

Consumer Protection Office Case Example: Updating Services

Members of the Midland City Council raise concern about the services of an existing city agency.

Background

At a recent meeting of the Midland City Council, several council members again raised their concern that the services of the city's Consumer Protection Office (CPO) deserve review and updating, perhaps expansion, in light of the many developments in this area of citizen needs and interests, beyond those prevalent when the office was established two decades ago. Other members expressed support. There was no partisan debate, so the council approved a resolution directing the city administrator to appoint a planning committee to review and recommend possible directions as a basis for discussion within the council for updating and enhancing the services of the CPO, including the possibility of its being renamed to reflect a more contemporary mission.

Composition of the Committee

After conferring with the council members who initiated the resolution, with the director of the CPO, and with several aides, the city administrator appointed a core group of six persons, to be "assisted" by personnel from the office of the city attorney and the city's Weights and Measures Unit. The core group would consist of the administrator's executive assistant as chair, the director of the CPO and two of its program managers, the staff person in charge of the Better Business Bureau (BBB), affiliated with the chamber of commerce, and a representative from one of the several interested citizen and nonprofit organizations (after consultation with key council members). Leaders of the outside organizations were consulted by the administrator to ensure their interest and willingness to be represented. The committee was to develop liaison relations "as appropriate and feasible" with the county's Public Health Department and the state's Consumer Affairs Office. (Both underwrite some of the current activities of the CPO and sponsor programs relevant to the planning group's charge, but none were to serve as actual members of the group.) The administrator thought it desirable that the group develop some linkages with particular county and state agencies and other organizations, but it would be inappropriate for these outsiders to participate directly in determining municipal services, and it also would be too time consuming. Furthermore, adding more participants would make the group unwieldy for the work at hand.

Because there had not been differences among council members along partisan lines on this matter, and it was clear that the council expected a largely internal working group to prepare initial proposals in a short time, the composition of the committee was independently decided by the administrator. Under such circumstances, he customarily proceeds in this way after obtaining the viewpoints of the persons having the most interest in the matter at hand. He designated his executive assistant to chair the group because she was experienced in handling such assignments efficiently and effectively, and the administrator wanted to underscore the importance with which he regarded the group's task. The "assistance" expected from other city offices was understood to mean that they could be called on for particular purposes, perhaps attend certain sessions relevant to their areas of work, but not otherwise join actively in the planning work.

Planning Charge

The charge to the committee was stated in a short memorandum from the administrator to the four city personnel he had appointed (with copies to other city offices) and in an equally brief invitational letter to the two noncity persons who had been designated. Both the memorandum and the letter included excerpts from the council minutes: one sentence stated that the executive assistant would serve as chair and provide "guidance." Two sentences encouraged open-minded and energetic efforts by participants. One sentence requested a briefing in two months. And a closing statement requested that a report be readied for the administrator's review "within three months" and for possible submission to the council "if it appears that your work has reached that point of readiness."

The administrator's contacts and communications made clear that it was neither expected nor desired that the committee prepare detailed program development or change designs for this initial report. Instead council members appeared interested in some charting of endeavors that the office might undertake that would be responsive to new circumstances that did not exist when the CPO was founded years ago. At that time, concern had focused on fraudulent sales practices, unregulated door-to-door selling, alleged discrimination in credit and loans, and landlord-tenant contracts, often resulting in adversarial proceedings. As one councilwoman stated, "Although we are still dealing with some of those problems, we are facing new ones." Now there seemed to be a groundswell of interest in healthful nutrition, product safety, advertising claims, and home-based ecological and conservation practices. Particular interest was also expressed in the office's recent venture into conflict resolution rather than adversarial methods.

◆ ◆ ◆

At this point, the reader may wish to pause and engage in a brief exercise. Examine the CPO example, disassemble the charge, and list its elements, including its substance or aims, scope or limits, sources of authority, and determinate aspects. When you are finished, compare your work with the presentation of the chair at the committee's first meeting.

◆ ◆ ◆

Consumer Protection Office Case Example:
The First Planning Committee Meeting

The chair opened the meeting with a welcome and introductions, followed by the distribution of an agenda, her disassembly of the charge, and a draft of an initial work plan (which the reader will see later as the committee carries out its agenda). She reminded the committee that an informational packet about the CPO had been mailed or distributed to each member by the director. The members acknowledged receipt of the program summaries, the annual report, and service statistics, and stated that they had read the material in preparation for the meeting.

Review and Interpret the Charge

The agenda was accepted with agreement that items could be added as "we interpret what we're supposed to be doing." The chair directed the group to the first item on the agenda—review and interpret the charge—by reading the features of the charge, which she extracted from the administrator's memorandum and conversations.

Substance "We have been asked to address several conditions, including healthful nutrition, product safety, advertising claims, and home-based ecological and conservation practices. The council also wants to explore suggestions for further development of mediation and conflict resolution methods rather than relying on adversarial methods."

Aims "To review and recommend possible directions or endeavors the office might undertake that would be responsive to circumstances greatly changed since its establishment."

Scope and Limits "The committee is not expected nor is it desirable to prepare detailed program development or change designs. The charge is determinate in at least three other ways: the composition of our committee is set—representatives of other city and county departments may serve in a consultative or liaison role as needed; the administrator wants a briefing in two months; and he wants the report submitted in three months."

Sources of Authority "We are accountable to the administrator and the city council. The committee must also be mindful of the electorate to whom the city council and most city employees are accountable."

Discussion of the Charge

After reading the charge, the chair invited comments. All members expressed enthusiasm and welcomed the opportunity to be creative in shaping the future of the CPO without being burdened by program details, but they felt a bit overwhelmed by the range of items in the charge.

One member asked how healthful nutrition found its way into the charge. The director of the CPO reported that two council members, who were advocates of wellness and illness prevention, heard about a nutrition program while attending a regional conference for city officials. After some discussion, the committee concluded that it would not consider ventures that duplicated the nutrition programs of the county Department of Health, the Department of Public Welfare, Head Start, the two local hospitals, the local HMOs, the senior services center, the community college, and adult basic education. However, all but one of the team members agreed that false advertising about the nutritional content and benefits of food, supplements, vitamins, and drugs ought to be included in its work. The citizens' group representative said that was the job of the Food and Drug Administration (FDA). The CPO director noted that both his office and the council members had received complaints about such advertising found on food packaging and in the media. After a lively discussion, the group acknowledged that a local program would be more visible and accessible than a federal program, and among other things, CPO could build on the work and materials of the FDA. The chair noted the decision for the record, and on her copy of the work plan she penciled in, "Look into false advertising re nutrition and develop a proposal."

The chair then distributed a handout that directed the group's attention to several other aspects of the charge that required clarification:

1. Is the council almost inviting the committee to reconsider the CPO's mission, and not merely its service activities?
2. What do officials mean by product safety? False advertising? Home-based ecological practices and conservation? Mediation and conflict resolution? What should be included or excluded within each of those areas?
3. Although the committee is not expected to prepare detailed program development or change designs, what must be included in the proposals? The chair told the team members that they probably would not have enough time to finish the first two items during today's meeting, so she scheduled the discussion of the last item for the third meeting.

The chair knew that the CPO director had discussions with several council members during the last year and asked him to comment on the first two questions. He reported that the council was giving the committee a "lot of latitude," and he and his staff welcomed the opportunity to broaden the CPO's mission. They had been working on initiatives to update the work of the CPO and had been looking into innovative programs in other cities. Several council members had called him about constituent complaints concerning product safety (for example, hazardous toys and baby furniture, tanning salons, drain cleaners, defective tools, and off-road vehicles), and truth in advertising (for example, long-term care insurance for the elderly, investment opportunities, and telemarketing practices). Council members representing low-income districts were particularly concerned about constituents who were victims of rent gouging. He believed that the committee should develop a proposal to have the council consider mediation and conflict resolution methods. The citizens' group representative believed that it also would be useful for the CPO to study rental fees and publish comparative analyses of rents and particular features of rental housing, thereby empowering consumers to make informed decisions as they go about seeking and securing rental housing. The chair intervened by thanking and complimenting both for their contributions but expressed reservations about zooming ahead into the design of service programs before the team had completed its review of the charge.

The representative from the BBB reported that his office received similar complaints, and before the chair could interject a comment, the group was off and running on a spirited exchange about what the role of the BBB was versus what the future role of the CPO might be in handling such complaints. The chair reined in the buoyant discussion by asking the director and the BBB representative to present a report on these complaints in two weeks, and they accepted.

The chair informed team members that they were running out of time. She asked them if they were prepared to accept the charge as presented and clarified with the understanding that some elements required further clarification at the next meeting, and the group accepted. In the time remaining, the team turned to the chair's draft of the work plan (discussed when this case example continues later in the chapter).

◆ ◆ ◆

Examine and Document the Results of the Review and Interpretation of the Charge

A planning team may emerge from its first meeting with a clear understanding of its charge, or one or more aspects may need further clarification. The substance of the charge may be ambiguous, its scope uncertain, or its aims contradictory. The charge may not be complete or sufficiently clear to commence planning. Officials may not be able or may not want to be more specific or directive about certain elements for any number of reasons (for example, lack of expertise, ambiguity of the problem, or concern about curtailing the planners' creativity).

Even if the charge is complete and concrete, it is subject to varying interpretations. Planning participants always proceed from their own definitions of the situation, and they bring in and act on their own notions, concerns, apprehensions, understandings, and misunderstandings. These become elements in their collective efforts to grasp the meaning of the charge presented to them, and their changing definitions continue to play out in the process. That is why some of the sources of uncertainty about the charge can be attributed to the planning participants and their interpretations of the charge.

The initial review and interpretation of the charge may lead to the conclusion that work needs to be done during and outside team meetings to achieve a determinate understanding of the charge. This task must have high priority as the team decides its next steps and develops a work plan.

Develop an Initial Work Plan

After the introductory review and interpretation of the charge and during the first meeting of the planning team, members must develop an initial work plan for the immediate tasks that must be addressed between and during the next two or three meetings. Work plans are formulations developed by team members that provide shared understandings of what needs to be done, who needs to do it, when it will be done, and how it will be done. These understandings are needed to ensure that work proceeds in an orderly way, that things to be done are identified and assigned to move the effort forward, and that teams meet their due dates and deadlines.

Although the specific nature of the initial work plan varies from one planning endeavor to another, there are common start-up chores that must be addressed by those involved in planning new service programs or changing existing ones. The leader or the entire team may develop the work plan by listing and clustering the substantive, procedural, and housekeeping matters that require the team's immediate attention. The initial work plan should include an agreement on the immediate tasks that need to be carried out by someone on or off the team, deadlines for their completion, the assignment of a note taker for this and subsequent meetings, an agenda and time for the next meeting, some plan—if not a decision—on the focus and schedule of future meetings, and a time frame for the whole planning venture (unless this has already been fixed, as in the CPO example). The planning team may need to confer with officials to determine the financial and staff resources to be allocated to the planning effort, including but not limited to such matters as the level of effort required of staff, availability of support staff, use of consultants and volunteers, support for travel, honoraria for key informants, duplication, food and beverages for group meetings of the team or service recipients, and equipment. The fund application and instructions for completion must be obtained as soon as possible if external funding will be sought to support the new or changed program. Whether or not external funding is sought, from the outset planners must know what officials or funders want in the program plan document that must be submitted. A review of the requisites of the program plan document is therefore essential. (This is discussed in a subsequent section of this chapter. See Chapter Eight for a more complete discussion.)

Some of the immediate tasks to be addressed in the preliminary work plan and the next set of meetings often emerge from the initial review and interpretation of the charge:

- Formalize a determinate understanding of the charge (if it could not be completed at the first meeting).
- Interpret mandates that have a bearing on the charge.
- Determine how the condition came to the attention of officials.
- Determine who the important stakeholders are in the planning effort and outcomes.

The extent to which these matters need to be addressed varies according to the planning venture (new program or changed program) and the composition of the planning group (for example, whether planners are only insiders or if they include outsiders in relation to the unit doing the planning, whether planners are privy to the "goings on").

The CPO case example continues with the first meeting, where the chair has distributed a draft of the initial work plan for the group's consideration and review. See Table 3.1.

◆ ◆ ◆

Consumer Protection Office Case Example: Continuation of the First Planning Committee Meeting

The chair directed the committee's attention to the preliminary draft of the initial work plan and asked the members to review and approve or modify it. One member asked the chair to "walk the group through the work plan," and others nodded in agreement. Discussing the items in order, the chair anticipated that the team would need one or two more meetings to formalize its understanding of the charge and reiterated what had been just agreed on—that members would come to the next meeting with further suggestions for defining the focus of false advertising, product safety, home-based ecological and conservation practices, and mediation. One member asked whether ideas should be presented in writing, and after a brief discussion the committee agreed that verbal presentations would suffice.

The chair proceeded to the meeting schedule and recommended that the committee should meet twice a week for at least two hours per meeting. She used a sketch pad to work backward from the deadline to outline the general tasks that had to be addressed. "We were asked to report to the city administrator in twelve weeks.

TABLE 3.1. DRAFT OF THE INITIAL WORK PLAN.

Tasks	Meeting #1	Meeting #2	Meeting #3	Meeting #4
1. Review, interpret, and formalize an understanding of the charge.	X →	X		
2. Set schedules.				
a. Set agenda and schedule for the next meeting.	X			
b. Decide meeting schedule for the next three months.	X			
c. Brief administrator on progress in two months. →		Approximately at the eighth week		
3. Select a recorder and decide on procedures for writing summaries.		X		
4. Develop orientation procedures.				
a. Provide an orientation to CPO programs and a review of the packet mailed to members.		X		
b. Provide background information and rationale for the CPO planning effort.		X →	X	
c. Provide an orientation to BBB.		X		
d. Provide an orientation to citizens' groups.		X		
5. Explore whether others should be involved as consultants, key informants, experts; explore roles and relationships with other agencies.			X	
6. Identify external mandates that have an impact on the planning effort.			X →	X
7. Determine how to proceed with the planning effort and assignments.			X →	X
8. Determine the elements and format of the proposal to be submitted to the administrator and the council.			X →	X
9. Develop an overall work plan.			X →	X

During the eleventh week, we will have to review and approve the final draft to make sure the secretary has enough time to type the changes and duplicate the report. Therefore the penultimate draft must be prepared, copied, distributed, and reviewed around the tenth week. Counting this week, that leaves us about nine weeks to get oriented, study a few problems, and recommend possible CPO directions to the council." After checking their calendars and commitments, the group agreed to meet Tuesdays and Fridays from 9 to 11 A.M. The chair volunteered to serve as the recorder and distribute summaries of discussions, much to the relief of the others.

◆ ◆ ◆

The director of the CPO believed that it was important to provide further background information about his discussions with the council, because it would enable the team to understand where the council and the CPO "were coming from," and he welcomed the opportunity to inform the group about the work of the CPO at the second meeting. There was agreement that everyone ought to understand the purposes and work of the organizations represented on the committee. The chair realized that she had forgotten to include an opportunity for the CPO staff to report on what they had learned about innovations in other cities. All agreed to include such a presentation in the third or fourth meeting to stir creativity.

Item number 5 (regarding the use of consultants and the relationships with other agencies) on the proposed Draft of the Initial Work Plan (Table 3.1) elicited different points of view. Some said that the list should be open and should be developed as the team went through the planning process, and key informants and others could be sought on an as-needed basis. Others wanted to have representatives from organizations that deal with false advertising, product safety, and conservation come to meetings early on to make presentations, so "we don't duplicate what's already being done." As a compromise, the chair asked members to "take it a step at a time. Come to the third meeting with your list of significant others, a brief statement of what they do, and how they are essential to or might help our effort, and then let's take it from there." The committee accepted the remaining items of the work plan, and the chair and the director of the CPO volunteered to prepare and circulate drafts of their respective assignments prior to the designated meetings.

Formalize a Determinate Understanding of the Charge

As indicated earlier, by the end of the team's first meeting, planners may have had only a general impression of the charge. They must then formalize a determinate understanding of the charge and specify the condition and the people that are of concern to officials. Planners may be required to work with official conceptions of the problem, they may be given some latitude to entertain other perspectives, or they may have to solicit others' conceptions of the condition, including professionals, volunteers, and prospective beneficiaries of the service. Planners may also discover divergent perceptions of the condition among themselves, and they will have to reconcile their own as well as others' differences. Even when a problem appears to be concretely described, it is subject to varying interpretations. Whatever the case may be, planners must arrive at a determinate understanding of the charge that includes a shared definition of the condition and the target population.

Returning to the CPO case example, you will see how the committee addressed the matter of home conservation and ecological practices.

◆ ◆ ◆

Consumer Protection Office Case Example: The Second Planning Committee Meeting

The chair began by reminding the group that they had agreed to do some thinking about home-based ecological and conservation practices and asked the representative from the citizens' group to offer one of his ideas first. He believed that the CPO should expand its landlord-tenant relations program to focus on energy conservation in low-income rental housing. He informed the committee that the utility company conducts home energy audits, makes recommendations, and offers assistance to reduce energy consumption. The citizens' group representative was of the opinion, supported by some experience, that some landlords of low-income housing were not taking advantage of the utility's program and would not invest in weatherization as long as tenants were paying the rent and the heating bills. He believed that the committee should have the council consider a proposal that would encourage landlords to participate in energy conservation, perhaps relying on incentives, mediation, and conflict resolution methods. Low-income tenants would benefit by having more income to meet other needs. Because the CPO had been involved in landlord-tenant relations from its inception, he believed that the development of a proposal focused on energy conservation in low-income rental housing was appropriate for the CPO. Residents with low incomes or on public assistance were consumers, and often vulnerable ones at that, and the CPO had an obligation to protect and assist them. Some members started to envision a CPO program, but the chair pointed out that the council did not want detailed program proposals—it wanted food for thought. In addition, depending on what the team discovered about the alleged problem in the next phase of planning, it could decide to drop it or go forward with it. "Right now, the team has to decide whether this interpretation falls within the purview of our charge and if we should proceed to the next step with it."

The BBB representative was hesitant about including his colleague's suggestion in the formal interpretation of the charge. He did not want the team to have a public re-lations problem by inserting an "accusatory" statement into the public record of the charge, which would appear to imply that all owners of low-income housing have been dragging their feet about energy conservation. The chair reminded the committee about the city's open meetings and public records statutes and ruled that an informal, under-the-table charge was not acceptable. She also told the committee that the coun-cil had demonstrated leadership in energy conservation by allocating funds to weath-erize the city's low-income housing units. Again, she clarified the charge. "We can offer alternative proposals. The council wants ideas. It does not want detailed program pro-posals." After agreeing on tactful wording, the committee decided to include the sug-gestion in the scope of its charge.

The director of the CPO urged the committee to include in its interpretation of the charge the inappropriate disposal of household toxic wastes that contribute to health hazards and groundwater contamination. Too many residents were disposing of motor oil, radiator fluid, chemicals, oil-based paint, and insecticides by pouring them into the ground. In a recent incident, children playing in a shallow pool of water after a rainstorm became ill. A study revealed that their symptoms could be attributed to solvents that someone had poured into the gully. Recycling of household solid waste such as newspapers, cans, plastics, and glass also should be considered. The com-mittee agreed to add these items to its charge and work plan.

◆ ◆ ◆

These are just some of the features of the written charge and the oral explana-tions of officials that require interpretation by the planners. The foregoing dis-cussion illustrates how planners have to unravel a charge to determine what they are being asked to do. The questions indicate that planners need to do some check-ing and backtracking to focus the problem and the population of concern be-fore they can proceed. Planners must strive to arrive at some reasoned interpretations of their charge, and these interpretations ought to be concretely stated for affirmation or refutation by officials as the process unfolds, as well as in the final report (see items number 4 and 16 in the requisites section later in the chapter). Ordinarily, it is not necessary to be obsessive about clearing everything with officials, but it is important for planners to know whether they have discre-tion and over what matters.

If the charge is incomplete or uncomfortably ambiguous, planners should for-malize their interpretation of the charge and send it to the decision makers. A cover memo might explain that a charge was recently issued, and in the interest of being responsive to the request, the planners have formulated a memorandum of their understanding. This memorandum might state that the planners will assume that their interpretation of the charge is correct if they do not hear from the officials who issued it. Sometimes planners have to "manage up" (Austin, 1989). They may well have to maneuver decision makers into formulating a more complete charge that has a reasonably clear beginning direction. Planners have to minimize the possibility that they will be held accountable for expectations not communicated, or only ambiguously communicated. If planners are to be held accountable, it is wise to leave a paper trail that can be referenced. Such maneuvering is commonly known as—cover your derriere, or CYD.

Interpret Mandates That Have a Bearing on the Charge

Mandates were identified earlier in the chapter as external orders or requirements that are sources of authority and that might compel an organization to plan. Here the focus is on how a review of mandates might help planners arrive at a more determinate understanding of the charge and the planning effort. This discussion of mandates should not be read as matters that must be addressed up-front by planners, before they can do anything else. Nor should it be interpreted as defining the scale of work that is required in a planning process. Some mandates are made known to planners or discovered by planners at the outset, some in the course of the work, and still others after programs have been in operation.

Funders impose requirements pertaining to financial and staff resources. These requirements have such obviously significant importance for program planning that participants should make them explicit at the outset and should be mindful of them throughout their work. Constraints often include restrictions of service to people with particular characteristics and problems, ceilings on the amount of a grant or award, the number of years a program will be supported, reductions in the amount of support over the duration of the program, requirements for local matching funds, or restrictions on the types of staff or equipment that will be funded. These and other types of requirements imposed by funders constrain the use of resources and require careful preparations to implement.

The continuation of the CPO case example demonstrates how funders' mandates have implications for the charge and the planning effort.

◆ ◆ ◆

Consumer Protection Office Case Example:
The Third Planning Committee Meeting

The director of the CPO reported that the state consumer affairs office and county government underwrite some of the current activities of the CPO. He advised the committee about jurisdictional responsibilities and the legal and financial consequences of changing or terminating some of the existing services of the CPO. He informed the committee that some state funds are granted on the condition of local intergovernmental cooperation, and he distributed a synthesis of this information to the members.

The chair reminded the group that within two years a state law would go into effect that would prohibit the disposal of grass clippings, leaves, and brush in landfills. Residents would have to start composting and would need instruction about the process to prevent offensive odors and the disposal of garbage that does not degrade easily, which might attract insects, rodents, and other animals, and that could contribute to health hazards. The committee thought this was a splendid idea, and it agreed with a member who said that the CPO might have to change to the CEPO: Consumer and Environmental Protection Office.

◆ ◆ ◆

Some mandates that are pertinent to the planning venture can be determined and declared from the outset, and steps should be taken to collect and examine essential documents to determine what types of requirements exist and the aspects of the charge, the program design, or the planning processes that are affected. Source documents may include program-enabling legislation and other statutes; codes, standards, rules and regulations; judicial decisions; grant applications, award notices, and contracts; and position statements of significant interest groups. Some source documents may not be available because they are out of print or their requirements are being revised or challenged. Therefore planners may need to seek exchanges with key organizational informants to obtain their interpretations of what is required.

There are ways of surmounting the complexity and uncertainty about directives and constraints. Some local and regional planning bodies, as well as colleges and universities, provide limited technical assistance to staff members from service organizations. In large organizations, there are often staff familiar with grants, contracts, relationships with funders, insurance reimbursements, and related matters. They can be sought out to demystify some of the expectations, to interpret policies, and to read the fine print and read "between the lines." Large funding bodies often have personnel (grants officers) who are assigned to applicant and recipient agencies in designated regions with responsibility to facilitate compliance with funding requirements and to interpret policies and expectations. Persons who are new to program planning are encouraged to seek advice and assistance before, during, and after developing the plan from consultants or personnel in other organizations who have a record of achievement with these tasks.

Mandates that directly impinge on the plan for a new program, or for a change in an existing one, should be concretely stated in the appropriate place in the final report (see item number 15 in the requisites section later in the chapter), including both the source and the nature of the requirement. Among other reasons, such citation helps those who are responsible for reviewing and approving the plan to point to its derivation from the mandates and its congruence with them, and it aids those who will be assigned to the work of implementation as they seek to ensure that all important requirements have been satisfied.

Determine How the Condition Came to the Attention of Officials

Planners may have to backtrack from the issuance of the charge and examine the factors that influenced officials to commence planning. Social problems and undesirable social conditions are recognized by administrators of human service organizations under a variety of circumstances. Influential or outspoken individuals, groups, or associations may urge that it is timely and legitimate to direct public attention to a problem because its nature or seriousness can no longer be tolerated. Changes in social attitudes and political priorities toward a social problem are affected by its incidence (the number of new situations in an area during a specific period), prevalence (the existing number of situations in an area during a specific period), changes in standards of living, and threats to life or well-being. The availability and utility of new solutions to old problems may motivate officials to initiate planning (for example, psychotropic drugs and their impact on community placement of the mentally ill). Belief that a problem can be corrected and that decision makers are likely to be responsive have a bearing on problem recognition. Sometimes service organizations attend to social problems and conditions only when presented with an opportunity to address them (for example, new funding or political resolve). Occasionally, officials are able to create opportunities to address problems that they are ready to recognize (for example, increased willingness to cooperate with organizations that serve the same target population).

Social problems and undesirable social conditions find their way to the top of organizational agendas in several ways:

- Reports from staff who have some ongoing responsibility for monitoring a problem or condition

- Requests, urges, demands, and petitions of special-interest groups or concerned citizens
- Media coverage that raises public consciousness about a problem or condition
- Government officials who use their influence or authority to direct attention and resources to their priorities
- Funding bodies that provide monies as incentives to service organizations to address a condition or social problem
- Social science studies

Desirable social conditions, such as effective use of leisure time, community or neighborhood cohesion, self-actualization and personal growth, ethnic and race relations, assimilation of refugees, and accessibility to the performing arts, are championed by church, political, civic, and business leaders and special-interest or advocacy groups.

Concerns about program effectiveness and efficiency come to the attention of administrators in several ways:

- Program staff discover and report important service delivery problems in the course of providing services.
- Ongoing monitoring of an organization's program operations reveals major shortcomings.
- Governmental and funding agencies require changes in program features as a consequence of program reviews.
- The complaints of program participants or other organizations reach a level that cannot be ignored.
- Professional, governmental, and scientific studies provide assessments of problems, evaluations of programs, and recommendations for improvement.

Determine Who the Important Stakeholders Are

In many planning ventures, it is essential to determine who the important stakeholders are in the planning process and outcome, as well as the balance of support and opposition among staff, board members, service recipients, officials of other organizations and community groups, and others. It is important to begin arranging collateral assistance or liaison relationships or to reconsider the composition of the team. The following continuation of the CPO case example illustrates how planners may pursue this task and why they have to incorporate it into their work plan.

◆ ◆ ◆

Consumer Protection Office Case Example: Continuation of the Third Planning Committee Meeting

As the committee discussed the "significant others" who should be involved in the planning venture, one member focused on the council's desire to move toward mediation and conflict resolution. He believed that the Legal Aid Bureau and members of the bar and the judiciary might have some questions about the CPO's movement into "legal territory," or if they supported the idea, they might want some ownership of a conflict resolution program. He suggested that someone ought to "touch base" with them and find out what they thought about the idea. The chair of the committee volunteered to confer with the city attorney to get his reading on whether any preliminary contacts should be made with the legal community prior to a public discussion of these matters at a council meeting. The BBB representative said, "While you're there, I suggest that you check with him about the legality of publishing information about rental properties and rental fees. There may be some liabilities the city should know about."

◆ ◆ ◆

Such complex decision making about representation and stakeholders is not universal to all planning ventures. However, the planning charge may not be carried out effectively and planning goals may not be achieved if important stakeholders are not consulted or involved in the planning effort in some way.

With the help of officials and initial appointees to the work group, stakeholders can be identified by exploring several questions: Who are the key players or spokespersons in the community associated with the condition, problem, or issue that is the substance of the charge? Who are the persons within and outside the organization that will be affected by the group's work? Which departments within the organization and agencies in the community will be affected by the group's work? What is the nature of the stakeholders' investment or interest in the matters that the work group will be addressing? Some terms are useful in identifying stakeholders. Who has a lot of *sunk costs* in the program or issue? Sunk costs are one or more of the following: long-term involvement, substantial financial or staff investments, organizational identity that is associated with the program or issue, and "psychological investments," for example, "This is our baby. We gave birth to this program." Who are the gatekeepers? "Whose toes will we be stepping on?" "Who has a lot to gain from our efforts?"

In identifying stakeholders and deciding on the type and level of their involvement in the planning project, planners should be mindful of stakeholders with several agendas that may or may not conflict with the planning team's ability to carry out its work. For example, in one situation, shortly after the planning project began, the representative of an influential stakeholder informed the group that his boss supported the development of several components of the program, but he would not support one component under consideration. If the group pursued the unfavorable component, he would withdraw support for the whole program and would advocate for its rejection with officials. In another situation, one stakeholder in a planning project supported and contributed to it, but she also maneuvered herself and her unit into a position to be administratively responsible for the new program. In some planning projects, some stakeholders are critical to its success, and they must be involved regardless of their agendas.

This concludes the discussion of the initial work plan and the tasks that might flow from the review and interpretation of the charge. There is another matter that must be addressed before planners can move onto the next stage of planning.

Review the Requisites for the Completed Program Plan Document

This section focuses on the main components that a report of a completed program planning process should include and present in a well-organized written document—the plan—for official review and approval. These components provide a critical end-of-the-process lighthouse for planning teams, and therefore for their work plans. These requisites tell a team where it should end its work, complementing whatever is in the charge. However, the team should not wait until the very end to draft its report. The requisites should be used to guide the incremental drafting of interim reports or sections of the final report as planning unfolds, and the final plan document for submission should increasingly pull the planning team to the end. It is essential for the planning team to give early attention to the features of the plan that they ultimately will be required to detail in a document, and the incremental drafting of the report should be included in the overall work plan for the whole planning effort (see Chapter Eight).

After a brief discussion, the requisites are listed with citations of the several formats in which they are prepared and presented (for example, straight text, diagrams or displays, standardized forms). This is followed by discussion of the sources, formats, and uses of these components, as well as how their preparation facilitates the planning process. Finally, the meanings, variations, and applications of each component are discussed.

Why These Are Requisites

The final plan to be submitted should be a single coherent document that makes it possible for organizational officials to understand all important aspects of the program plan being presented and to make decisions about the proposals it contains. As discussed previously, the process of producing the report itself is the documentation, and each of the components and their explanations are the specifications. Each of the requisite components is important and probably necessary for effective decision making. This list of requisite components incorporates the kinds of basic plan information that are now generally required among organizations, funders, and other bodies that determine whether a given program plan can win approval and be implemented.

Plans for New Versus Changed Programs

There are no distinctions here between what is necessary for presentation of entirely new service programs and what is necessary for changes in ongoing programs. Some changes to existing programs may seem so minor as to need little or no documentation, but this can be decided only by the officials responsible for approving any change. Changes in ongoing programs are often of considerable scope and involve many or most of these requisites. Furthermore, planners may fail to reckon with the implications of proposed changes for other parts of the organization and its services, or with those of outside regulatory bodies or constituencies. It is therefore strongly recommended that every plan report include attention to all of the requisites, adjusting the extent of explication appropriately. See Exhibit 3.1 for the complete list of requisites for program plan documents.

Sources of the Requisites

In terms of authentication, all requisites are drawn from a broad span of contemporary program and related materials. These include standardized outlines and proposal requirements that are routinely set forth by funding bodies (United Way; foundations; and local, state, and federal governments and their major departments). Similar requisites are defined by licensing and regulatory bodies. These kinds of funding and authorizing bodies are alike in that they receive many proposals and applications from several organizations. They have long since found it necessary to inform applicants about the details of what they need to know so that submissions meet minimum standards of completeness, format, and length. Adherence to declared requirements helps ensure that reviewers understand all materials, and competing requests can be judged on their substantive merits. Further, the volume of applications received for review—especially by government agencies and large foundations—necessitates some uniformity of presentation (with variations or additions appropriate to specific areas of interest).

EXHIBIT 3.1. REQUISITE COMPONENTS OF COMPLETED PROGRAM PLAN DOCUMENTS.

1. "Executive summary" or synopsis of entire document (and title page)	T
2. Citation of authors, contributors, and source(s) of plan materials	S, T
3. Table of contents or outline of plan document	S, T
4. Summary of charge or authorization for the plan (and its effort)	T
5. Statement of the problem or condition to be remedied or optimized and summary of its evidence or needs assessment	T
6. Statement of the specific service goals and objectives to be achieved	T
7. Identification of the particular target population to be served, as delimited	T
8. Description of the services to be provided (to achieve the service goals)	D, T
9. Calendars, schedules, charts, and time lines for service phases and cycles	T, C, D
10. Relationships to other service programs (and those in other organizations?)	T, C
11. Procedures for monitoring program processes and assessing results	T
12. Inventories of the resources required to conduct the program	T, S, D
13. Organization's capability to host and conduct the program	T
14. Program reporting and accountability requirements and procedures	T, S
15. Applicable statutory, regulatory, code, certification, and other requirements	T, S
16. Plan review and approval steps and implementation recommendations	T, S

Note: Supplementary and technical materials are usually appended. *T* indicates a text document; *C* indicates a chart; *D* indicates another type of display; *S* indicates that standards exist.

Most of these requirements have direct counterparts for decision making within the host organization, especially when it is large and well established. (For example, How does this new program comport with our mission and mandates? How should it be meshed with our other services? Will this program change require more or different resources, and if so, which ones?) For both insiders and outsiders then, the question is this: What do we need to know in order to understand and evaluate the plan about which we must reach a decision? These are among the reasons for the widespread adoption of these requisites among service organizations.

Outside financial support—and perhaps collaboration or authorizations—are frequently expected or required for both new and continuing programs. Because these kinds of information (and more) must be made available to obtain outside approvals or funding, economy of effort requires preparing and presenting most of it when plans are submitted for official internal review.

Variable Formats, Terms, and Phrases

Each service organization and each funder or other external body declares its own content outlines, format requirements, actual forms, and other terms in which it requires proposals to be prepared. The common characteristic is standardization among all proposals to be submitted. The apparent diversity in the formats and terms among these bodies may obscure their underlying similarity of content. Diversity is perhaps greatest in their formats and in the kinds of technical materials that must be included (an area of fast-developing conventions, if not yet standards). But budgets, for example, have long since converged toward almost identical structures (although persons new to budgeting may not recognize this). Expectations for graphic displays of schedules, flowcharts, and time lines have become common, but not yet standardized.

The language and perhaps the order of such materials may be different, with one body subsuming certain matter under different headings or giving it greater prominence. Generic terms are used here for the components, because the many distinctions do not make significant differences.

Usefulness of the Requisites for Planners

The requisite components list clarifies that all essential steps in planning are directed at preparation of a document, and this is the product needed for review and decision making by others. The aim of planning is to produce the plan report as product, so these product requirements should guide planning thought and procedure. Attention to these requisites during all stages of the planning process can help participants better understand how work on both substantive and procedural tasks will eventually take definite form within a composite but coherent plan document. The order of the items in the list clarifies the necessity for the overall plan to be unified. (In Exhibit 3.1, the statement of the problem, item number 5, is followed by the formulation of program goals and objectives, item number 6, clarifying the necessary connections between these elements.) The specification of the formats in which one plan component after another is best communicated can aid in understanding how each part of the emerging plan will take concrete expression and have its place in direct relation to all other parts.

A final argument for the requisites is their value in facilitating implementation after a plan is approved. In order for those undertaking implementation to be able to conform to all important elements of the plan, sufficient information must be included in the document that will guide them. (See Chapter Eight for a discussion of the information items that may appropriately be carried over to the implementation process). Plan documents will vary in the amount of detail presented on each component. In general, the more the better, provided it is clearly and succinctly stated.

The following is a continuation of the CPO case example, which explains what the committee decided about the requisites of the proposals to be submitted to the council.

◆ ◆ ◆

Consumer Protection Office Case Example: Continuation of the Third Planning Committee Meeting

At one point during the third meeting, the chair directed the committee's attention to one of the remaining items on its initial work plan: determine the elements and format of the proposal to be submitted to the administrator and the council. She and the director of the CPO had met between meetings and were prepared to present their recommendations.

She began by recalling discussions during the first two meetings in which clarifications were made about the council's expectations: the team was responsible for proposing "possible endeavors and approaches" to stimulate the council's review, thinking, and decisions, and "detailed program proposals were not necessary." "We don't have to settle on these versus those programs. We can even present competing alternatives. This will reduce the need to reconcile or resolve what may be important differences of opinion or pragmatic choices dictated by CPO resources." The team was pleased with this approach, but the BBB representative wondered if an alternative could be presented, even if only one person supported it. The chair praised him for raising a good point but suggested that the matter could be resolved if and when the team encountered such a situation down the line. The members agreed, and she proceeded with the presentation of the recommendations prepared by the CPO director and her.

"The chair's briefing of the administrator during the eighth week should focus on work accomplished, the direction the committee is taking, problems, possible difficulties, and an outline of the written report. The written report should begin with a summation of the charge as it was presented to the team by the administrator, followed by a section that describes the mission and current services of the CPO with emphasis on its mandatory programs and services. The rest of the report should focus on four topics: (1) the concerns and complaints of citizens and officials, (2) relevant services provided by local organizations, (3) services provided in comparable communities, and (4) prospects for the CPO in Midland. A summary of how the committee conducted its work over the course of three months, including frequency of meetings, persons and organizations involved, methods of investigation, etcetera, could be inserted in the Appendix."

After the committee discussed the recommendations, it came to the following two conclusions:

Number one. Sections of the report would be written while work was in progress. The chair agreed to write the charge and the section on methods for the Appendix. The CPO director agreed to draft a statement about the CPO and assigned a staff member to develop sections on model programs in other cities and relevant services provided locally. The other writing assignments would be based on who worked on which aspects of the charge, which could be determined as early as the next meeting.

Number two. The details of what should be included in the complaints, concerns, and prospects sections would depend on what the team discovered and what it proposed. However, general agreement was reached on several matters. The complaints and concerns section should briefly state the nature and the consequences of each condition or problem, its magnitude (if it could be known), and the characteristics of those affected. The prospects section should provide the council with a description of the proposed services, the staff qualifications essential to the provision of services, some notion of the target population, the number of people who might be served with a minimal staffing plan, and some rough estimates of costs.

The director outlined what the members were facing. "So far, we have agreed to tackle mediation and conflict resolution methods, false advertising, product safety, high rental fees for housing, home-based ecological practices and conservation, and within the latter category we have included energy conservation in low-income housing, groundwater contamination, composting, and recycling of household solid waste such as cans, glass, and paper products—eight items in all. If we were to write only one single-spaced page for each complaint and concern and two pages for each proposed service, the report would be twenty-four pages long. Council members are swamped with reports, and they do not 'weigh by the pound' in evaluating proposals." After a brief discussion, team members agreed to limit the report to approximately twenty-five pages.

◆ ◆ ◆

Develop an Overall Work Plan for the Whole Planning Effort

After a team achieves a determinate understanding of its charge, obtains background information, identifies mandates, recognizes stakeholders, reviews the requisites for the program plan document, and completes other elements of its initial work plan, it can proceed toward an overall work plan for the whole planning effort. Work plans are intrinsically dependent on the nature and scope of the task at hand, on the context in which the work is carried forward, and on the persons who compose the team engaged in that task. Insofar as the charge that authorizes the planning process is concretely detailed in any of its fundamental aspects (for example, definition of the problem, the kind of service to be planned or changed, deadlines and due dates), these automatically serve as elements of the work plan. All other elements must be formulated to some sufficient degree if team efforts are to remain focused, directed, coordinated, and timely. The more complex the task, the more extensive the work plan must be.

Work plans are almost invariably formulated in a progressive manner and amplified during the process, but never completely detailed. They cannot be highly detailed until participants have immersed themselves in the planning effort and have identified numerous elements necessary to its achievement. The degree of detail or specification appropriate for a work plan should be sufficient to ensure optimum use of participants' time and skills, to provide clear directions for work and coordination, and to assess progress toward task goals. Work plans should remain open to change, extension, and adaptation as experience develops, more matters are determined, work is completed, and the unexpected is encountered. To this end, work plans have to be periodically redeveloped during and between each stage of planning and specified as planning unfolds. The work plan can be used to nudge the team if it bogs down, keep it on course, and take stock of how things are going as the group moves through the stages of planning.

By the end of the first set of meetings, the planning group should develop a fairly concrete and comprehensive work plan that includes the major steps between the review and interpretation of the charge and the submission of the completed plan document to officials. There are limits on how far ahead a team can look and how specific it can be in developing its work plan. Not all intervening steps need to be identified, but they do need to be identified to the extent that the beginning and the end are really linked, thus establishing the means-end nature of planning processes. To get a general sense of their work, teams may rely on the essential tasks in each of the stages of planning (outlined in the Part Two Opener). For example, depending on the particular planning venture, at some point the team may have to determine the methods to study the problem, interpret the findings of the problem analysis, interpret needs, set priorities, formulate goals and objectives, and design a new program or redesign an existing one.

The following continuation of the case example shows how a planning team might begin to develop its overall work plan.

◆ ◆ ◆

Consumer Protection Office Case Example: The Fourth Planning Committee Meeting

To facilitate the team's development of an overall work plan, the chair gave each member several nine-inch by fourteen-inch work sheets, which listed the remaining weeks of the planning effort across the top (week three, week four, and so forth). Some of the tasks and deadlines had already been included by the chair, based on one of the concrete directions embedded in the charge (for example, three-month deadline) and on what the team had agreed on in its first three meetings:

1. CPO director and BBB representative present report on citizen complaints and concerns—week three.
2. CPO director presents draft description of CPO programs (with emphasis on mandated services) to be included in the final report—week three.
3. CPO staff engage in modest effort to gather and synthesize information on false advertising re the contents and benefits of food, supplements, etcetera, and report to team—week 3.
4. Chair contacts city attorney and if necessary the Legal Aid Bureau—weeks three and four, respectively.
5. Committee reviews draft of relevant services by local providers and model programs in other cities—week five.
6. Chair briefs the city administrator on progress, alerts him to difficulties—week eight.
7. Team to focus on mediation and conflict resolution methods, false advertising, product safety, high rental fees for housing, home-based ecological practices and conservation (energy conservation in low-income housing, groundwater contamination, composting, and recycling of household solid waste). Concrete tasks, specific assignments, and deadlines for completion to be determined.

The chair led the team in a discussion of the division of labor and the tasks that had to be addressed. The team agreed that members should be assigned to specific areas rather than having everyone work on all eight major areas.

The director of the CPO and the BBB representative reported that their statistical reports about citizen complaints and concerns pertained only to false advertising, high rents, and product safety. Information about problems related to energy conservation in low-income rental housing, improper disposal of hazardous household waste, composting, and community failure to recycle would have to be obtained elsewhere. The problems that might be addressed through mediation and dispute resolution also needed to be addressed. The investigation into these problems was divided among the members, with suggestions as to who could provide the information, and time frames were established for reporting back to the committee. The chair reminded the group that it was asked to chart some endeavors that the CPO might undertake. "We don't have to study any problems in depth, and we can rely on information that is in current reports or files."

The BBB representative volunteered to examine the reports from other BBBs in similar-sized cities and check into the backlog of cases in small claims court because that might have some implications for a dispute resolution program directed toward consumers and businesses. He estimated that that could be done by the fourth week. One of the CPO staff members was assigned to obtain information and prepare a report on health problems, groundwater contamination, and improper disposal of household hazardous wastes by the fifth week. The other CPO staff member was assigned to determine (within two weeks) whether any county, state, or federal agencies, including the FDA and the State Bureau of Licensing and Regulation, had any programs related to the eight areas or whether they had superordinate control over those areas. The chair volunteered to obtain some information about mediation and conflict resolution centers in other cities. The BBB representative volunteered to consult with the utility company to determine whether it could shed any light on the participation of owners of low-income rental housing in its energy conservation program, and the citizens' group representative agreed to draft by the fourth week a statement of the problem based on the experience of groups and organizations he represented.

The chair remarked that during earlier meetings, the group had offered some general suggestions for services that might be appropriate for the city of Midland, but concrete tasks related to developing and proposing those services had not been determined and assigned. She suggested that the committee would have to begin drafting such proposals by the seventh week, and that would give the team at least six meetings to propose and agree on the "new approaches and endeavors" requested by the council and to draft the final report. The members agreed to a division of labor and the proposed timetable.

After the team finished listing, clustering, and scheduling its planning activities, the chair complimented the group for its accomplishments, including the tasks in the initial work plan. She ended the meeting by reviewing what had been agreed on at that day's meeting and at earlier meetings and reported that she would have the overall work plan typed and circulated at the next meeting.

◆ ◆ ◆

The overall work plan must address the subtasks unique to the planning endeavor, their assignment to team members or others, and deadlines for completion. After the work plan is drafted, the team should mull it over and evaluate whether it is complete and realistic, and members should be given an opportunity to amend elements over which they have discretion.

Looking Ahead: Expect Changes in the Charge, Mandates, and Policies

This section addresses the nature of charges, mandates, and policies and how they impinge on subsequent stages of planning. The discussion of the initiation of program planning could well leave the reader with a sense that mandates, policies, commitments, and charges are unchanging. But this is almost never the case, even when organization policymakers set forth very clear, detailed, and determinate objectives for the planning effort and call for only one review of the results before expecting to take action. Officials typically modify, extend, redefine, even reverse major elements in the policies or charges that they set forth. The charge might be amended to greatly speed up (or prolong) the planning deadline or to impose still other midstream changes.

Authorities outside the organization doing the planning might declare a change in a mandate or policy that then requires a change in an internal policy and the planning charge, sometimes drastically intruding on work under way, other times nullifying major parts of a plan on its initial submission. For example, the funder's authorization may be altered to redirect a new program's primary focus toward a mere segment of the recipients as they were originally conceived, or a policy may be modified that reduces the scope of the program by half.

All of these changes cause great dismay among those working diligently under the initial understandings. Are the decision makers being arbitrary? Have they any idea of the havoc they are creating? Should we really keep working at this thing, or should we try to resign in protest? Staff may become disillusioned when changes are made or constraints are imposed on the planning process while it is under way. Unless these shifts are anticipated from the outset and planners make allowance for them in their initial (and subsequent) plan submissions, such shifts can be extremely frustrating and can be viewed almost as reneging on good faith commitments. One of the key responsibilities of the leader, and the other team members as well, is to scan the decision environment and bring back to the group information that may affect its work.

Why do decision makers cause such difficulties and create such frustrations? There are two main sets of reasons why it is wise to anticipate changes from the beginning and to prepare for constructive responses to them during the planning process. One set of explanations takes into account developments outside the organization that can be neither controlled nor fully anticipated at the time the initial charge is defined. Funding sources are continuously modifying their priorities, their fiscal and policy commitments, and other conditions that powerfully affect program plans. (And the reasons for these changes are, in turn, caused by unforeseen developments in the funding sources' own environments, including legislative or political twists and turns.) Other outside influences on the planning process include changes in scientific knowledge and technology (especially in the health and ecology areas) and population and economic developments. There is no way that an organization's policymakers can (or should) shield their personnel from the impact of such changes in the larger community and society.

A second set of explanations for changes in the planning process are intrinsic to the nature of service programs, their development (including planning), and their adaptation. If the decision makers knew in advance all of the major features of the new program to be developed (or changed) and implemented, there would be little need for planning as such. Somehow these features would be embodied in the process of their initial decision making. Even the most farsighted board or other policy group cannot possess such infinite wisdom, so if they were to call for no changes during the planning process, they would simply be binding themselves to whatever the planners would propose—an obviously intolerable relinquishment of responsibility.

What usually happens is that plans—whether preliminary or final—immediately help decision makers clarify important matters that require rethinking or change and therefore a resumption of the planning process. In fact, persons involved in planning usually discover in the course of their work that many aspects of the mandate, policy, or charge—as well as the problem or need toward which they are directed—are hard to grasp or to codify in a plan. They find that many new issues arise that call for rethinking the endeavor in part or in total and that proposed solutions seem to present new dilemmas that require further review. As noted throughout the chapters, human problems are fraught with uncertainties, dilemmas, and contradictions, and interventions designed to address these problems also present many intransigent complexities.

Given these conditions, persons who undertake planning new programs or making major changes in ongoing programs should adopt a problem-exploring approach as an integral and deliberate part of their work toward developing solutions to fulfill a charge. They should search for the points and areas that—given the circumstances of their place and time—clearly raise new issues of policy import or seem likely to deserve (if not require) further attention by those who defined their charge initially. This anticipates a give-and-take or back-and-forth sequence between decision makers and planners. By this means, planners can constructively shape their first submissions so as to provoke careful reexaminations of the problem definition as well as renewal of the charge to submit a plan for tackling it. Mutual trust and respect are nurtured, frustration is reduced, and all parties can gain a shared sense of significant accomplishment.

◆ ◆ ◆

Chapter Four explores the analysis stage of planning. It is at this stage that planners tackle problem analysis and needs assessment. This is when they start to gain an understanding of the nature of the problems facing the prospective recipients of the service. Planners address several questions: What are the manifestations of the problem, including its features, consequences, magnitude, and distribution? What are its causes? How is the problem experienced by those who are affected by it? What are the characteristics of those who are affected by it?

CHAPTER FOUR

ANALYZING PROBLEMS AND ASSESSING NEEDS

The second period of planning is the analysis stage. Its primary activities—problem analysis and needs assessment—are aimed at unraveling and understanding the nature of the problem and the needs of the people experiencing them. The completion of these activities also serves other purposes: to guide the formulation of program goals and objectives, program design, and resource allocation; to provide officials and funders with evidence that problems and needs exist; and to legitimate requests for funds.

This chapter focuses on the eleven tasks associated with problem analysis and needs assessment:

1. Find out what the planners already know about the nature of the problems and needs.
2. Decide what more has to be known about the problems and needs and the people experiencing them to plan or improve a service program.
3. Plan the approaches to needs assessment.
4. Decide the methods for carrying out the problem analysis and needs assessment.
5. Assign investigative tasks.
6. Collect data.
7. Analyze the data and prepare initial findings and supporting data to present to the planning group.

8. Analyze the initial findings and supporting data, and determine the needs that will be translated into program goals and objectives and targets of intervention.
9. Analyze opportunities for intervention.
10. Determine priorities.
11. Write the preliminary draft of the problem statement.

In many planning projects, especially those focused on new programs, all of these tasks must be addressed. In some projects, some tasks do not have to be carried out because the problem analysis and needs assessment have been completed by another entity. For example, local and regional agencies, often known as the Area Agency on Aging; organizations affiliated with United Way; and central planning units in state agencies conduct studies and then distribute the findings to service providers and local units of state government to enable them to plan effectively. In these situations, planning teams may not have to engage in tasks 3 through 6, but they certainly must address tasks 1 and 2 and probably have to adapt tasks 8 through 11. The nature, scope, and quality of these studies vary, and they may not be sufficiently congruent with the purposes of particular planning projects. So it is up to planners to decide which tasks must be addressed for their planning project.

Before addressing these tasks, the chapter will clarify the meaning of three key concepts, introduce the elements of problem analysis and needs assessment, and provide a case example that will illustrate the discussion.

Key Concepts

Conditions are real-world events, matters, and circumstances, both human and non-human (for example, infant mortality rates and parts per million of a toxic chemical in the water supply), and these change over time. All can be objectively observed and measured with varying degrees of certainty, reliability, and validity. Each condition has underlying causes that, unlike the conditions themselves, may or may not be known or observable (for example, gulf war syndrome and fetal alcohol syndrome). Only some conditions give rise to perceptions of problems and needs.

Problems and *needs* are both in the eyes and minds of those who perceive, experience, assess, or assert them. Both refer to kinds of conditions, but both vary with the valuational and perceptual orientations of the observers. Problems are manifestations of observed or asserted conditions about which there is concern and a basis on which this concern rests (for example, the condition violates some social values, it is experienced as an adversity, or it departs from some accepted standard). Need refers to something that is essential or desired to maintain well-being (for example, self-esteem, companionship, and food) or something that is necessary to relieve a state of deficiency or deprivation (for example, poor nutrition, inadequate job skills, and homelessness) (United Way of America, 1982, pp. 8–9; Mayer, 1985, pp. 127–129; York, 1982, pp. 56–57; Gates, 1980, pp. 101–118).

The Elements of Problem Analysis and Needs Assessment

Problem analysis is a discovery and learning activity directed at understanding and describing the nature of the problem that is of concern to planners. Planners may ascertain the nature of the problem by addressing the following questions: What are the manifestations of the problem, including its features, consequences, magnitude, and distribution? How is the problem experienced by the persons who are affected by it? What are the characteristics of the persons who are affected by it? What factors either contribute to the problem or are barriers to its solution?

Needs assessment is also a discovery and learning activity. It is directed at interpreting what is necessary or desirable for a particular set of persons based on these factors: knowledge of a problem or experience with a problem, the findings from the problem analysis, or direct measures of need. Thus problems become translated into needs, but regardless of how they are determined, needs are then addressed in program objectives and by a service program. For example, children who are being abused (the problem) are at risk (consequence), which translates into a need for protection. Protection of these children can be accomplished through daily lengthy visits of a parental coach and counselor, placing the child in foster care, court-ordered attendance in parenting and anger management classes, or other services. The problem of adverse drug reactions among the elderly may be translated into a need for correct usage of drugs. This need can be met through provision of information about medications in a health education program, assistance in medication management, and drug audits by pharmacists at the time prescriptions are filled. Problem analysis and needs assessment are complementary and integrally related activities. Sometimes these tasks are carried out concurrently and at other times sequentially. In this chapter, the terms *investigation, inquiry,* and *exploration* are used to refer to both activities. The complex relationship between problem analysis and needs assessment is discussed later in the chapter.

Assessing Need for Services: A Cautionary Note

As used here, need refers to something that is judged essential for well-being or something that is required to relieve a deficiency or deprivation. Need has also been used to refer to the services intended to satisfy it (need for nutrition education, vocational training, or shelter). For that reason, some needs assessments have focused on the need for services instead of the needs of the persons experiencing the problem. The major pitfall in assessing needs for services is that the lack of services and resources (solutions) is conceived as *the problem*. This perspective then leads to the formulation of program objectives in terms of services to be provided, and it results in the selection of solutions that have not been customized to the needs of prospective recipients.

There are other pitfalls to this approach. Services that staff prefer may predominate in assessing the needs of prospective service beneficiaries and the various ways to meet them. Sometimes a service introduced as but one means of helping individuals in need becomes the only way to help them. Even if some important needs are being met by current services, staff who are asked to assess need for services are sometimes not given the opportunity to look at other related needs that may have developed or that were not identified within the initial set.

Nevertheless sometimes planners are required to assess need for a particular service, because that is what funders want from organizations seeking financial support (for example, one local Area Agency on Aging just wanted to know how many elders needed home delivery of hot meals). While fulfilling the proposal requirements of the funder, it is recommended that planners also direct their efforts to assessing *needs as attributes* of persons or segments of a community (for example, assess whether elders have proper nutrition and what the barriers are to getting them nutritious meals and then decide which service is appropriate, such as Meals on Wheels, congregate meals, or food stamps). The decision about a particular service should be addressed later in the planning process, after the findings from the problem analysis and the needs assessment have been explored and as program goals and objectives are being formulated. This position is recommended whether funders require an assessment of need for services or not. (See the section on Approaches to Needs Assessment later in this chapter.)

Introduction to the Case Example

In this chapter, the case example focuses on delays in service (a program operational problem) and on sexual assault of children (the social problem) to illustrate the discussion of the elements and steps of the analysis stage. The focus of the example is on planning change in an existing program rather than on planning a new program because changing an existing program is more common in the work life of the staff in service organizations. The case example shows that problematic program operations, and any proposed changes, cannot be considered apart from the problems and needs of abused children. The case example is presented in segments. The first segment includes information on the auspices of the program, the types of services provided, the recipients, the presenting problem, the charge to the planning work group, and other background information. Segments that describe the activities of the work group will follow in the discussion of particular elements and steps. The case example preserves some realities of planning, but in the interest of readability, many of the complexities associated with planning services for sexually abused children have been omitted. (A sexual assault may or may not be substantiated at the time of referral to an agency. But to avoid the awkward use of *victim or alleged victim, abuse or alleged abuse,* and *perpetrator or alleged perpetrator,* the following case example just uses the terms *victim, abuse,* and *perpetrator* to mean one or the other.)

◆ ◆ ◆

The Counseling and Advocacy Center Case Example: The Waiting List Problem

This organization wanted to figure out how to facilitate service to traumatized children without adding to their trauma with long waits for service. It also needed to figure out how to meet the requirements of its grant to provide crisis management services in a timely manner.

Background

The Counseling and Advocacy Center (CAC) is a program under the auspices of a nonprofit organization that provides outpatient mental health services to children and their families in a county with a population of two hundred thousand people. The organization was awarded a grant for three years to develop and start up the CAC—a program for sexually abused children and their families. One program director (PD) and four counselors are responsible for its operation. The CAC provides four types of services: crisis management; supportive services to the victim and family during judicial proceedings and law enforcement and protective services investigations of the alleged abuse; clinical assessments of victims and their family situations; and long-term counseling to the victim and family, including the perpetrator, if he or she is a family member and is assessed to be appropriate for a community-based service.

During the first year of operation, 250 victims and families were admitted to the CAC. Most of them were referred by Children's Protective Services and law enforcement agencies. Some were referred by health and social service organizations, and a few were initiated by parents. The referrals include both substantiated and unsubstantiated cases of abuse. (In substantiated cases, there is sufficient evidence to validate the claim that abuse occurred).

Approximately eighteen months after the CAC was established, the program found itself with a significant waiting list of referrals. The PD was concerned about two matters: the consequences of service delays for victims and their families and the fact that the program was not fulfilling its commitment to provide timely crisis management services after the discovery of the sexual assault, as stipulated in the terms of the grant from the foundation. The PD decided to discuss her concerns with the executive director.

The Charge

Shortly after that, the executive director issued the following written charge to the PD: "As we recently agreed, you will chair a work group composed of your staff and Dan from Administrative Services. Your group will explore the factors that are contributing to service delays and propose budget neutral solutions, including plans to deal with the waiting list problem. Due to the urgency of the situation, these tasks must be completed ASAP. I have spoken with Dan. He is ready to give you a large block of time to retrieve data from our management information system and assist in the analysis of the CAC's operations. Let me know if I can help."

Preparations for the First Meeting of the Work Group

The PD met with Dan to orient him to the CAC's admissions practices and to do some groundwork in preparation for the work group's first meeting. The PD informed Dan that she and the four counselors rotate into "admissions officer of the day" once a week. "We deal with phone calls to screen and accept referrals, complete a one-page referral form, and schedule admission interviews between carrying out other counseling tasks. Two hours of the day are set aside for admission interviews that are scheduled and posted two weeks in advance. Counselors schedule initial interviews in any appointment slots that are open on a first-come-first-served basis." After this orientation, the PD asked Dan for his help in some explorations of relevant CAC statistical reports. The PD prepared a memorandum that summarized their findings and her analysis of the characteristics of the cases on the waiting list. The written charge and the memorandum were distributed before the first meeting, with a note asking staff to come prepared to discuss both items and their experiences with the waiting list problem.

◆ ◆ ◆

The rest of the story about the work group will follow in segments in later discussion of the tasks of the analysis stage. The case example will illustrate the discussion. The following section deals with the usual first task for planners in the analysis stage.

Find Out What Planners Already Know About Problems and Needs

During the initiation stage, planners typically begin to share some of what they know about the problem, as they formalize a determinate understanding of the charge, including a shared definition of the problem. At this point in the analysis stage, however, planners should have a concentrated and structured discussion on this matter to take advantage of their expertise and achieve some initial common understandings about the problems and needs.

In some planning ventures (for example, those centering on perceived difficulties with ongoing programs), staff already know a lot about the problem (or think they do) by virtue of their experience, education, and training. Staff may not have to design a study to determine the nature of the problem and needs, but they should find appropriate ways to examine them and test the validity of what they think they know.

Planners may be inclined to bypass the analysis stage when the project is focused on a proposed change in an ongoing program, because the problem appears to be easily understood and amenable to a quick fix, and that may be so. For example, waiting lists are sometimes viewed as problems that do not warrant substantial analysis ("just hire another staff member"). However, there's usually a lot more to this than meets the eye. A decision to omit the problem analysis and needs assessment should be made very carefully.

There are several approaches that planners can take to structure their discussions of what they already know about the problem. If external funding is being sought, planners should immediately consult the funder's guidelines for developing a proposal, so they can focus on what officials want to know about the problem and the kind of documentation that is required. (Planners should have already reviewed and flagged these guidelines during the initiation stage of planning if they were available.) Planners would be wise to use the funder's informational requirements and guidelines to inventory what they already know or have and to follow them exactly from the outset. For example, a state public health department's guidelines for developing the problem statement in proposals for pregnancy prevention included specific informational requirements: description of the service area, including an area map; estimates of need for women below the poverty level; data on estimated demand for services by teens and minorities; data on teen pregnancies; documentation of teenagers' and minorities' failures to use existing services; and waiting times for health care appointments. Assume that some nurses from a county public health department formed a planning committee to develop a pregnancy prevention program. Given the nature of their contacts with patients, they probably know a lot about teenagers' and minorities' failures to use existing services, because they have to deal with its tragic aftermath (for example, low birth weight, birth defects, infant mortality).

The discussion of what planners already know about problems and needs (and what more they need to know) can also be structured by relying on the elements of problem analysis and needs assessment presented earlier: What are the manifestations of the problems and needs, including features, consequences, magnitude, and distribution? What are the causes? How is the problem experienced by the persons who are affected by it? What are the characteristics of the persons who are affected by it? After the planners address these questions, they should substantiate the validity and reliability of what they know with documented facts and independent sources of information.

The continuation of the case example illustrates some of these matters and shows how the work group approached some of them at its first meeting.

◆ ◆ ◆

The Counseling and Advocacy Center Case Example: The First Work Group Meeting

The meeting was devoted to the customary tasks of the initiation stage of planning—reviewing and clarifying the charge, scheduling work group meetings, developing a work plan and a division of labor. The members agreed to meet for two hours every Monday and Friday for the next four weeks, if necessary. They discussed the PD's memorandum that was circulated before the meeting and their experiences with the waiting list problem.

The Features of the Problem

The PD reported that she had been monitoring the delays in service from the outset. During the first fifteen months of operation, staff arranged an initial interview with most of the referrals within a week. During the sixteenth month, a few families had to wait about two weeks before their first interview. "As we approach the end of our eighteenth month of operation, we find ourselves with ten referrals waiting for service. It will take a couple of weeks before the first ones will even be interviewed, and some have not even been scheduled. We receive about five referrals per week. Thus in another two weeks, we could have twenty referrals waiting for service, and that's intolerable for these persons."

Consequences of Delays in Service

Dan, the administrative services staff member, asked why the staff were so concerned about apparently short delays in service. The senior counselor served as spokesperson. "Sexual assault is particularly distressing, and its discovery often precipitates a family crisis, especially if the perpetrator is a parent, live-in partner, or other family member. Sometimes the nonperpetrating parent denies that abuse occurred. Some families want to cover up the problem and welcome the delay to pressure the victim to recant or withhold disclosure. The victim may continue to be at risk. Some situations become volatile, when family members want to lash out in a lethal way. Many families can't cope or don't cope well. Thus the victim and the family need assistance soon after the abuse is reported rather than waiting for an extended period." Dan appreciated being informed about the likely consequences of delays in service and understood the staff's diligence in finding a solution.

Characteristics of the Cases on the Waiting List

The group reviewed the PD's memorandum that summarized the characteristics of the referrals on the waiting list. The information was taken from the one-page form that is routinely completed on all cases at the time of referral.

- Eight referrals involve familial perpetrators, and in four of these cases, the abuse has been substantiated. The perpetrators consist of two fathers, one stepfather, and one live-in partner.
- In the four substantiated cases, the victims are between eight and fourteen years of age. They were able to discuss the abusive incidents during interviews with protective services investigators. One of these cases involves several incidents of abuse and serious sexual misconduct.
- The victims in the unsubstantiated cases are four years of age or under.
- To the best of our knowledge, none of the family perpetrators had prior involvement with the Children's Protective Services Unit regarding allegations of child abuse.
- The two remaining cases involve two older children, who reported being molested at a park by an older teen.
- All of the victims are females.
- One is African American, and the others are white.

Factors That Might Be Contributing to the Problem

The PD reported that as the waiting list problem became apparent, she had conferred with staff to find an explanation for it. "Our records show that the waiting list was not caused by a sudden increase in referrals, by the unavailability of staff due to illness or vacations, or by an increase in recipients' failures to keep appointments. However, one counselor reported problems scheduling her weekly rotation into the admissions office. She checked her activity logs that confirm some missed rotations, which she believes contributed to the waiting list problem. We need to take a closer look at this rotation arrangement."

◆ ◆ ◆

The rotation agreement will be discussed later in this chapter as the case example work group decides what more it needs to know about the nature of the problem.

The preceding segment of the case example shows that the PD already had some understanding of the features and magnitude of the waiting list problem and the characteristics of the cases on the list. The counselors had some understanding of the ways in which family problems can be exacerbated by delays in service. The PD and one counselor had some knowledge of a contributing factor.

Planners can ascertain what they already know about the nature of the problem and needs in several ways:

- They can share knowledge.
- They can apply standards, norms, or regulations in analyzing the problem to make normative judgments about need (for example, the counselors relied on their professional knowledge and experience to make normative judgments about the needs of victims and families—protection for victims and support for families to minimize disorganization).
- They can explore, reflect on, glean insights from, and document their own experience and the experience of others with the problem (for example, the senior counselor reported on the staff's experience with incest cases—perpetrators who are family members).
- They can distribute and discuss relevant file information, statistics, or other kinds of reports that the organization has in hand (for example, the PD prepared a summary of the characteristics of the cases on the waiting list).

In this way, planners can rely on their own expertise and the expertise of others in determining the nature of the problem and needs. Regardless of the approach, someone should be designated to record the work group's key points, observations, and initial findings. Planning groups should develop a cumulative record to draw upon when it is time to draft the problem statement in the final program plan document. (See Chapter Three, Exhibit 3.1, requisite item numbers 5 and 7, and see Chapter Eight.)

The Relationship Between Problem Analysis and Needs Assessment

This is an appropriate place to revisit the relationship between problem analysis and needs assessment and to further clarify what it means to assess needs and how it is done. Getting information about the features and consequences of a problem will enable planners to make determinations about need. Examining the features and consequences of the problem in the case example will illustrate the point. The PD's memorandum included information about such features as the length of time that families were on the waiting list, whether the cases were substantiated or not, the relationship of the perpetrator to the victim, prior sex offenses of the perpetrator, and the sex, race, and age of the victim. The PD extracted this information from the referral forms because she knew that some of it would be useful in determining which families and victims are more vulnerable and traumatized than others and therefore more needy. The senior counselor described the different consequences of delays in service for victims with different characteristics. As a result, planners decided to explore some matters rather than others, because they anticipated that it would help them assess needs and in turn formulate program remedies.

Understanding a problem and the related need may be a straightforward, uncomplicated matter. Substantial time and resources are not necessary to learn about them and figure out what should or could be done (for example, children who are abused need protection; individuals whose homes have been demolished by a flood need shelter; people with low incomes who cannot pay their heating bills need help in paying those bills). But other conditions can be enigmatic, requiring intricate analyses. This generally occurs when large-scale and long-range solutions are sought rather than small-scale and short-range solutions or when underlying rather than manifested conditions are the focus of planning.

Decide What Else Planners Need to Know About Problems and Needs

After sharing what they know about a problem, planners may discover that they know a lot. They may also learn that other organizations, government departments, or researchers have completed a problem analysis and needs assessment, and their findings can be used to guide the planning process. As stated earlier, in these situations planners must decide which tasks of the analysis stage must be addressed and which ones can be set aside.

Conversely, after sharing what they know about a problem, planners may discover that they know very little or that they have divergent perceptions of the problems and needs, partial understandings, and preconceptions or convictions (for example, the hypotheses about an increase in referrals, no-shows, and staff absences from the office as causes of the waiting list were not supported by the CAC's activity reports and file data). In such cases, planners often realize that further investigation is required to sort through these complexities and explore subjects that are not adequately understood. This is a challenging task, because planners cannot explore all of the facets of a problem. However, there are several approaches that planners can take to decide what more they have to know and to delimit the focus of their investigation.

Again, if external funding is being sought, planners must structure their investigation to satisfy the specific informational requirements that funders want in the proposal's statement of the problem and needs. If funders do not have specific informational requirements, readers are advised to try the following.

Planners can rely on techniques for generating ideas in groups (for example, brainstorming) and on the use of work sheets to record answers to the following questions: What do we want or need to know? Why do we want to know it? How will we get the information? and How will we use the information? (Public Management Institute, 1980, pp. 24–25; Van Gundy, 1981, pp. 75–146). These questions help narrow the agenda and should be directed toward the nature of the problem—that is, its features, consequences, causes, magnitude, distribution, and the experiences and characteristics of those affected by it. The following portion of the case example illustrates how this approach might be used. In this segment, the work group used these questions and some work sheets to structure their inquiry into the relationship between incest cases, missed staff rotations into admissions interviews, and the waiting list. These questions were also used to assess the impact of a program operational difficulty on the problems and needs of abused children and their families.

◆ ◆ ◆

The Counseling and Advocacy Center Case Example: Continuation of the First Work Group Meeting

All of the counselors reported that at one time or another, their schedules did not allow them to set aside a block of time for admission interviews. They also had to postpone and reschedule admission interviews, but none of the counselors could recall the exact number and when they had occurred, except for the last week. A couple of counselors even had to cancel admission interviews. The discussion then turned to the factors that hindered staff in their rotation into admissions, and staff shared their experiences.

The discussion focused on the admission and assessment of incest cases, which are more complex and require more time in the early stages of service than other cases. These cases typically require collaboration with the Children's Protective Services Unit of the Department of Social Services, the police, physicians who provide medical examinations, the prosecuting attorney's office, and the juvenile court. This collaboration often includes participation in a weekly meeting focused on interdisciplinary assessment of victims and their family situations and joint service planning. Court hearings and other legal proceedings associated with these cases are also time consuming and unpredictable—counselors and others who are called to testify often must "hurry up and wait," or they are on the witness stand much longer than anticipated. All of these duties result in difficulties in setting aside blocks of time for admission interviews.

The work group decided that these matters merited further exploration. The PD distributed some work sheets and led a brainstorming session focused on four questions: What do we want to know? Why do we want to have this information? How will we get this information? How are we going to use this information? The results as recorded and edited by the PD are presented in the following sections.

What Do We Want to Know?

The brainstorming session turned up six areas of inquiry:

1. Has there been an increase in incest referrals? If there has been an increase, when did it occur?
2. Of the fifty admissions periods that should have been scheduled during the last ten weeks, how many were not scheduled? Of those that were scheduled, how many were postponed or canceled? When did these unscheduled admission periods, postponements, and cancellations occur? Did they coincide with the emergence of the waiting list?
3. Do some counselors have more missed admission rotations than others? When did they occur?
4. Are incest cases evenly distributed among counselors?
5. Has there been an increase in staff attendance at interdisciplinary assessment and joint service planning meetings?
6. Has there been an increase in court appearances? What has been the frequency of attendance and appearance for each counselor?

Why Do We Want to Know This Information?

The brainstorming session turned up three reasons:

1. To learn whether incest referrals have increased and how many missed interviews have occurred

2. To find out whether there is support for the group's speculation that staff activities related to incest cases contributed to the backlog in admissions

3. To get information about each counselor's caseload and activities, which would enable the group to assess if counselors with more incest cases have more difficulty scheduling their rotation into the admissions office

How Will We Get This Information?

Dan will extract and compile relevant information from the CAC's Staff Activity Reports and Admissions Statistics for each of the last ten weeks.

How Are We Going to Use This Information?

If there is a connection between the waiting list, missed staff rotation into the admissions office, and possible increases in incest cases and related staff activities, the work group will know what to target for change. The work group can then make informed recommendations about adjustments in staff assignments.

As the time for adjournment approached, the PD complimented the members for their insightful analysis of the waiting list problem, summarized the group's discussion, and reviewed the work plan. The group agreed to meet at the end of the week to receive Dan's report. The PD also wanted to discuss the kinds of cases on the waiting list, because she believed that it was necessary to set priorities for admission. The PD recognized that she was "pushing it," but the waiting list problem called for a speedy and concentrated effort.

◆ ◆ ◆

This approach (using a few pragmatic questions) has merit because it requires the planners' immediate and disciplined attention to the rationale for the information they want, the methods for obtaining it, and its anticipated use in the planning process. These steps are particularly important in making sure that planners do not stray into a "fishing expedition" that has little or no validity for the development of the service plan.

Other approaches for exploring and deciding what should be the focus of the investigation include consultations with experts, inquiries to comparable programs elsewhere, and reviews of health and social research conducted by various bodies (for example, in examining research on child sexual assault, planners might conclude that abused children have some universal needs, but the types, magnitude, and distribution of abuse would have to be studied locally to figure out the design and scale of the program).

Those Elusive Causes: Which Ones to Explore

Planners may have different perspectives, hypotheses, or convictions about causes (for example, the emergence of the waiting list was initially ascribed to the unavailability of staff due to illness or vacations; an increase in referrals, no-shows, and incest cases; and related staff activities). These differences are not necessarily troublesome, because problems are rarely well understood by relying on only one among several conceptions. The purpose here is to raise the consciousness of planners about their conceptions of any problem and their bearing on the focus of the investigation. Our own conception of any problem influences our response to it, setting off our inclinations to perceive and act on the problem in a particular way that often overlooks other (valid) perspectives. The planners' awareness of their conceptions of the problem provides opportunities to entertain other viewpoints and to decide whether the inquiry should focus on additional or different barriers to meeting needs.

In planning new programs, it is likely that some attention must be given to a causal analysis of social conditions or problems. In planning a change in a current program, a causal analysis may not be necessary, because it probably was carried out when the program was established. However, instead of assuming that this step can be bypassed, planners should explore whether the program change requires a review or a redo of the causal analysis. For example, a juvenile detention center decided that it had to modify its educational and counseling program to better serve a newly emerging critical mass of residents—preteens and early teens who were involved in predatory behavior and aggravated assault. Their defiant behavior in the detention center also challenged the coping skills of the staff. So the staff decided to take a closer look at the juveniles' social histories to see if they could have a better understanding of what was behind this behavior. A review of their case records revealed that in many instances these juveniles led unsupervised lives and were unaccustomed to having someone telling them what to do. On the basis of their analysis, the staff developed a behavioral management program of clear expectations, consistent limits, a highly structured plan of daily activities, and a structure of rewards and consequences for appropriate and inappropriate behavior. It is clear that in planning some program changes, it is necessary to carry out a causal analysis of the social problem of concern. There might be additional factors that contribute to the development of a social problem or condition. Regardless of the focus of the planning venture—program change versus a new program—there are some common steps that planners can follow in deciding which causes they should explore in an investigation in order to keep it within reasonable bounds.

Step One: Propose and List Hypotheses About the Causes of the Problem. Hypotheses about causes of social problems can be derived from the planners' knowledge of human development and behavior or from their understanding of the particular problem or concern. For example, let's assume that you have some expertise in gerontology, and as part of a planning venture, you are designing an investigation into the factors that contribute to adverse drug reactions among the elderly who use prescription and over-the-counter drugs. As you propose hypotheses about the causes that should be explored, you might draw on our knowledge of aging, elders, and drug usage. You might explore short-term memory loss, because you theorize that some elders lose track of how much medication they took and when they took it. You might also explore whether they are inappropriately deferential to physicians as authority figures and are reluctant to ask questions about dosages, side effects, and adherence to drug regimens. Perhaps some elderly patients do not understand the interactional effects of mixing alcohol with over-the-counter and prescription drugs. These and other hypotheses about causes can be developed by reflecting on the planning team's knowledge and experience regarding the population and problem of concern. If the planning team needs help in proposing hypotheses about causes, it can consult experts or the professional literature.

Another approach that planners can use, either in addition to or instead of thinking about causes as determinants of problems, is to do a search for the factors that contribute to or sustain a problem or the factors that are barriers to correcting problems (see Mayer, 1985, p. 129; Kettner, Moroney, and Martin, 1999, pp. 76–80). This approach has merit because it directs planners toward factors that are *observable, accessible,* and *manipulable* and away from fruitless efforts to distinguish ultimate, primary, or "the real" causes of problems that cannot be readily discerned. Furthermore, the identification of these factors enables planners to translate them into needs that can be met by a service program. In the CAC case study, as applied to the problem of abuse, it is reasonable to say that the nonperpetrating parent's denial that "anything ever happened" is a barrier to correcting the abuse. When children are at home alone, that contributes to their vulnerability to abuse. In both instances, the factors are manipulable, and they can be translated into needs (protection and supervision) that can be met through a service program (home visits, counseling, child care, placement of the child, or removal of the perpetrator depending on the gravity of the situation). In applying this approach to the CAC's operational problem, it is reasonable to say that an increase in staff appearances in court caused the staff to miss their regular rotation into admissions, which contributed to delays in service provision. The assignment of every counselor to provide each service is a barrier to correcting the waiting list problem.

The absence of what is desirable or essential for well-being, and states of deficiency and deprivation (unmet need), can be interpreted as barriers to problem resolution or as factors that contribute to and sustain problems. So hypotheses about causes of social problems can also be based on the planners' insights about possible unmet needs, as derived from their understanding of the population and the problems of concern. To illustrate this approach to proposing hypotheses about causes, assume that you are a member of a group that is planning a study of unemployment in your community. In planning which causal factors to explore, you could think about and list the absence of factors that are desirable or essential for employment or the states of deficiency or deprivation related to unemployment. The following list illustrates this approach. It's certainly not definitive.

- *Transportation:* Public transportation is not available. Public transportation exists, but bus routes and schedules to manufacturing plants are not convenient for unemployed persons living in the inner city. The unemployed persons do not have access to a car. Or they do have access to a car, but the car needs repair, insurance, or a license plate, or more than one of these. The unemployed persons do not have a driver's license.
- *Child care:* The unemployed persons can't afford a sitter, or they can't find a sitter.
- *Education and training:* The unemployed persons lack a high school diploma, or they lack vocational skills, or they lack skill in reading, writing, speaking, or calculating.
- *The marketplace:* There is a lack of low-skill jobs. There is discrimination.

This is another example of the convergence of problem analysis and needs assessment, and of their complex and interdependent relationship. As planners decide which hypotheses about causes should be explored, they have an opportunity to plan the assessment of need. The exploration of unmet needs as causes can yield findings about factors that can be translated into needs that can be satisfied through a service program (Mayer, 1985, p. 129).

Up to this point, the discussion has assumed that planners are free to consider a wide range of conceptions of social problems, or they will when they are free to do so. Several factors suggest that these assumptions usually are not warranted. The planning charge and mandates have already been cited as factors that have a strong bearing on planning processes and outcomes, because they may prescribe particular conceptions of the problem. Organizational auspices may have a bearing also, in that particular viewpoints are preferred or some may be unacceptable, as when some church-sponsored agencies believe that sexual relations among unmarried high school students are moral problems, and therefore, teaching the use of contraceptives is inappropriate. The primary function of the organization also limits the perspectives that it can consider. For example, a planning agency—some community councils and coordinating agencies, departments of county and state government—can consider varying conceptions of a problem. However, a service organization with a substantial investment in counseling services is unlikely to entertain conceptions that would move it away from those services. It may be appropriate for an organization to be selective in how it perceives and deals with a problem. Organizations may be obligated or have chosen to focus on segments of a target population or particular manifestations of a problem (for example, young children who have been sexually abused by a family member).

The professional education and training of staff, and their allegiance to particular schools of thought, influence their theoretical preferences, and this has a profound effect on how they view problems, causes, and solutions. For example, some physicians take a biologically deterministic perspective in diagnosing and treating illness, whereas others also recognize psychological and spiritual determinants and treat patients accordingly. Some professionals take an economic and societal perspective on adolescent drinking (for example, persuasive positive images of consumption in alcoholic beverage advertising), but others take a social and psychological perspective (for example, consumption experiences of parents or teen feelings of inadequacy) (Harms and Wolk, 1990).

Doctrinaire allegiance to one perspective will restrict the range of services that can reasonably be considered appropriate to meet a given need. In addition, the persistence of some problems, increases in their scope or severity, and the failure of current programs to correct them are compelling reasons for entertaining other perspectives and other solutions. When the consciousness of planners is raised about the significance of their own or their organization's conception of the problem, it may contribute to a healthy skepticism about the efficacy of social programs and a heightened sensitivity to the complex and changing needs of current or prospective recipients. Of course, it is easy to advise someone to disregard partial or flawed conventional understandings, but it is hard to follow this advice when there are occupational, social, and organizational incentives to follow the party line or accepted "truths." In addition, support from officials is necessary if planners are to depart from conventional perspectives. However, the alternative—complacency—may not only be a disservice to recipients, but it may lead to organizational atrophy. The bottom line is that within the limits identified in the previous chapter (mandates; funder's requirements; organizational mission, policies, and commitments), planners have an obligation to recipients and the community to reconsider and modify or disregard prevailing conceptions that are partial or flawed and therefore fail to attend to the complexities of problems.

Step Two: Sort Through the Hypotheses and Decide Which Ones to Explore. Deciding which causes will be explored during the investigation is a crucial task in the analysis stage of planning, because it directs planners' attention to needs and enables planners to target interventions and consider alternative solutions. Unlike some types of social research, where knowledge is desired for its own sake, studies of problems and needs that are conducted as part of a planning effort must be directed toward identification of factors that are observable, accessible, and manipulable by service programs and their planners. Other kinds of factors are typically too elusive to devise intervention approaches that are appropriate and feasible for a particular organization.

Another example will illustrate how planners might use these criteria to select factors that should be further explored. This example focuses on a committee from a women's center that is planning a shelter for women who remain in abusive relationships with their spouses or partners. Assume that the staff are exploring several hypotheses about factors that contribute to this situation, and they have to decide which ones they will investigate further. Their list of hypotheses includes these: the women who abuse substances are dependent on their partners for drugs. The women were socialized to violence in their families of origin. The reference group norms for both the women and their partners support abusive relationships. The women are financially dependent on their partners. The women are isolated from their friends and family. The women lack the necessary legal assistance and social support to file charges against their partners. As the subjects for inquiry are proposed, planners can exclude some because they are not within the parameters of the organization's mission, policies, commitments, capabilities, resources, and investments in particular services and staff competencies (for example, the agency doesn't have the resources and staff competencies to establish a shelter for abused women and their children that includes women who abuse substances). Some factors may be observable and accessible but are not manipulable by the service organization (for example, socialization to violence in families of origin). Some factors may be observable, but not easily accessible and manipulable (for example, the norms of the reference groups of the women and their partners). *Feasibility* is therefore a criterion in deciding what will be investigated. The planners may conclude that the service organization does not have and cannot gain sufficient leverage over some factors. Therefore there is no point in exploring them.

Step Three: Decide How the Hypotheses Will Be Explored. The methods for exploring hypotheses about causes, and about other aspects of the problem analysis and needs assessment, are discussed later in this chapter in the sections on Approaches to Needs Assessment and Methods of Problem Analysis and Needs Assessment.

What is the significance of this discussion for program planning? The conception of the problem merits serious attention, because it has a profound impact on the design of the problem analysis and the needs assessment. The determination of causes is linked with the determination of needs that will be selectively included in program goals and objectives and as targets of the service program. How you think of the problem influences how you deal with it.

Determine the Magnitude and Scope of the Problems and Needs

Magnitude refers to an estimate of the number of persons who have a particular problem or need. *Scope* refers to the number of existing cases of a given condition in a specific population and area during a specific period *(prevalence)* or the number of new cases of a condition in a specific population and area during a specific period *(incidence)*. Data about magnitude and scope are essential to decide the amount of change that is desired and possible (program objectives) and to estimate the units of service and resources required to deal with the problem. Data about scope enable planners to assess whether there is differential need among segments of the population, and if so, planners can recommend that particular groups of persons should be targeted. Quantitative measures of magnitude and scope can also be translated into measurable outcome statements that can be used to evaluate the effectiveness of the service program.

Planners can use different population segments to estimate the magnitude and scope of problems and needs. Estimates can be based on the *service population* (the segment of the child population that has been abused *and* has been receiving services), the *target population* (the segment of the child population that has been abused and for whom services are intended), or the *population-in-need* (the segment of the child population that has been abused). Studies of the *general population* (all children in a community) or determinations of the *population-at-risk* (the segment of the child population with significant probability of being abused) are rarely conducted by planners in a service organization, not only because such information may not be essential to plan but also because service organizations almost never have the resources to carry out such studies. If data about large segments of the community are needed, planners often rely on basic information (for example, about health, education, crime, housing, transportation, and employment) routinely collected and widely available from governmental institutions (see the section on Use or Reanalysis of Existing Data).

The focus of this aspect of the investigation may depend on whether planners are working on changes in an existing program or a new program. For example, in planning a change in an existing program, the inquiry into magnitude is likely to be confined to the organization and focused on service statistics, or on staff or recipients' experiences (as in this chapter's case example). Sometimes precise measures of magnitude are not necessary to plan changes in programs. The insightful observations of a few staff or the bad experiences of a few recipients may be enough to direct planning of changes in a program (for example, in one situation, the complaints of six mastectomy patients were sufficient to establish and direct a planning committee to improve the educational and counseling aspects of postoperative care). However, in planning a new program, it may be necessary to find out the magnitude and scope of the problem in the community. The resources and time available to conduct the study, the accessibility of different segments of the population, the representativeness of a segment of the population, and the organization's sphere of operations greatly limit the approach and level of effort expended on finding out the magnitude and scope of the problem.

One might ask whether it matters that planners have an exact measure of the magnitude of the problems and needs. The level of effort devoted to ascertaining the problem's scope should be guided by the required accuracy of the estimates and whether scale of need is likely to be matched by an appropriate level of resources. For example, complete estimates may not be necessary if there is a funding ceiling on particular conditions and services—of all parents who need child day care, probably only a certain number can be served, so there is no point in inquiring about all families who need day care. However, some problems may require complete estimates—the number of children who need special education in public schools given comprehensive governmental mandates and service provisions. Accurate—but not necessarily complete—measures are useful in the design stage of planning in determining the program's required units of service, staff resources, and location of services. Accurate measures are also essential in evaluating programs, as in making comparisons of magnitude and distribution over time to find out whether services are successful or if the problem is getting worse.

Sometimes a good measure is politically rather than objectively and rationally defined. Advocates may use big estimates or numbers to provoke a social response, because they fear small numbers might justify inaction. Conversely, small numbers could be used to argue for the manageability of a problem and that it will not cost so much to deal with it (Stone, 1994, pp. 30–31).

Find Out the Distribution of the Problems and Needs

Problems and needs are often differentially perceived, experienced, distributed, and reported, according to variations in sex, race, age, income, occupation, education, religion, marital status, location of residence, and other characteristics (Hatchett and Duran, 2002; Shapiro, 1994; Cleary and Demone, 1988; Barusch and Spaulding, 1989; Broman, Neighbors, and Taylor, 1989; Stone, 1989). Consequently, it is imperative to know the characteristics of the persons who are experiencing the problem in order to learn its distribution among different subgroups of the target population, to direct services toward those in need, and to design services that are responsive to the characteristics of prospective beneficiaries. The particular sociodemographic and other characteristics of interest to planners vary depending on the nature of the problem and the planners' initial understandings of the people who are experiencing it. In this chapter's case example, the characteristics of interest include the age, gender, and race of the victim, the nature of the case (incest, substantiated and unsubstantiated), the relationship of the perpetrator to the victim, prior abuse offenses of the perpetrator, the reactions of the nonperpetrating parent to the disclosure of abuse, and whether the victim can discuss the incident.

In designing the investigation, inclusive criteria should be used to ensure that the diversity of the organization and the community or prospective target population are represented in the study. Planners must avoid gender-restrictive approaches and interpretations of conditions that fail to take cultural diversity into account. Some groups believe they have been overstudied, and they resent the failure of officials to keep the implied promise of studies—that someone will do something about their problems. Planners should approach such groups with sensitivity and perhaps with the help of group representatives.

Recap

Up to this point, the chapter has addressed what planners have to know about the nature of problems and needs: their features, consequences, causes, magnitude and scope, distribution, and the characteristics of the people who are experiencing the problem and are in need. Several steps were identified to help planners decide what they need to know and why. As the group decides the focus of its investigation, it should document them on a work sheet that can be used in subsequent steps of the analysis stage (for example, to check if there is a method of data collection for every item to be investigated, to assign investigative tasks, to assess whether all the data the group wanted were collected, to guide the selection and preparation of data that have been collected and that should be reported back to the team).

Plan the Approaches to Needs Assessment

As the planners decide what more they need to know about problems and needs, they must also choose the approaches and methods that they will use to obtain the information. This section focuses on four approaches to the assessment of needs—

measuring normative, comparative, perceived, and expressed need (Bradshaw, 1977). The next section deals with methods that planners can use to carry out the investigation. Regardless of the approach, the assessment of needs must result in the discovery of factors that can be translated into program objectives and targets of the service program.

Assessing Needs Normatively

Normative need refers to a condition of a population that falls below a standard held by a community or prescribed by knowledgeable people such as professionals and scientists, or by those in authority, including elected and appointed officials in executive, legislative, and judicial branches of government (Mayer, 1985). These experts and authorities, as well as lay, consumer, and special-interest groups, rely on experience, science, surveys, public pressure, social indicators, statistical patterns, professional judgment, and official policies to establish desirable standards that are compared with the norms, practices, or patterns that exist. Normative definitions are often quantified, formal, and public standards that are subject to public scrutiny and debate, and they often identify goals worthy of community pursuit. Normative definitions change as a consequence of the dissemination of information, development of knowledge, scientific discoveries, changes in societal or community values, public policies, or changes in a group's definition of its standard of living.

Some examples of normative standards include nutritional requirements for maintaining well-being, the minimum number of prenatal visits to an obstetrician, the timing of essential immunizations for infants and children, federal minimum income requirements for a family of four, elementary and secondary school curriculum requirements, housing codes, and highway safety and pollution standards. Taking a look at a few of these will illustrate how planners assess needs normatively. Housing codes are used by inspectors and planners to assess the quality of a community's rental housing stock and to plan educational and enforcement programs. Highway safety and transportation councils monitor traffic accidents, including their causes, frequency, location, time of occurrence, and the characteristics of the drivers. They use these data to identify statistical patterns that enable them to make normative judgments about highway safety (for example, accidents at a particular intersection exceed the accident rate recorded for similar intersections). Discovery of these patterns enables councils to target highway safety programs toward particular communities or drivers (for example, teen drinking and driving) or to focus on particularly hazardous street or highway conditions.

Normative approaches can be used to assess need for services when that is necessary. For example, there are pediatric standards for the timing of particular immunizations for infants and children (for example, measles vaccinations at twelve to fifteen months and then between four and six years). In tracking reportable diseases, officials can assess need for immunization. Public health departments assess this need when children first enroll in elementary school—parents must submit documented proof of immunizations to school officials. In one situation, 3 percent of the children were not in compliance with immunization requirements. Although these children were healthy at the time of enrollment, they were normatively defined as being in need of immunization (services). However, the assessment did not stop there. As pointed out earlier, planners must stay focused on the needs of the target population. In this case, officials "looked behind" the lack-of-immunization problem to get the "rest of the story." They discovered that these children were from immigrant families. (What are the characteristics of those who are experiencing the problem?) They discovered language barriers and families leery of government institutions and officials. (What are the barriers to meeting needs?) A customized outreach health promotion program was developed to reach immigrant families that were mostly clustered in one neighborhood. This example illustrates that assessments of need for services can be approached normatively, as they often are in epidemiological health studies. However, discovery of need for services should be the point of departure for further assessment, not the end of the assessment.

When planners assess needs normatively, they often analyze existing data about a community or a segment of the population (as in the previous examples). The results of the analysis are then evaluated to determine whether the community or population measures up or falls short of the pattern, standard, norm, or criterion in question. Shortfalls are interpreted as indicators of need that can be targeted by a service program. Normative definitions of need can be troublesome when there are different and conflicting standards due to variations in value orientations, political ideology, and interpretations of data and experience.

Assessing Needs Comparatively

Comparative need, or *relative need,* refers to the condition of individuals, a community, or an area that falls significantly below the average or generally accepted level of that condition among comparable groups, communities, or areas (Mayer, 1985, p. 128). Comparative data are useful in identifying differential need (for example, high rates of infant mortality and morbidity among women with low incomes). Comparative measures are sometimes used to give high priority to people or communities that are relatively less well off or deemed to be at higher risk than others (for example, a health clinic in a rural area developed a special health program for migrant workers, because they had high rates of diabetes compared with other low-income families in the county). Comparative measures are also used when there is a desire to introduce equity or eligibility as a criterion in the allocation of resources or when predictions of demand for a new service can be based on the experience of a comparable community or population group. Sometimes relative need cannot be assessed, because data that enable comparison have not been or cannot be easily collected (for example, data about the elderly who are isolated, living alone, and are lonely). Even if data are available, they may not be organized and easily retrievable, or planners may not know which characteristics should be used in making comparisons when little is known about a problem. For example, much of the data about adverse drug reactions among the elderly is buried in patient records in physicians' offices.

Need for services can be assessed comparatively if that is necessary. For example, there are standards for the number of prenatal visits that pregnant women should make to their obstetricians. For healthy patients with a normal pregnancy, the standards are one visit to the doctor every month for the first twenty-eight weeks, every two weeks from twenty-eight to thirty-six weeks, and every week thereafter. Officials can determine the need for prenatal services by comparing the degree to which women from different racial, ethnic, age, or socioeconomic groups have the appropriate level of prenatal care. However, as in the immunization example, officials should also analyze the barriers to, factors associated with, and consequences of inadequate prenatal care.

Assessing Perceived Needs

Perceived need refers to the views or wants of those who are experiencing a problem or those who speak in their behalf. They include family members, representatives of voluntary associations (for example, church, immigrant, and neighborhood associations, court and prison watch groups, self-help groups), and specialized advocacy organizations (for example, Multiple Sclerosis Society, Mothers Against Drunk Driving, Vestibular Disorders Society, and organizations in local communities advocating for citizens with retardation). Perceptions of need can be assessed through interviews, surveys, petitions, complaints, or group meetings.

Measurement of perceived need is the preferred approach when it is essential to have the participation of current or prospective beneficiaries in order to understand how they experience problems and are affected by them. In the CAC case example, the work group could have assessed perceived need by conferring with some parents and victims about their experiences with the program's referral and admissions process and delays in the provision of crisis management services. Some parents who experienced delay could have been interviewed, or part of the meetings of the mothers' therapy group and the adolescent support group could have been used to elicit this information.

Program planners have a responsibility to solicit and be sensitive to the prospective beneficiaries' definitions of the situation and the bearing that their views may have on use of services and service delivery design. Interactive methods (for example, focus groups or key informant interviews) of exploring perceived need are especially useful in helping planners overcome professional blinders by structuring an open approach to the assessment of needs. Taking a look at a domestic assault example will illustrate how planners sometimes discover needs fortuitously when measuring perceived needs. This time, assume that you are a member of the investigative team and are interviewing a woman who was abused. Toward the end of the interview, your respondent blurts out that she refused to file charges against her partners, because she feared retaliation, at which point you experience a thunderbolt of insight: Why should she have to assume the burden of prosecution? She needs to be supported and protected before, during, and after court proceedings. (Some states now have domestic violence statutes in which law enforcement agencies assume the burden of prosecution.) This example illustrates that needs are sometimes discovered incidentally as the problem is being explored. Planners must be vigilant and seize the insightful moment when it presents itself. Planners should "collect" these insights about needs that are discovered in the course of the investigation and present them to the group for further assessment.

There are some populations-at-risk that cannot or do not speak for themselves (for example, elders in nursing homes, the homeless, illegal aliens, and individuals with mental retardation), and planners must seek out others who can speak for them. In some instances, they are members of advocacy organizations and associations that independently carry out normative and comparative assessments of need or interpret the perceived needs of the target population. (You do not have to worry about seeking them out. The advocates know who and where you are!) As some of these advocates voice their perceptions of need, planners often are faced with the paradoxical situation of being the focus of another organization's planning efforts.

If planners were to rely only on normative and comparative assessments of need, their decisions would be made independent of the prospective recipients of the service. Sometimes planners do not have much choice in their approach to assessment for all kinds of reasons, and in some planning ventures that may not matter. But sometimes it does matter and planners do have a choice.

Why does it matter? Declining to involve prospective recipients or their advocates may be perceived as an act of superiority by insensitive bureaucrats, and it might result in a "we-they" situation. This would be an unfortunate circumstance, especially if the successful implementation of the program is contingent on the motivation and cooperation of the target population or its advocates. Furthermore, given the culture of participation and empowerment, people expect to be involved in decisions that have consequences for them. So planners are encouraged to consider whether it is essential or desirable to solicit the perceived needs of prospective recipients or their advocates. (The ways in which this can be done are discussed later in this chapter in the sections on Small-Group Methods and Surveys.)

Several factors influence whether individuals or groups consider a condition a need and how the need is defined: the standard of living, the expectations of a community, knowledge of one's own conditions and community conditions, and individual experiences. Not everyone who has a problem may be in need. For example, some may be managing well in spite of their problems. Some may be receiving adequate services or help from friends or relatives. Others may be experiencing a problem, may feel a need, but may have low expectations that it can or will be met. Changes in any of these factors may lead to changes in a person's perceptions about what constitutes a need that should be met through provision of service. Individuals who are asked to report their needs may exaggerate them or may be reluctant to engage in self-disclosure. For these reasons, perceived need, by itself, may not be an adequate measure of need.

Earlier in this chapter, planners were cautioned about the pitfalls of assessing need for services and defining problems in terms of lack of services. Asking lay people to assess their need for service is appropriate when respondents are informed about and can evaluate their own or others' conditions, understand the nature of services and the differences among them, and make a judgment that certain conditions can be ameliorated through the provision of specific services. For example, an agency conducted an assessment of need for respite services among parents who were providing in-home care for their children with disabilities. The staff believed that parents knew enough about their situations to decide what help they needed. However, it is likely true that few lay respondents can satisfy these conditions. The findings from assessments of need for services may be of dubious value, particularly when prospective recipients are asked about their self-perceived need for services. For example, the answers to questions about the need or desire for more training for better jobs, or for increased or improved community services, are predictable.

Assessing Expressed Needs

Expressed need is a perceived need that is acted on when members of a target population request a service. Expressed need can be measured through an analysis of service statistics—how many persons ask for help. Unmet need can be assessed by the numbers of applicants on a waiting list or of those who seek but do not qualify for or who cannot obtain assistance. If officials keep records on applicants, planners may be able to develop profiles and descriptions of their problems, needs, and characteristics (which is what the PD did in the CAC case example).

Measures of expressed need underestimate the extent of need and may have to be supplemented with other measures for a more thorough estimate. In the CAC case example, the PD may have a poor estimate of the unserved abuse cases. Staff from the referring organizations may have decided that there was no point in referring cases that could not be promptly accepted for service, and discouraged parents may have sought help elsewhere. Some persons do not express their needs because they have had too many frustrating experiences with provider organizations, they are unable or reluctant to admit being in difficulty, or they are wary of losing control of their lives to staff. Sheer ignorance of available services, misunderstanding of who is eligible, and the costs (stigma, time, energy, fees) of seeking and receiving help are other reasons that assistance is not sought. But measures of expressed need are easy and inexpensive to obtain and provide some quantitative evidence of demand for assistance or a given service.

Combining Approaches to Needs Assessment

The discussion of each of these approaches cannot convey the complexity with which they converge and combine in the real world of planning. Planners may have to use several approaches to make a valid assessment of needs. Each approach has its advantages and limitations for use in identifying and assessing needs relevant to a service program, and each provides only a partial perspective on needs. If different approaches to needs assessment yield similar findings, planners can use the consensus to make a compelling case that this is a need that merits attention. Convergence among findings obtained through different approaches should also ease formulation of program objectives about target populations to be given priority for services. However, sometimes there is divergence in findings about perceived needs among different respondents or among different measures of need. In a subsequent section, there are some guidelines for priority setting that may help planners deal with these dilemmas.

Decide the Methods for Carrying Out the Problem Analysis and Needs Assessment

A variety of quantitative and qualitative methods exist that draw on well-established social research techniques that are useful when planners conduct problem analyses and needs assessments. Descriptions of these techniques and their advantages and disadvantages have been well documented (Witkin and Altschuld,

1995; Soriano, 1995; Gilmore, Campbell, and Becker, 1989), and manuals for conducting needs assessments have also been developed (Public Management Institute, 1980). The following is a summary of the features of the major methodologies, along with some observations about their usage. Remember that here the exposition of the tasks is linear, but in the real world, planners are more likely to consider methods while they are figuring out what they want to know. It is unlikely that planners would first list everything that they wanted to know and then figure out how to get it.

Use or Reanalysis of Existing Data

The organization that initiates a planning effort is an important and abundant source of information about problems, needs, and the people who have them, especially in planning changes in existing programs. Most human service organizations have service statistics and staff activity reports that include information about recipients, service provided, waiting lists, terminations, referrals to and from a program, placements, no-shows, workloads, and more. Recipients' records, management and recipient information systems, and reports to and from licensing, regulatory, funding, and accrediting agencies are other sources of information. Because staff members and recipients (and often their significant others) have experience with the condition of concern and the current service program, they can easily serve as key informants during individual or group interviews. Other sources of information include exit interviews with recipients, analysis of findings from satisfaction and exit surveys, home visits, follow-up contacts, as well as examination of critical incident reports (for example, accounts of personal injury, misplacement of files, medication errors, and isolation of acting-out offenders in a detention facility). Information and sources within the organization should be exploited before or instead of going elsewhere. Not only is it practical and feasible, but the organization might be the source of the best and most useful information. Furthermore, it may be necessary because few organizations have sufficient resources to undertake extensive studies. Sometimes planners must go outside the organization for information (which is likely in planning a new program). However, before embarking on their own investigation of a problem, they should examine the wealth of data that are accessible, underused, and inexpensive or cost free to retrieve. All sorts of reports, studies, and data can be obtained via the Internet from sites developed by governmental and nonprofit organizations. (See Resources for Planning Service Programs for a selective list of sites. A few of those listed are gateways or have links to many other sites.)

Virtually all governmental jurisdictions (local, state, federal), school districts, institutions such as hospitals and universities, federated state and national organizations (for example, Child Welfare League of America), and local planning organizations (for example, United Way) routinely collect and report data on social conditions, trends, services, and the like. The available data pertain to many areas of concern: employment and the labor force, housing, health, education, crime, mental health, poverty, and the characteristics of the people affected. The U.S. Census Bureau provides data on the characteristics of the population and households that can be retrieved through the Internet. Government reports are also available across the nation in public libraries that are designated as repositories of government documents. Many governmental and nonprofit organizations regularly report statistics on the characteristics of their beneficiaries and the services that were provided to them. In addition, there are private not-for-profit organizations (for example, Children's Defense Fund, Brookings Institution) and chambers of commerce that routinely describe and assess social conditions and place their findings in the public domain (for example, the *Kids Count* publications of the Children's Defense Fund and *American Demographics,* a monthly publication of Dow Jones & Company).

Many kinds of data can be accessed and applied in several ways:

- Using existing independent data and organizational service statistics to estimate the population-at-risk that qualifies for service but is not currently receiving it
- Extrapolating estimates of the magnitude of a condition or the characteristics of the population in need from one area to another similar area (for example, the incidence rate of child abuse in one county might be used to estimate the incidence in a similar county)
- Identifying trends in population characteristics or social conditions
- Comparing areas or communities with similar characteristics
- Combining and reanalyzing these data sets to suit one's planning purposes

Sometimes planners can develop proxy measures of a problem when direct measures are elusive or lead to low estimates (for example, the number of adverse drug reactions among the elderly might be estimated by extrapolating information from medical records about falls and accidents). Existing data can be used to learn about normative, expressed, and comparative need. For example, minimum-income standards for a family of four can be obtained from federal government reports—normative needs. The number of patients seeking medical attention for sexually transmitted diseases is reported by departments of health—expressed needs. The academic performance of students in different districts is reported by departments of education and local school districts—comparative need.

Adequate solutions to problems and needs may already be in place in the community. It is essential to take stock of existing services before planning major improvements, and certainly before planning new programs. This process is known as an *inventory of services*, which is defined as counting or estimating and assessing existing services relevant to a planning venture and the target population in a particular locale (Mayer, 1985, p. 127). Inventories are required by some funding agencies as a part of the grant application process. They want to avoid misapplication of resources and duplication of services and to assess whether there are appropriate levels of cooperation among programs that serve the same target population. (See Chapter Three, Exhibit 3.1, requisite item number 10, Relationships to Other Service Programs, and see Chapter Eight).

Six dimensions are suggested in conducting inventories: *quantity, quality, adequacy, appropriateness, acceptability,* and *accessibility* (Mayer, 1985, p. 130; Suchman, 1967). Quantity refers to the known or estimated measures of each service that is used or needed by the target population. Quality refers to the standards to which a program adheres in meeting the needs of the target population. Adequacy is a measure of the extent to which the target population was meant to be served and was actually served by the program (Flynn, 1992, pp. 78–79). Appropriateness addresses whether the services or resources that are provided through a program are fitting of a particular purpose or suitable for a particular need, condition, or characteristic of a target population. Acceptability refers to the degree to which a service is pleasing, satisfactory, worthy, or agreeable from the perspective of the service population or those who speak in its behalf. Accessibility refers to the ease with which segments of the target population can reach and use services. (Accessibility is discussed more fully in the chapter on developing the essential program components, Chapter Seven.)

Information about or measures of some dimensions of service programs are easier to obtain than others. Information about quantity and accessibility can be gleaned from Web sites and public documents such as monthly, quarterly, or annual reports or descriptive program brochures. However, the variation in information systems and service statistics among organizations, and duplicated counts of persons who are service recipients in several organizations, make it difficult to estimate the service population. Information about some aspects of quality can be obtained by finding out whether the organization or its programs are accredited, licensed, inspected, or otherwise regulated and by assessing the education, training, certification, and licenses of staff (for other measures of quality, see Martin and Kettner, 1996, p. 42). Information on the other dimensions is not routinely collected by human service organizations, and planners are highly unlikely to invest resources to measure adequacy, appropriateness, and acceptability.

Some dimensions of inventories can be easily counted, estimated, or assessed in small communities, because all or most other organizations and programs offering similar services (or to the same populations) are known to one another, and contacts for updated information would not be burdensome. However, in metropolitan areas where many and different types of services are usually available for people with particular problems, an inventory may be challenging. The level of effort expended on an inventory will vary with the time, persons, and funds that are available to carry it out, the condition that is of concern, the services that are likely to be offered, the detail that is essential, whether it is required by funders, and staff knowledge about providers and the service system (Hagedorn, 1977, pp. 93–94).

If planners must inventory relevant community services, it is advisable to use sources in the public domain and to conduct short, structured interviews with organizational officials, in person or over the phone, to elicit information that is accessible instead of investing substantial time in developing a survey or questionnaire. Some organizations have staff members whose responsibilities include provision of information to others (for example, public relations or marketing directors, management information personnel, or program evaluators). In many communities, some information about services can be obtained by relying on information and referral services, consumer affairs and advocacy organizations, some funding and planning agencies (for example, United Way and Area Agency on Aging), directories of human services developed and provided by libraries, and county and state government agencies. However, these directories may be incomplete and difficult to interpret, and they are often out-of-date. For-profit providers and church-sponsored social ministry programs are not always included in these directories.

Small-Group Methods

There are several small-group methods of obtaining original data about a problem and felt or normative needs. Focus groups (Krueger, 2000), and structured group interviews (Delbecq and Van de Ven, 1977) are inexpensive to plan and carry out. These methods provide eight to ten key informants with opportunities to share knowledge, perceptions, and experience; to describe conditions; and to report needs and preferences for services and how they should be delivered. Key informants may include service recipients or their significant others, representatives of populations-at-risk, staff members, volunteers, and professionals, meeting within their own or across participant groups, depending on what planners want to accomplish. Each participant group has more or less to contribute to the inquiry depending on its focus. For example, staff and professionals are likely to have a grasp on the prevalence of a condition and valid knowledge of its features, but representatives of the population-at-risk can be expected to have valid and unique understanding of their experience with a condition. Care must be taken in composing groups to ensure appropriate representation.

If several panels of meetings with different cohorts are planned, the meetings should be completed within a short time to minimize problems with the validity and reliability of the information. The degree of structure and the direction of interaction in group meetings vary depending on the particular group method used. However, it is advisable to plan a method for questioning, listening, recording, summarizing, and interpreting.

Small-group methods are underutilized means of analyzing problems, assessing needs, and exploring alternative modes of service. Experience shows that both the initial skepticism and the lukewarm attitudes of the planners and the participants toward these methods typically give way to confidence in these approaches and satisfaction with the group experience.

Surveys

Surveys rely on standardized questionnaires or interviews to elicit information about perceptions of problems or felt needs. The realities of life among most service organizations suggest that surveys are not appropriate or feasible means of analyzing problems and assessing needs. There is a high probability that the staff of most human service organizations do not have the minimum expertise to conduct a reliable survey. Only experienced survey centers or experts can solve troublesome sampling problems, hire and train interviewers and coders, and organize, analyze, and interpret data. Not only are surveys costly, but they often elicit data that require further investigation or that provide no direction regarding which services would be most appropriate and efficacious.

The authors' experiences with umpteen research projects, needs assessments, and consultations testify to the difficulties and costs of getting reliable survey-type information that is useful in learning about needs and planning programs. Mailed questionnaires are particularly problematic when prospective respondents are alienated, resistant, or have poor reading skills. The response rate is likely to be low, and the types and range of questions that can be asked are limited. Telephone or face-to-face interviews guided by an interview schedule provide opportunities for the interviewer to explain questions and to probe for clarification. However, these interviews are costly and require extensive training of interviewers. A survey interview can be useful in a needs assessment if it is carefully limited in scope and provides the opportunity to adequately explore a need or a problem.

There are situations where existing data in combination with information from surveys or small groups are desirable, as in modifying and extending an existing service. Suppose officials learned that a given service was not reaching the intended target population as well as it should or that the population was now believed to be larger than originally estimated. With little effort, one could probably specify the likely unserved population using public data sources and then employ a small-group method or a focused, efficient, and reliable respondent survey designed to reach the underserved, the resistant, and the uninformed. Planners know they are out there, and the question becomes how to adapt the service to make it acceptable and accessible to as many of them as possible.

Health and Social Science Studies

Information about problems and needs can also be found in studies published in professional, health, and social science journals, especially those with a focus on a particular condition, service, or target population—speech pathology, retardation, crime and delinquency, genetic counseling, rehabilitation of people who are blind, elders, or adolescents. These journals can be found and accessed in many public university libraries through user-friendly on-line computer-assisted searches, sometimes with some coaching by library staff, or through customized computer searches carried out by staff, sometimes for a modest fee. (Call the university reference librarian in your area for particulars.) A literature review is likely to yield a few studies whose findings provide understanding of a problem and preclude or influence aspects of the investigation by the planning group. For example, a literature review might reveal that children who are sexually assaulted have common needs. By knowing this, planners probably could omit this aspect from their inquiry and focus on more locally relevant matters (for example, types of abuse, magnitude, characteristics of victims and families). These studies usually describe the research methods used by the investigator. Although many research designs are complex and not easily replicated by staff in service programs, planners may find some ideas on how they can explore problems and needs. Sometimes a literature review must be conducted because funders want it included in the program proposal.

Choose and Combine Methods Carefully

Within each of the four major methodologies, there is a range of techniques and procedures, detailed in numerous texts, manuals, and handbooks on social research (Babbie, 2001; Westerfelt and Dietz, 2001; Krueger, 2000; Miles and Huberman, 1994). If planners need guidance, they can consult these works or an expert. Only a few of these techniques or procedures are likely to be used in any particular planning effort. Economy is essential, considering that most of the staff become involved in program planning beyond what they ordinarily do on a daily basis. As planners mull over the methods that should be used to conduct the investigation, several factors are likely to influence their selection: the purposes of the problem analysis and needs assessment, staff and financial resources, time frames, the competencies of the planners, the accessibility of respondents, the availability of data, and the level of precision of the measures of need that are required.

Some needs assessments are very complex. In one study, several methods of inquiry were used, and a participatory approach engaged stakeholders, such as service providers and beneficiaries of the assessment. These stakeholders served as volunteers in the development and implementation of the study. Such involvement ensured completion of the project, ownership of the findings, and a commitment to implementation. However, there were challenges and struggles—disproportionate workloads and participation among committee members, the length of time to complete the project (twenty months), and insufficient understanding of research methods, among others. Readers who may want to adapt this participatory model are advised to consult Balaswamy and Dabelko (2002).

Sometimes planners use a contingency and sequential approach in selecting and implementing methods of inquiry. One method of inquiry is completed before others are considered or carried out. The findings from the initial investigation may be sufficient to guide planning, and further study may be unnecessary. Or the findings may be used by the planners to select appropriate subsequent methods of study or to modify the preliminary plan of investigation. For example, planners may begin a study by extracting information from patients' records, and after completing a preliminary analysis, they may decide that group interviews are not appropriate, but follow-up interviews with key informants are essential. Concurrent implementation of two or more methods of inquiry may be necessary or desirable, but as stated in Chapter Three, it is advisable for planners to take a problem-exploring approach and to make decisions based on what is discovered as the process unfolds.

Assign Investigative Tasks

Once the planners decide how they are going to get what they want to know, they must update the work plan by figuring out who is going to do what and by when they are going to do it. The assignment of investigative tasks should be approached systematically by referring to the work sheets that the group has been using to guide the planning of the problem analysis and needs assessment. For example, refer to the CAC work sheet and examine the list of information the group wanted under the question "What do we want to know?" Also note how the group intended to obtain the information and that Dan was designated to get it.

The group should scan the list of the investigative tasks that it decides to pursue. Some of the steps for carrying out a particular task may still need further analysis and development by the group or by individual investigators (for example, the group might want to decide the criteria for selecting the composition of a focus group and the focus questions, but individual investigators could well decide the procedures to be followed in extracting numerical data from a report). The group should consider the competencies, resources, and time required to carry out particular investigative tasks and assign persons accordingly.

Data collection tasks are usually carried out individually by the members of the planning group or other responsible persons (for example, professional or support staff, student interns, or volunteers). Each investigator should have a focus to direct data collection and should be assigned a particular investigative task (for example, retrieve demographic data about victims of sexual assault and perpetrators from crime reports; conduct group meetings with parents of victims to learn about their children's situations; extract information about abused children from case records). Fishing expeditions are not recommended.

Collect the Data

The particular data collection tasks and steps vary depending on the method and approach. If planners need help, they can consult the works identified earlier or consult an expert. The purpose here is to provide some guidance in collecting data for use by a planning group.

Investigators must strive to get the essence of what each data source reveals with an eye on what the group wants to know and how the data might be used in the group's deliberations. It is important to assess at this point that the group has completed its work properly and that what it wants to know has been influenced by what officials and funders want to know and what they want included in the final program plan document. Data deemed irrelevant should be filtered out right away. As the relevant data are discovered, it is likely that more data will be gathered and recorded than the individual investigators will report back to the group. This result is understandable and unavoidable regardless of the method of data collection (for example, extracting numerical data from a census table or the organization's information system, gleaning information from a research report, or recording responses during individual or group interviews). It is not possible to determine the adequacy and sufficiency of the data and winnow them as they are being gathered and recorded piece by piece. An initial determination of adequacy and sufficiency can be made only after the investigator is finished and examines what has been collected in relation to what was supposed to be accomplished. A complete evaluation of all collected data cannot be carried out until the group has reviewed the initial findings of the individual investigators.

The source of each data set must be documented. Officials and funders want to know the sources of the information used as evidence about problems, conditions, and needs. As investigators winnow the information to be presented back to the group, they may inadvertently leave out important matters and may have to backtrack.

Analyze the Data and Write Up the Initial Findings

The discussion begins with two examples that illustrate what investigators might face at this point in the planning process. Assume that one member of the work group was charged with responsibility for estimating the number of children who were sexually assaulted during a given year in a particular county. Also assume that she decided to obtain information about the magnitude of this problem from municipal police departments and the county sheriff, the juvenile court, and protective services. She may discover that their reports about magnitude are not comparable. There are often variations in the way cases are classified and counted, and different time periods are used to report information (for example, monthly, quarterly, calendar year, budget cycle). She is also likely to learn about the variation among the agencies in the specific information that is kept about the characteristics of victims, which makes it difficult to estimate magnitude among different groups of victims. She is likely to have duplicated counts. Now that she has completed her investigation, she has to figure out what the numbers represent and how the estimate of magnitude should be made. Should she make a conservative estimate? Should she display the data from different sources in comparative fashion? Should she rely on one agency's figures because it has quality controls in its information system and has the most reliable data? Whatever she decides, she must analyze the data, estimate magnitude, and figure out how to report her estimate and explain the basis for it.

Assume that another group member was assigned to conduct a group interview with teen victims of sexual assault who experienced delays in service provision. She was charged with finding out their self-perceived needs and the consequences of these delays. She is likely to have a collection of notations about these matters. There is likely to be convergence and divergence of experiences and perspectives. The content of these qualitative data need to be studied, labeled, and organized so that they can be interpreted, summarized, and presented back to the group for its consideration.

These examples show that after completing the collection of data, individual investigators are likely to have unordered sets of numerical or qualitative data, or both, that must be studied, coded, organized, and analyzed. The specific techniques and procedures for accomplishing these tasks vary depending on the methods used by investigators (for example, qualitative data require a content analysis; numerical data may have to be disassembled, recalculated, and standardized in percentages). The focus here is on some general but practical guidelines for analyzing the data, transforming them into initial findings, and preparing them in a write-up to present back to the planning group. The term *initial* is used to distinguish these findings from those that must be agreed on by the group. Also, some initial findings may be divergent or contradictory and must be reconciled by the group.

1. Sort through and cluster similar, complementary, and related data. Sort through and cluster divergent or contradictory data (Miles and Huberman, 1984, pp. 213–219). Data are the objective and subjective facts (for example, the number of sexually abused children documented in police reports, the posttraumatic experiences and feelings of sexually abused children).

2. It is not desirable nor is it necessary for individual investigators to report to the group everything that was gathered or recorded. Whenever possible, *data* should be transformed into *initial findings*. This can be accomplished by analyzing the data for patterns, themes, trends, relationships between the factors investigated, and whether the hypotheses posed by the group were supported or rejected (for example, rental housing units in census tracts populated by low-income minority groups have the highest rates of housing code violations; some in-home accidents among the elderly can be attributed to adverse reactions to prescription drugs; the teen mothers' discussions during group meetings revealed hopelessness).

Data must be interpreted in terms of the information sought and the questions posed when the problem analysis was planned. For an example of how this can be done, refer back to the CAC example, in which the staff listed the information they wanted under the question "What do we want to know?" Notice the first item on the list: "Has there been an increase in incest referrals? If there has been an increase, when did it occur?" Now scan the list of Dan's findings presented in the following section, The Second Work Group Meeting. Note the correspondence between this list and the what-do-we-want-to-know list. In particular, note item number 2 of Dan's report of the initial findings: "Just before the admissions scheduling problems started, the number of incest cases referred to the program increased." The list of wanted information was used to direct the investigation and now to guide the transformation of the data into initial findings.

3. In the real world of problem exploration, some discoveries are made by accident, and they do not fall neatly into the preplanned investigative questions. Planners may have to invent categories for reporting these discoveries.

4. The initial findings and a *summary of supporting numerical data* or *supporting qual-*

itative data must be documented in a *write-up* for presentation back to the planning group by its individual members or others doing investigative work in its behalf. Initial findings often turn out to be "the" findings reported in the problem statement of the program plan document.

5. The write-ups may include a narrative, a series of one-liners that report findings, an outline that can be followed during a briefing at a meeting, or some combination of them. Some critical incidents, case vignettes, or a summary of a typical case or situation might also be included. Numerical and qualitative data that support the findings have to be summarized, condensed, or presented in tabular displays (in the interest of simplicity, the term *write-up* includes charts and displays). For example, narrative records of what was learned during interviews or a focus group must be summarized into a comprehensible and usable form. Data extracted from recipients' files, census tables, or organizational reports must be condensed in narrative form or presented in charts or tabular displays.

6. These write-ups should be submitted to the chair or other designate, so that the responsible individuals can plan the meetings at which the initial findings and supporting data will be presented to the group. The write-ups give the group something it can "put its hands on" as it tries to collectively comprehend and work with what was learned. These write-ups are essential in facilitating the group's analysis of the initial findings and supporting data, the determination of needs, and the preparation of the problem description in the program plan document.

Analyze the Initial Findings and Determine Needs

Those responsible for planning the meeting at which initial findings and supporting data will be presented must examine the write-ups and in consultation with each investigator figure out how the information might best be presented to the group (for example, assemble and distribute the write-ups as submitted, merge parts of some write-ups, summarize the main points on flip sheets, prepare transparencies for use with an overhead projector, prepare a chart or a table, prepare a Power-Point presentation). The sequence of the presentations by each investigator, and the approach to the analysis of the findings and the determination of needs must also be planned. All of this should be set forth in an updated work plan and presented to the group for its review and agreement at the outset of the meeting. Planners should bring their problem analysis work sheets to the meeting so that the group can refer to them at essential points in the proceedings. A copy of the officials' and the funders' requirements for the problem description should also be brought to the meeting so that the group can begin its documentation of problems and needs accordingly.

Several matters should be addressed at the outset of this meeting to focus the group on the work that must be accomplished next.

1. The chair should recollect the charge issued to the group, where it had started out, and what it had accomplished so far. Sometimes members get so narrowly focused on each of their investigative tasks that they lose sight of the big picture. This recollection helps the group reset its bearings on the course of planning.

2. The chair should also remind the group about its overall purpose at this stage of the planning effort—that is, to understand and describe the nature of the problem, including its features, consequences, causes, magnitude, scope, distribution, and the characteristics of those experiencing the problem and how they are affected by it; and to determine needs. The group should be asked to keep an eye on these elements during its deliberations, because officials and funders require them to be addressed in the problem description of the program plan document. One of the planners should be assigned responsibility for recording the conclusions from the group's analysis, the results of its discussion, and what it wants included in the narrative of the problem statement.

3. The work plan for the meeting should be presented to the group for its review and approval.

It is time to return to the case example to illustrate how planners might go about analyzing the findings and supporting data and determining needs. The work group is at its second meeting. Dan has been asked to present his findings from the analysis of incest cases and related staff activities. (The example is illustrative, not definitive.)

◆ ◆ ◆

The Counseling and Advocacy Center Case Example: The Second Work Group Meeting

Dan distributed a summary of his findings and presented them to the work group.

1. Of the fifty admissions periods that should have been scheduled during the ten weeks that were studied, eight periods were not staffed. More would not have been staffed had some counselors not compensated by scheduling an additional admissions period for the following week. Problems with the scheduling of admissions interviews started at approximately the same time as the program started to develop a waiting list. The scheduling problems started during the seventeenth month.

2. Just before the admissions scheduling problems started, the number of incest cases referred to the program increased.
3. When the scheduling problems started, staff attendance at interagency meetings increased.
4. Staff participation in court hearings and legal proceedings also increased.
5. Incest cases are evenly distributed among the counselors.

The staff discussed Dan's report and concluded that the increase in incest cases and related staff activities probably contributed to the missed rotations into admissions. The demands of incest cases had not been fully appreciated until they reached a critical mass and a shift occurred in the composition of the caseload to a higher proportion of incest cases. The missed rotations into admissions eluded early detection because they were distributed among the four counselors during a six-week period. The PD directed the discussion toward further analysis and interpretations of the findings. The senior counselor led with the following comments.

"Every counselor has responsibility for admissions, crisis management, supportive services, assessment, and long-term counseling with all kinds of cases. Staff were deployed this way for two reasons: at the beginning, when there were only a few staff, everyone had to do everything. And the final plan for the CAC optimized continuity of care to the victim—that is, to the extent that it was possible and desirable, the victim could count on working with one counselor the whole time. I believe that many parents and victims need and value timely help with a crisis more than the victim needs continuity of assistance from one counselor. Some need both, and we can decide which cases do."

One counselor followed up on her colleague's comments. "We need to be more efficient in dealing with incest cases. Under our present arrangement, we all are dealing with the same representatives from the collaborating agencies, and we even run into each other during the interagency joint assessment and service planning meetings. We need to consolidate some of these activities. Otherwise all the staff will be bogged down with these cases. To deal with the waiting list and minimize service delays in the future, we may have to develop specialized staff roles, such as a crisis counselor."

The staff were in general agreement with these observations. The PD remarked that the group apparently wanted to reconsider the program's original operational objectives regarding continuity and make some staffing adjustments. The group agreed to table further discussion of these matters until the next meeting, when it would consider the criteria for preferential selection of cases from the current and any future waiting list.

◆ ◆ ◆

In this segment, the work group interpreted the findings in light of their experience. The need for a timely response was affirmed; continuity for all victims was questioned; and efficiency, consolidation, and specialization in operations were deemed essential. The PD linked the group's interpretation of the findings to the need for change in the CAC's operational objectives and adjustments in program operations, foreshadowing the tasks of the next stages of planning.

◆ ◆ ◆

The Counseling and Advocacy Center Case Example: The Third Work Group Meeting

Before the meeting, the PD asked members to review the memorandum that she had distributed at the first meeting, which contained the description of the characteristics of the cases on the waiting list. The description was based on information taken from the one-page form that was completed at the time of referral for each of the ten cases on the waiting list. Every member of the work group also had a set of the individual forms. The PD asked the group to assess the needs of these cases and reflect on the needs of cases not represented among the current referrals, to decide which ones warranted preferential selection for service.

The counselors decided that severity of the abuse, regardless of the perpetrator, should be a prime factor in placing referrals high on the waiting list. Several elements should be considered:

1. What the nature of the abuse was (for example, sexual touching versus penetration)
2. If the abuse included physical violence, force, the use of a weapon, threat to use a weapon, ritualistic or sadistic abuse
3. If there was more than one perpetrator
4. If there was more than one incident of abuse

Children who experience such abuse are often the most traumatized and warrant preferential treatment. The PD remarked that some of this information is not always discovered at the time of referral, but during counseling. As the group examined the forms of the ten referrals, it concluded that at least one case clearly met the severity criteria and should be placed at the top of the list.

The counselors agreed that high priority should be given to meeting the needs of victims in substantiated cases of abuse committed by family members or live-in partners. The problem is out in the open and accessible to intervention. The family has to deal with substantial emotional turmoil and threats to its stability. The perpetrator may be facing legal action, and sometimes there are threats of retaliation. Furthermore, the interagency teams are geared up to serve these families. Excluding the severity case, there were three of these cases on the list.

The counselors had differences of opinion about priorities for victims in unsubstantiated incest cases. In these cases, protective services officials strongly suspect abuse but can't prove it. The alleged perpetrator denies the charge, and the nonperpetrating parent is in denial or is ambivalent, but some accept the referral to CAC to get help in dealing with the allegations and the uncertainty. In some of these cases, the child suppresses the initial disclosure or is too young to be a credible informant, and the perpetrator has access to the victim. In these circumstances, the child is virtually defenseless. Two counselors believed that it was imperative to serve these children and their families, to monitor the family situation, and to give the child some protection. Two other counselors thought that the CAC should not take on the functions of protection—that is the responsibility of protective services. The PD suggested that a compromise could be worked out depending on other characteristics of these cases and advised the group that she would consult with the director of the Children's Protective Services Unit about this matter. Meanwhile, the staff should not admit such cases that are currently active with protective services. Of the four unsubstantiated incest cases on the waiting list, none were active with protective services.

One counselor suggested that cases with the following combination of characteristics would be viewed as less needy for CAC services: the abuse was less intrusive (for example, touching), the perpetrator was not a family member, the parents were supportive, and the victim was an older child or adolescent who could be taught methods of self-protection. Such cases usually do not require immediate attention and can be managed in a few educational group sessions or referred elsewhere. Two of these cases were on the waiting list, and the group recommended that the parents should be encouraged to enroll their children in a local agency's support group. Another counselor suggested that some older children and adolescents whose perpetrators were not family members, who disclosed abuse that had occurred several years ago, and whose parents were supportive could wait for service a little longer.

The PD summarized the group's deliberations. "Considering the needs and criteria we discussed, there are eight cases that have high priority and two that can be referred elsewhere. As we think about adjustments in the deployment of staff to better cope with incest cases, we need to consider whether those adjustments will enable us to initiate service to these high-priority cases. The discussion also suggests that we need to fine-tune our program goals and objectives in line with the priorities we just discussed and inform our constituencies accordingly."

◆ ◆ ◆

In this segment, the group addressed the needs of particular cases and decided which ones merited preferential attention. Some differences were expressed about who should meet the needs of victims and families in unsubstantiated cases. The PD linked the group's deliberations to the CAC's program objectives and the proposed adjustments in staffing.

The previous segment of the CAC case example provides these guidelines for analyzing the initial findings and supporting data and for determining needs:

1. The work sheets used by the group to plan the problem analysis and needs assessment and to assign investigative tasks should be the points of departure for the analysis of the initial findings and supporting data and the determination of needs. For example, one of the work sheets might show that the planners wanted an estimate of the magnitude of the problem and that they had identified sources of information on which to base the estimate. The work sheet would also show why they wanted the estimate and what they planned to do with it. The chair could use the information on this work sheet to help the group recall what it had planned in relation to this particular investigative task. Then the chair could ask the investigator who was responsible for this task to report her initial findings and walk the group through the supporting data. This approach can be used with each investigative task and investigator. In this way, the group can systematically "audit" what it had planned to investigate, what was actually investigated and discovered, and whether it can use the findings as intended (for an example of how this can be done, see the work group's discussion of its findings).

2. The group should evaluate the initial findings and supporting data to determine whether they are adequate to describe the nature of the problem and determine needs.

3. Once the initial findings and supporting data have been presented, quickly scan them to see what the group has and what jumps out (Miles and Huberman, 1984, p. 213). Needs that are obvious can be readily determined (for example, children who experienced severe abuse were given highest priority).

4. Make another pass through the initial findings and supporting data; sort through them and look for similar, complementary, or related findings; and cluster them (for example, the findings from needs assessed comparatively may correspond with those assessed normatively, or data extracted from recipients' files may complement the observations of key informants). Assess whether the findings support the hypotheses that were explored. (For example, do the file record data support the speculation that incest cases and related staff activities contributed to service delays?)

5. Determine needs normatively. Evaluate the descriptions of the problem in the write-ups and as presented by the individual investigators. Evaluations can be based on standards, norms, regulations, experience, and professional or scientific knowledge and judgment. Normative determinations of need require a judgment by planners about the findings (for example, housing stock is inadequate, income is insufficient, employment practices are unfair, disciplinary measures are inappropriate, elderly are insecure in their own homes, and attitudes are intolerant).

6. Determine needs comparatively. If possible, compare the findings of different segments of the population that were included in the investigation to see if there is differential need among subgroups (for example, compare men and women, different racial groups, or different age groups).

7. Determine self-perceived needs. If members of the target or service population or their representatives were involved in the problem analysis and needs assessment, evaluate their contributions and decide which self-perceived needs should be addressed.

8. Interpret the findings and determine needs. Interpretations are inferences directed at discerning *meanings* that are hidden, elusive, or perplexing. Often planners must rely on interpretive judgments about needs that are implicit in the findings about the features, causes, consequences, magnitude, and distribution of the problem (Gates, 1980, pp. 119–120). For example, the findings from an investigation into the problems of unemployed, low-income, single mothers in a Head Start program led to the interpretation that they needed hope for a promising future and a vision for achieving it. A special program was established in which staff with low caseloads provided substantial emotional and instrumental support to help mothers sustain their efforts to achieve educational and employment goals. Interpretation can be facilitated by entertaining different theoretical explanations for the findings or by looking for underlying themes or patterns.

After the group carries out these steps, it is likely to have an unordered collection of descriptions of the problem and needs. This collection must be sorted, clustered, and compiled to facilitate the group's decision making: Which parts of which problems and which needs experienced by which people should be the targets of a new or changed service program? Often, if not typically, these choices are difficult to make, because there are too many needs, too many individuals who have them, and the resources and services to meet needs are too limited. Opportunity analysis is another approach to deciding the features of the problem and needs that will be the focus of program goals, objectives, and intervention.

Analyze Opportunities for Intervention

Opportunity analysis is a method of distinguishing those features of the problem and needs that are observable, accessible, and manipulable by means of a service program that the organization is likely to use. Some features provide opportunities for problem resolution, some more than others, but others do not provide such opportunities. Some might be excluded from attention because they are not within the parameters of the organization's mission, policies, commitments, capabilities, resources, sunk costs in particular services, and staff competencies and ideologies (for example, in one program similar to the CAC, nonfamily perpetrators are excluded from service). Some aspects may be observable, but not accessible and manipulable (for example, the unmotivated nonperpetrating parent who is in denial in an unsubstantiated case of incest). Feasibility is therefore an important criterion in decision making. The planners may conclude that the service organization does not have and cannot gain sufficient leverage over some aspects of the problem. The perceived or demonstrated degrees of effectiveness of services to deal with a particular aspect are other criteria used in deciding which aspects will become targets of goals and objectives. Planners "grade" problems in terms of the possibilities of improvement.

After completing the opportunity analysis, planners may still be left with more needs than can be feasibly addressed in a changed or new program. Consequently, concurrent with or following the opportunity analysis, planners must set other priorities to facilitate selection of those needs that will become the focus of program goals, objectives, and intervention.

Determine Priorities

In determining priorities, needs are weighed according to criteria so that they can be ranked in order of preference for the allocation of program resources. Several criteria have been developed to help planners in their decision making (Salvatore, 1975, pp. 34–35).

Availability of Resources and Cost of Service

The level of resources (funds, staff, equipment, facilities) required to deal with one need as opposed to another is also used in deciding which needs will become the targets of program goals and objectives. For example, a school for children with developmental disabilities decided that some students who were at risk of medical emergencies would be excluded from community and camp outings because the required nursing staff and special equipment were beyond the school's budget. In the CAC case example, the administration discontinued provision of service to divorcing spouses who were making counterclaims of abuse. Such cases took an inordinate amount of staff time, proved to be costly, and the benefits were questionable. Staff had difficulty ascertaining the validity of the alleged abuse and were being manipulated by each spouse and opposing lawyers to advance one or the other party's interests. In this way, planners grade problems not only in terms of the possibilities of improvement but also in terms of their associated costs (Liss, 1993, p. 109).

Community Concern and Expectations

The emergence or visibility of a problem may lead to a critical mass of community and political concern and expectations that planners and service providers should attend to the problem (for example, the salience of natural disasters, illegal immigrants, teen pregnancy, youth-perpetrated violence, and domestic assault during the early 1990s versus the salience of drugs, AIDS, and homelessness during the 1980s). Political and related factors also influence priority setting and the meeting of needs. For example, "The *Philadelphia Inquirer* reported an agreement between United Way and the Catholic Archdiocese of Philadelphia whereby agencies that in any way offered birth control, abortion counseling, or services opposed by the Church were to be excluded from United Way funding" (Perlmutter, 1988, p. 96).

Severity

Needs can be ranked according to severity, which can be judged by the size of the population that has the condition, whether the condition may lead to wide-scale and divisive community conflict (for example, racial incidents), or whether the condition threatens life, health, or safety—regardless of the number who have the condition. In deciding priorities, planners may grade the actual troublesome state and the consequences of no improvement (Liss, 1993, p. 125). For example, CAC counselors graded severity based on the nature of the sexual abuse; whether physical violence, force, or weapons were involved; and the number of perpetrators and abusive incidents. Counselors were also concerned about family disorganization, suicide among teen perpetrators, retribution, and the victim's ability to cope if service provision was delayed.

Compensation for Prior Neglect

Problems or needs that have not previously received sufficient attention or resources may be given priority to compensate for prior neglect or inequities in allocations. When planning committees, in retrospect, become aware of their failure to recognize a condition or respond to it adequately, compensatory allocations may be awarded to bring a program up to capacity or to fund new services (for example, some neighborhoods in minority or low-income communities with few or no parks and recreation programs have received compensatory funding; some communities with toxic waste dumps whose health hazards have been neglected for years have received targeted funds for cleanups).

Who Sets Priorities

Planners seldom have unlimited discretion in setting priorities. They may have to follow prescriptions contained in a legislative mandate or policy directive (for example, women who are pregnant or who have children two years of age or less have priority for nutrition programs). Priorities are also set by governing boards, executives, program directors, or governmental department chiefs and may well reflect any or several criteria discussed here. Sometimes it is essential or desirable to set priorities consensually through participation of staff, board members, service recipients, community interest groups, or some combination of them.

Write the Preliminary Draft of the Problem Statement

Once priorities have been set, the group should have concluded the process of determining which part of which problem and which needs experienced by which people should be the targets of a new or changed service program. Now the group must decide the specific documentation of these matters that should be included in the preliminary draft of the problem description. This documentation is necessary to guide the group in formulating program goals and objectives, and in designing the service program. The preliminary draft is one way the group can carry its work forward. The completion of this draft at this point in the planning process also serves another purpose.

As stated at the outset of this discussion of the analysis stage, the writing of the different sections of the program plan document should be done as the planning process unfolds. So the conclusion of the analysis stage is a good opportunity to write the preliminary draft of the problem description that must be included in the submitted program proposal prepared according to specific guidelines established by funders or officials. (See Chapter Three, requisite item numbers 5 and 7, and see Chapter Eight). Unless officials and funders stipulate otherwise, the documentation should address the description of the problem and needs, including their features, causes, consequences, and magnitude; the characteristics of those in need; and a recommendation for the highest priorities to be addressed through the changed or new program. The challenge for planners who are competing for limited resources is to provide documentation that is factual, persuasive, compelling, and maybe even stirring.

The group can contribute to the development of the preliminary draft in several ways: flag specific sections of the write-ups to be included in the working draft; compose some vital text on the spot during the meeting; recommend text that should be composed after the meeting; identify particular numerical data to be included in narratives or in charts or tabular displays; charge the writer of the problem statement with responsibility for a faithful rendering of the essence of the group's conclusions about problems and needs.

During the analysis stage of program planning, the preliminary draft of the problem statement is usually shared just with the members of the planning group as an essential base for its subsequent work. Although it is not customary, there are times when an oral or written update may have to be submitted to officials, because it is required by the charge or because guidance and approval are needed for the next steps in planning. Sometimes there are unexpected, unflattering, or incendiary findings (for example, evidence of racial or gender discrimination, or of poor staff performance). This is not to suggest that troublesome findings should be withheld or modified. Officials and planners have an obligation to learn whether the investigation was complete and adequate, and if so, officials must report the findings responsibly and be prepared to handle fallout.

The group might find it helpful to share the results of their investigation with other staff or volunteers to assess congruence with their impressions and understanding of the problem. Occasionally, current or prospective recipients, or their spokespersons, agree to participate in the investigation if they receive a summary of the findings in writing or at a public meeting. It may be worthwhile to give stakeholders opportunities to review the findings. In so doing, they take some ownership of the planning effort and its results, and suggestions for later stages of planning are likely to be offered. However, review by officials is always essential before findings are reported to others inside or outside the organization.

The completion of the tasks of the analysis stage is a significant event in the life of a planning group. Much hard work has been accomplished. The chairperson should recognize this milestone with some sort of whoop-de-do and expressions of appreciation for the contributions of the members, which is likely to boost group morale for the hard work that lies ahead.

◆ ◆ ◆

Chapter Five delineates the tasks that are required to develop program goals and objectives, including reviewing the guidelines for setting goals and objectives; translating needs into goals; turning goals into concrete objectives; formulating process and output objectives; and organizing and documenting program goals and outcome, process, and output objectives.

CHAPTER FIVE

SETTING GOALS AND OBJECTIVES

This chapter focuses on the tasks in developing program goals and objectives:

- Review the boundaries and guidelines for setting program goals and objectives.
- Translate problems and needs into program goals and program outcome objectives.
- Formulate process objectives and output objectives.
- Specify program objectives—outcomes, processes, and outputs.
- Organize, check, and document all program goals and outcome, process, and output objectives.

As the tasks are discussed, the relationship between program goals, program outcome objectives, process objectives, and output objectives are explored. Before addressing these tasks, the chapter discusses frameworks for goals and objectives, introduces a reliable framework, and explores the nature of the goal and objective setting process.

Frameworks for Program Goals and Objectives

Program goals and objectives are usually developed in accordance with frameworks prescribed by funders or officials of human service organizations. These frameworks serve two key purposes: they oblige planners to carefully think through what they want to accomplish and how it is to be accomplished; and they provide a structure for formulating, relating, organizing, and documenting written statements of program goals and objectives in funding proposals or program plan documents.

Another purpose for the use of a goals and objectives framework by funders, government departments, and boards of voluntary agencies is to hold organizations accountable for achievement or nonachievement of their commitments. Most service programs do not have the resources to conduct rigorous, extensive evaluations of program outcomes for recipients. Systematic assessment is one means of examining the validity of objectives. However, more modest assessments of outcomes can be conducted through a variety of measures, including focus groups, postservice and satisfaction questionnaires, and single-case designs. Formulation of program outcome objectives and of the means for assessment of their achievement orients service providers toward program development and what they should be doing. This inevitably leads to questions about the means of achieving goals and objectives—namely, the program's services. In this way, a goals and objectives framework accompanied by a plan for assessment helps revitalize programs and makes them more responsive to the needs and characteristics of service beneficiaries.

Organizations and their programs are being held accountable not only for the stated recipient outcomes but also for what they promised to do in the course of pursuing these outcomes—that is, their efforts and outputs. As these commitments become embodied in program funding applications, they become specific, de facto contractual obligations that the organization accepts on behalf of the program, extending to its operations as well as its outcomes for recipients. Major elements of this framework are now intertwined with budget explication and justification requirements, program monitoring and reporting procedures, and mandatory assessment or evaluation requirements.

Other developments also have placed demands on service providers to specify the outcomes of their work with a higher level of precision than was expected before. Staff in government departments are expected to develop annual plans that document program goals and objectives and their achievement, including any plans for funding "outside" programs and projects that must be reviewed and approved by officials in the executive branch. Annual program goals and objectives are also required by boards of trustees of school districts, historical and arts societies, libraries, and museums. In programs for the developmentally disabled, practitioners are required to develop individual independent-living and work-activity skills objectives linked to program goals and objectives. Multidisciplinary early intervention teams in schools (some teams are required by law or regulation) are specifically required to set program and student outcome objectives, and their achievement must be monitored at three months, at six months, or at annual intervals. Judges in family courts often order child welfare workers to specify the outcomes that birth parents have to achieve to regain custody of their children in foster care. All of these developments require service providers to work within goals and objectives frameworks and to be outcome oriented.

There are some variations in the requirements of these frameworks depending on the funders or officials who developed them. Goals and objectives are classified differently (for example, student learning outcomes versus student knowledge, skill, or attitude outcomes). Various names are used for similar types of objectives (for example, procedural, process, maintenance, operational, throughput). Different formats are used to show the relationship between types of objectives. And there are different expectations for the placement of the goal and objective statements in the program proposal. The specific requirements of funders and officials regarding these and related matters are often stated in the written instructions for completing the program proposal or on the funding application form. At the outset of this stage, the planning committee should review these requirements and should carry out its work accordingly. However, some funders and officials do not require a specific framework and let the planners decide this matter. (See Chapter Three, Exhibit 3.1, requisite item number 6, and see Chapter Eight.)

The focus now is on the elements of the framework, which shares a common logical and hierarchical structure with other frameworks. Readers should therefore find it easy to transpose its elements to satisfy the requirements of particular funders or officials.

A Recommended Goals and Objectives Framework

Figure 5.1 depicts the logical, hierarchical, and nested relationship of program goals, outcome objectives, process objectives, output objectives, and program activities.

In this framework, *program goals* (for example, children who have been sexually abused will experience a reduction in negative psychological and social consequences) are derived from the *problems and needs* determined through the planners' investigation (for example, sexually abused children experience self-blame, isolation, depression, guilt, anger, need for trust and security). Each program goal has to be specified in concrete measurable results that are wanted for the current or prospective recipients—*program outcome objectives*. For example, adolescents who are victims of sexual assault and who have withdrawn from customary social activities as a result of psychological complications—self-blame, shame, guilt—will

FIGURE 5.1. GOALS AND OBJECTIVES FRAMEWORK.

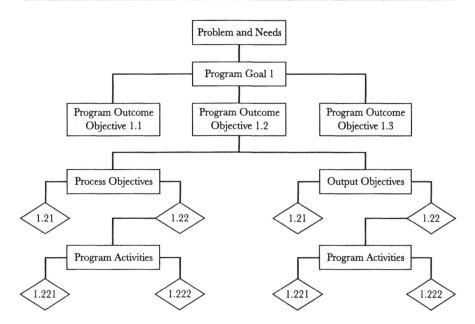

resume age-appropriate social activities, including family get-togethers, extracurricular school events and activities, peer relationships, and church activities. Achievement of the objective will be measured by comparing the frequency and types of social activities before and after the abuse, and after counseling. Program outcome objectives refer to achievements outside and after the program's process, must have real-world significance in relation to the problem and needs of concern, and presumably continue beyond the recipient's involvement in the program.

Each program outcome objective must have related process and output objectives. *Process objectives* pertain to the operational and procedural results wanted within the program that are essential to the achievement of program outcome objectives (for example, during the year 200X, support groups will be established and group counseling will be provided to adolescent female victims of sexual abuse). Achievement will be documented through staff activity reports and service statistics. *Output objectives* pertain to the quantity or amount of results wanted at or immediately following the outer boundary of the program process, or at the end of a program or budget cycle (for example, during 200X, thirty-two adolescent victims of sexual assault will receive supportive group services for two hours, once a week, for ten weeks). Achievement will be measured through service statistics. *Program activities* must be designed to achieve these objectives. For example, criteria must be established for determining who can benefit from supportive services, how groups must be composed, and what topics for discussion and group activities must be planned. Measures of the outcome, process, and output objectives must be established to assess results.

The program goal and related objectives of the framework are in a linear, interdependent, and nested hierarchical relationship in which each successive statement is both subordinate and instrumental to the one before it. Program goals justify and logically encompass program objectives. The program objectives give concrete meaning to the program goals by specifying the ends that are wanted and linking them to measurable evidence. The relationship between program goals and program objectives is discussed later in this chapter. Suffice it to say that planners must eventually produce a written set of statements of program goals and objectives, activities, and performance measures.

The Goal and Objective Setting Process

As we stated above, Figure 5.1 depicts the logical relationships among the elements of the goals and objectives framework. However, it does not depict the developmental process of goal and objective setting. The whole set of program goals and objectives are not formulated in a tidy, unidirectional, cascading flow beginning with a program goal, then moving down to the outcome objectives, then to the process and output objectives, and ending with the program activities. The actual process of setting many goals and objectives is a more dynamic back-and-forth process. A figure depicting the developmental process would have arrows going back and forth both vertically and laterally among the elements of the framework. For our purposes, we refer to this developmental process as a transactional process.

Planners start conceiving outcome, process, and output objectives after the nature of the problem and needs have been determined. Some of these objectives can be formulated in a linear, unidirectional manner. However, some outcome, process, and output objectives can only be formulated as the service program is being designed or after the design has been completed. Planners select outcomes that can be achieved by means of a service program that the agency is likely to offer. In fact, some outcome, process, and output objectives cannot be finally determined until the staffing plan, the units of service, and the budget have been approved. As planners design the program activities and formulate the related process and output objectives, they may realize that the outcome objectives were initially set too high or too low or that the recipient outcomes must be otherwise modified.

The sequence in setting program goals and objectives also depends on the nature of the planning venture (program change versus a new program), and on the discretion granted to the team in selecting solutions to the problem (the service program has been predetermined versus alternative service solutions may be explored). Planners need to decide which path they will follow in their work. However, program aims and results must be specified, whatever the approach and the nature of the planning effort. It is not possible and not necessary to capture the many complex ways in which the team can complete the tasks of the goal and objective stage. This chapter sets forth a logical, orderly way of addressing the tasks of the goal and objective stage of planning.

Review the Boundaries and Guidelines for Setting Program Goals and Objectives

The team's work plan should include a review of the charge and the mandates, as well as the organization's mission, relevant policies, and commitments. Planners should check whether there are boundaries and guidelines for the setting of program goals and objectives and proceed accordingly.

1. Are directives about program goals and objectives stated or implied in the planning charge? For example, a committee might be charged with responsibility for customizing and adapting a model service program to address local problems and needs. The model is likely to direct the committee toward particular recipient outcomes that can be achieved by this kind of service program. Other outcomes that could be desired for recipients must be excluded from consideration because the model is not designed to achieve them.

2. Are directives or constraints about program goals and objectives stated or implied in the mandates issued to the organization or the program? Some funding and accrediting agencies have umbrella goals or stipulations to which program objectives must be responsive. For example, one state agency on aging required service programs to pursue the goal of "least-restrictive alternative" in making decisions about the kinds of care to be provided to frail elders. In the CAC case example, the foundation wanted to support programs that helped victims and their families cope with the trauma of abuse and its aftermath (outcome for recipients). Accordingly, the foundation awarded the grant with the expectation that the CAC would pursue the process objective of timely provision of services soon after the abuse was discovered rather than waiting for an extended period.

3. Are there directives about program goals and objectives in the organization's mission statement or policies? Are there organizational commitments to and investments in particular programs, service delivery designs, beliefs, staff competencies, or even facilities that preclude the pursuit of particular program objectives or that indicate a preference for particular objectives?

These directives and constraints are usually embedded in narrative text. In order to deal with them in a workable manner, planners are advised to extract them and list them in a simple, abbreviated fashion on work sheets—just enough to know what you mean the next time you read what you wrote. Include a citation for the source of each set of directives and constraints in the event that the team has to refer to the original documents. After completing the review of the boundaries and guidelines for the setting of program goals and objectives, the team should have three documents in hand: the preliminary draft of the problem statement; the officials' or the funder's requirements for documenting program goals and objectives; and the work sheet of directives and constraints. If the planning effort is directed toward program change, the group should also have the existing statements of program goals and objectives in its possession. These statements must be assessed to determine whether they address the needs that were previously identified. Perhaps some program goals and objectives should be modified or no longer pursued, or additional ones should be formulated. With these documents in hand, the team can now proceed to the translation of problems and needs into program goals and objectives.

Translate Problems and Needs into Program Goals and Program Outcome Objectives

The team can take the next step in the program goal and objective setting process by reviewing the preliminary draft of the problem statement and deciding the features of the problem and needs that should be translated into program goals and outcome objectives. As stated earlier, program goals and outcome objectives refer to results intended for current or prospective recipients. The outcomes should address their *behavior* or the *problematic conditions* intended for change through a service program. Behavior refers to thoughts, feelings, words, or actions (for example, perceptions of low self-esteem, anxiety or depression, harsh exchanges between racial groups, child abuse, and recycling of hazardous domestic wastes). Problematic condition refers to levels of poverty, income, or education, or health, quality of justice, participation in the political process, or other circumstances that characterize a population.

A case example is used to illustrate this and other steps in setting program goals and objectives. In this chapter, it is the Parents' Respite Care Cooperative (PRCC). The PRCC is an association of parents who have children with developmental disabilities—moderate to severe mental retardation and physical disabilities. Both conditions present family members with challenges as they strive to provide in-home care for their child (for example, at the extreme, some adolescents function at the level of preschool-age children and need to be carried and fed). Motivated by a program in another city, the parents decided to come together to assess their situations and establish a respite care cooperative. A local agency agreed to guide the planning effort and assigned a staff member to assist them through this process. Assume that a committee composed of a few parents and the staff member has begun the goal and objective stage of planning, and they have just completed their preliminary draft of the problem statement. For now, just review the problems and needs. How the planning team translated some of them into program goals and outcome objectives will be discussed later in this chapter.

◆ ◆ ◆

The Parents' Respite Care Cooperative Case Example: Problems and Needs

This is the preliminary draft of the problem statement.

- Parents report that they are losing energy and interest in caring for their disabled children at home and complain of chronic stress, depression, and exhaustion. Many parents are considering residential placement for their children. Parents need some relief.
- Parents are not comfortable leaving their children with sitters and other usual child care providers. Because of this, parents and other household members do not engage in many customary social activities. Parents need care assistants who can deal with the unique care demands of their children.
- The child with the disabilities is at the center of family attention, and the other children are neglected. Children have several complaints: they can't get help with their homework; parents infrequently attend their school events; the family doesn't go to restaurants and doesn't take trips and vacations. Parents need opportunities to engage in customary social activities with their children.
- Some family members abuse the child with disabilities. Family members need opportunities to unburden their feelings about their situations in constructive ways. Some family members need to develop skill in managing difficult caregiving situations.

- There is alienation among parents, leading some to separation and divorce: spouses have little or no time alone together; mothers have most of the responsibility for caregiving even when the father is at home; fathers avoid responsibility for caregiving by investing themselves more and more in their work; spouses engage in angry exchanges and bicker about caregiving; spouses report absence or loss of affection.

The committee recognized that each family has some of these problems, but not others, and that there are fluctuations in the quality of their home lives and family relationships. Family strengths were also recognized (for example, love and mutual support, resilience, empathy, endurance, commitment, and resolve, among others).

◆ ◆ ◆

Program Goals

In terms of planning, goals and objectives are not the same. To ascertain their goals and objectives, planners often begin by stating the desired results for the current or the prospective recipients in general terms (the program goals); then through a process of specification (described later in this chapter), they decide on concrete program outcome objectives to give specific meaning to each goal statement. The objectives subsumed under each goal statement should define in concrete terms the particular changes that are intended to achieve that goal. That being the case, one might ask, "Why bother formulating program goals at all? Why not just prepare program objectives?"

Planners seldom have the capacity to translate problems and needs into statements of concrete results in one step. They tend to think in terms of goals rather than objectives until they have a better understanding of the problem or need and which of its features can be resolved through a service program. Goals give direction to breaking down, or getting a handle on, *selected aspects* of the condition, problem, or need. Planners conceive and state the intended results in a general way, and then through successive considerations, they select the objectives that represent the results that are wanted.

To illustrate the point, look at a statement listed in the PRCC case example: "Parents report that they are losing energy and interest in caring for their disabled children at home and complain of chronic stress, depression, and exhaustion. Many parents are considering residential placement for their children. Parents need some relief." As planners work on translating those problems and needs into one or more goals, their initial formulation might result in this statement: "Parents will increase their capacity to provide in-home care for their children with developmental disabilities." As planners examine their *working statement,* they often get an uneasy feeling and conclude that "we haven't got it right yet." What can planners do?

The team can backtrack to the preliminary draft of the problem statement, or even to the initial findings and supporting data, mull them over, and decide whether the goal statements address the substance of those matters. For example, one set of problems listed previously (stress, depression, exhaustion) suggests that the goal statement should be modified to include emotional and physical capacities to provide care. Besides backtracking, the work group can reconsider the goal statement itself by breaking it down or getting a handle on the meaning of some of its elements. For example, what about "increase their capacity"? What does that mean? Do planners really want to increase capacity? Or do they want to restore and sustain capacity? *Increase* implies improvement. *Restore* and *sustain* imply that capacity is adequate, but barriers to maintaining and expressing it have to be removed. Perhaps the committee wants parents to restore, sustain, and increase capacity. The goal statement only refers to the parents' capacity, but it should probably include the other children and extended family members. Perhaps some siblings or a grandparent living in the home also provide care, and their emotional and physical capacities also may need to be restored and sustained.

After considering these matters, the committee might have decided to concentrate on the parents. It might have reformulated the goal like this: "Parents will restore and sustain their emotional and physical capacities to provide in-home care for their children with developmental disabilities."

As planners make a few passes through the goal statement and reconsider the outcomes, they are able to formulate a statement that is a clearer and more satisfactory statement of the general outcome that they want to achieve. Although this statement does provide some direction in defining desired outcomes, it is still too general. What should planners do?

Program Outcome Objectives

Planners must proceed to transform each program goal into one or more specific desired and anticipated outcomes (now referred to as program outcome objectives) that denote future changes in the behavior or conditions of the target population. This will be covered later in this chapter, after we complete our discussion of process and output objectives, because the steps for specifying objectives are the same for all types. Before that, see the following segment of the PRCC case example, which illustrates the differences and the relationships between program goals and outcome objectives. Only some of the problems and needs identified by the PRCC have been translated into program goals and outcome objectives.

The Parents' Respite Care Cooperative Case Example: Program Goals and Outcome Objectives

For every goal, there is a specified and desired set of outcomes.

Program Goal A

Parents will restore and sustain their emotional and physical capacities to provide in-home care to their children with developmental disabilities.

Program Outcome Objectives A

Outcome objective one. After twelve months of participation in the PRCC, 80 percent of the parents will report experiencing relief from their caregiving responsibilities and increased participation in personal development and social activities, as measured by the couple's answers about these matters on the pretest and posttest questionnaire. Possible indicators of personal development are enrollment in a class or attendance at a lecture or presentation. Possible indicators of social activities are parental participation in other children's school events, participation in a bowling league, dining at a restaurant, and going to a movie.

Outcome objective two. After twelve months of receiving respite, 80 percent of the parents who stated on their PRCC applications that they had considered residential care for their children will report no longer feeling that way. Achievement of this objective will be measured by the couple's answers on the Annual Review Questionnaire.

Program Goal B

Spouses will improve their relationship with each other.

Program Outcome Objectives B

Outcome objective one. After twelve months of participation in the PRCC, 80 percent of the spouses with strained marital relationships at the time of their PRCC application will report improvements in anger management skills. Improvement will be measured by reviewing the couple's communication logs.

Outcome objective two. After twelve months of participation in the PRCC, 80 percent of the spouses who reported strained marital relationships at the time of their PRCC application will have developed, adjusted, and followed a written agreement regarding divisions of responsibility for caregiving. Achievement of this objective will be measured by documentation of a written agreement and by comparing the couple's answers about these matters on the Annual Review Questionnaire.

Outcome objective three. After twelve months of participation in the PRCC, 80 percent of the spouses who reported strained marital relationships at the time of their PRCC application will have jointly established and implemented training, discipline, and care plans for their child with a disability. Achievement of this objective will be measured by documentation of a written care plan and by comparing the couple's answers about these matters on the Annual Review Questionnaire.

◆ ◆ ◆

In these examples, program goals and outcomes are specified into the concrete results wanted for the prospective or current recipients of respite services. The objectives are the particular, measurable indicators or the kinds of results that planners want to achieve, whereas the program goals are too general to function in this manner. This is an illustration of how goals and objectives are in a hierarchical, nested relationship. Goals encompass and justify objectives, and objectives are the subsidiary and concrete specification of the goals.

Figuring out the specific outcomes to be achieved through a service program often results in the formulation of several objectives for each goal. According to Mayer, "Multiple objectives require special treatment because in all likelihood the decision maker will not have sufficient resources to maximize each. The relationship among them, therefore, must be analyzed to decide how to allocate efforts toward their respective achievement" (1985, p. 142). Mayer suggests that the relationship among program outcome objectives must be examined to avoid situations in which the pursuit of one objective detracts from the pursuit of others. He also alerts planners to other relationships between objectives (pp. 143–145). Outcomes may be additive in that the achievement of one enhances the attainment of others, and they may be sequential or simultaneous in timing. Program objectives may be independent in that the achievement of one is not related to the achievement of the other. Mayer suggests that when multiple objectives are additive, they can be combined or coordinated; when they are independent, they can be ranked in order of priority or feasibility; and when the pursuit of one objective interferes with the pursuit of another, it's important to maximize the positive effects of one objective and minimize the negative effects of the other. For example, participation in social activities with family members may interfere with the parents regularly having time alone together. Some planners manage the complexity among logically related outcomes by distinguishing levels of outcome, for example, ultimate—improved self-esteem; intermediate—appropriate assertiveness; and immediate—expressing dissatisfaction.

Program goals and outcome objectives are used in the design stage to guide consideration of a limited range of service or design alternatives, followed by the selection and development of one of them. As the solution is developed, the planning group relies on the program goals and outcome objectives to drive the design of the service program—that is, to make sure that it has the features essential to the achievement of the outcomes that are desired. Once the program is designed, the planning group must review its goal and objective formulations to ensure that they fit with the final program design decisions. Because planning is a discovery process, and planners are not prescient, some refinements or adjustments will have to be made in the initial statements of program goals and outcome objectives.

In some planning projects, the service strategy or some components of the service program are predetermined by officials or funders (for example, when they want to adopt or adapt a model program). In such a case, the prescribed strategy or components may predetermine the outcomes that can be achieved. For example, imagine that there are two agencies in two different localities that are seeking funding for nutrition programs for the elderly. However, in one locality the funder only wants to support Meals on Wheels, and in the other, the funder only wants to support communal meals—that is, meals that are served to groups of elders in a church or community center. Think about the outcomes that can be pursued in the second program that cannot be pursued in the first, and vice versa. Unlike the approach described previously, here the design drives the formulation of outcomes. Model programs often include model program goals and objectives, and planners adopt or adapt them to their local situation.

Formulate Process Objectives and Output Objectives

The next step for the planners is formulating process and output objectives.

Process Objectives

Process objectives denote the means by which the program outcome objectives are to be achieved. In planning a new or changed program, outcome objectives require companion process objectives, and each set must relate to the other. This interdependent linkage is essential to make certain that the achievement of program outcome objectives is operationally supported by the service program. Because program outcome objectives can be achieved in any number of ways, the process objectives provide direction about which sets of concrete means are to be carried out. This interdependence is illustrated in the next segment of the PRCC case example.

◆ ◆ ◆

The Parents' Respite Care Cooperative Case Example: Process Objectives

The PRCC developed the following process objectives:

1. In ten months, the first PRCC will have been formed and fully operating. Fully operating means (a) a steering committee established and functioning, (b) operating and governing procedures established and approved, (c) a parent appointed and trained as care manager, (d) parent-to-parent care training completed for parents of every child with a disability, (e) every participating parent involved in giving respite care—with an average of twelve hours of respite given per month, and (f) monthly meetings of the co-op for care exchange problem solving and mutual support initiated.

2. By the first month, participating parents will have been oriented to the program.

3. By the second month, a steering committee composed of one parent each from five families will have been selected to serve on a steering committee to develop a manual of program policies and a co-op handbook of respite care exchange rules, operating and governing procedures, and standards.

4. By the fourth month, the *Manual and Co-op Handbook* will have been completed by the steering committee and approved by the parents in the PRCC.

5. By the sixth month, at least ten families will have been recruited to participate in the first co-op.

6. By the eighth month, parent-to-parent care training will have been completed for parents of every child with a disability.

7. By the ninth month, participation in respite care will have been started and a parent appointed and trained as care manager.

8. By the tenth month, the members of the co-op will have started their monthly meetings for care exchange problem solving and mutual support.

9. After the PRCC has been implemented, each family will have used at least an average of twelve hours of respite per month by the sixth month of participation in the PRCC. Over this period, parents will have increased the frequency of respite per month up to the average. The achievement of this objective will be measured by examining the care manager's respite participation logs.

◆ ◆ ◆

If planners were too optimistic about the time lines, the initial number of applicants, or other matters, the outcomes wanted for parents would have to be revised (for example, an average of twelve hours of relief from caregiving per month, per family, by the sixth month of operation depends on the enrollment of at least ten families in the PRCC). Note that all of these objectives refer to what is to happen and not to what is to be gained by participating in respite care. Also note that these objectives prescribe some of the features of the program (for example, a steering committee, parent-to-parent training, a parent care manager, a monthly meeting). Process objectives are essential to guide the development of the service intervention in the program design stage of planning.

If the planning effort is focused on a change in an existing program, the team must formulate process objectives related to the program alterations that are wanted. These alterations may include eligibility criteria, an expansion of the service area or target population, the way services should be delivered, the flow of service beneficiaries through the program, the way staff are deployed, staff skills essential to the effective operation of the service program, an interagency joint assessment and service planning process for recipients, and others. The aspects of the program targeted for alteration (for example, the first-come-first-served admissions practice in the CAC case example) have to be transformed into the concrete modifications desired in the program's operations (for example, victims of a current severe sexual assault, and their parents, will have an initial interview with a CAC counselor as soon as possible after the referral, but no later than twenty-four hours). The focus here is not on all of the aspects of a program, but only on those aspects that have direct implications for recipients. The emphasis here is not on organizational changes, such as the introduction of computer technology or modifications in administrative structure or personnel policies that have no particular bearing on the recipients.

Alterations in process objectives sometimes require concomitant changes in the outcomes pursued on behalf of recipients. In the CAC case illustration, the work group decided that particular low-priority cases did not require an immediate response and crisis management services. Educational sessions and peer support groups were suggested as more appropriate service interventions for these cases. So the outcomes desired for them shifted from an exclusive focus on coping with the emotional turmoil of the abuse to focusing on skills in recognizing potentially abusive situations and behaviors and protecting oneself from them. As planners set program process objectives, they must be vigilant about their impact on recipients and the outcomes intended for them.

There are circumstances, however, in which process objectives do not necessarily have to be explicitly connected with program outcome objectives, nor can they be. For example, in planning a change in an existing program, the team may develop process goals regarding the installation and operation of a computer-assisted record-keeping process that does not affect objectives for recipients. However, program outcome objectives must always have process objectives. The program goals and objectives framework helps planners discriminate between different types of objectives and achieve relatedness when that is essential.

Program outcome objectives for recipients are often inappropriately expressed in terms of what the service provider intends to do with them, rather than what the recipients will be enabled to do or how they will be affected as a consequence of participating in the service program. For example, in formulating objectives about racial conflict in a high school, officials might be inclined to say, "Teachers will develop racially integrated discussion groups," rather than saying, "Students who have exchanged racial taunts and insults will (do such and such)." The first inclination refers to what teachers will do in the program, but the second begins to state an objective that students must achieve. Differentiation between process and outcome objectives is important for several reasons. Outcome objectives address the rationale for the service program and keep service providers focused on recipients. Outcome objectives direct program evaluations to the assessment of effectiveness—benefits to, achievements by, or changes in recipients. Furthermore, funders expect such distinctions, and these expectations are often prominently declared on the fund application form or in the instructions for completing the proposal. Some funders automatically disqualify proposals that fail to make discriminating formulations between program outcome, process, and output objectives.

It is not surprising that service providers can more easily identify what activities they intend to undertake than what they intend to help recipients achieve because identifying activities is under more staff control and has more certainty of achievement. However, if an organization wants to direct services toward particular outcomes that recipients should achieve and evaluate the impact of services on the achievement of these outcomes, then program outcome objectives are essential. In actuality, both types of objectives should be stated, but program outcome objectives should be directed toward behavior or social conditions of recipients, and process objectives should be directed toward facets of the program's operations. In program outcome objectives, the verbs should focus on the actions of the recipients or the changes in the recipients, whereas in process objectives the verbs should focus on the actions of the staff or the changes in some program procedures (for example, students will *learn* how to use a computer, and staff will *teach* them how to use it).

Output Objectives

Output objectives pertain to the quantity or amount that is produced at (or immediately just over) the outer boundary of the program process during a given time (for example, daily, weekly, monthly, annually, or at the end of a program or budget cycle). Output objectives may be set for the number of persons to be served, the number of services to be provided (for example, days of care, counseling sessions, health screenings, classes taught), or the number of goods to be produced or delivered (for example, holiday ornaments to be produced—sheltered workshop; food and gift baskets delivered—the Salvation Army; historical society publications). Output objectives are essential in deciding the scale of the program, the units of service to be provided, the staffing plan, and the financial resources required to implement the program. These objectives must be congruent with the outcome and process objectives. Returning to the PRCC case example will illustrate the point.

◆ ◆ ◆

The Parents' Respite Care Cooperative Case Example: Output Objectives

As the committee was formulating outcome and process objectives, it decided that it also had to consider the volume of work that the co-op should try to accomplish (that is, the number of families that should participate in the co-op and the average number of hours of respite that each family must contribute to achieve the desired relief). If the committee's estimate for the number of families and the average number of respite hours was too low, there may be too few respite caregivers and the level of relief may be too low to achieve the outcomes wanted. If the average number of hours of respite to be given was set too high, the provision of respite may be too burdensome, and the respite received may be insufficient to sustain participation in the PRCC. Clearly, output objectives must be congruent with outcome objectives.

In addition to providing respite, parents must develop and manage the cooperative. Therefore, in deciding on output objectives, the committee must also calibrate them with process objectives. For example, considering that some families in the co-op may withdraw their membership, how many families should initially be recruited to the co-op if it is to have ten families providing and receiving respite by the end of the first year of operation? Is it realistic to expect that in addition to providing respite care, members of the co-op will be able to meet monthly for two hours to attend to its administrative workings and to participate in support groups? These and other considerations led the committee to formulate the following output objective:

By the end of the first year's operation, ten families will have participated in the PRCC with an average of twelve hours of respite given per month.

◆ ◆ ◆

This output objective identifies the number of parents who must provide a particular level of effort to achieve the outcome objectives identified earlier. The process objectives that focus on the development of parents as caregivers and on the management of the co-op influenced the committee's decision about the number of families and the average number of respite hours to be given per month. If a paid staff member served as the care manager, organized and managed the monthly meetings and the parent-to-parent training, and otherwise served as the central person for the co-op, then the parents may have been able to give and receive more respite.

Planners formulate concrete outcome, process, and output statements through a process of specification, which refers to a detailed explication of the results wanted. It is therefore essential to know the properties of objectives and how they can be formulated, which is addressed in the next section.

Specifying Program Objectives: Outcomes, Processes, and Outputs

Program objectives are statements of specific, desired, anticipated outcomes, processes, or outputs. Well-formulated program objectives must be stated in concrete and measurable terms and must include the standards of performance by which attainment will be judged.

Specifying program objectives is a challenging task. As the committee strives to develop concrete, measurable program objectives, it is common to agonize over them: Are the stated outcomes concrete enough? Does each clarification need more concrete specification? Where do planners stop? Uneasiness and uncertainty about the adequacy of program objective formulations are inherent in program planning. One straightforward test is the "reasonable person's" assessment of their apparent validity and appropriateness—that is, as determined by the assessments of the planners, the organizational officials who review the program plan document, and the funders who review submitted plans. Persons competent in program evaluation are also capable of judging the adequacy of program objectives. However, there are some common standards for writing program objectives. Because outcome, process, and output objectives have some common properties, in the following section, they are all referred to as program objectives. The program outcome examples will illustrate the points, because these objectives are usually more challenging for planners to write than the others.

State the Program Objectives in Measurable Terms

The desired outcome, process, or output should be concretely specified, and indicators of achievement should be identified. Otherwise the program objectives will be arbitrarily defined and measured. In the PRCC case example, the committee developed several indicators of improved familial relationship.

◆ ◆ ◆

The Parents' Respite Care Cooperative Case Example: Measurable Program Objectives

After twelve months of participation in the PRCC, 80 percent of the spouses who re-ported strained marital relationships at the time of their PRCC application will report improvement in their relationships. Possible indicators of improvement are these: spouses regularly spend at least three hours a week with each other; spouses are not verbally abusive when they disagree on methods of behavioral management; or spouses do not interrupt each other during conversations.

◆ ◆ ◆

Look now at another outcome example, one focusing on the specification of "improved self-esteem." Does that mean that service beneficiaries will no longer make self-deprecating comments? No longer report feelings of inadequacy? Stop denigrating or belittling their accomplishments? Not give up in frustration (I can't do it), but show ability to sustain interest and effort? Be appropriately assertive when confronted with intimidating or controlling people? Care about their appearance? All or some of these?

Indicators of achievement must vary with the program setting, the characteristics of the service beneficiaries, and the nature of their problems and needs. For example, look at an indicator of self-esteem: service beneficiaries will be appropriately assertive when confronted with intimidating or controlling people. Assume that improved self-esteem is being pursued by a women's center in a community college. What does it mean to be appropriately assertive with that target population in that setting? It could mean to verbally challenge, state one's preferences, object, take exception, express discomfort or dissatisfaction, or any or all of them. However, improved self-esteem and appropriate assertiveness require different expression when high school students learn to deal with pressures to use alcohol or drugs or when employees learn to cope with an overbearing boss. Accordingly, the designs of the service programs to improve self-esteem and assertiveness among members of these groups must be customized (for example, confrontational tactics may be appropriate in a community college to deal with sexism, but not in a high school when dealing with a drug pusher). Striving for clarity about the outcomes that are wanted is important because it defines the focus of the program design stage of planning.

In specifying the desired behavior or condition, it is helpful to identify the circumstances that are associated with particular behavior, events, or conditions stated in program outcome objectives. Circumstances refer to a time, place, situation, or contingency. They are important to include in program outcome objectives because they define and specify the desired outcome or attach qualifiers to achievement. In the PRCC case example, the focus is on marital and familial relationships as affected by having to care for a child with a disability. In the community relations example, officials might specify that the service intends to reduce racial tensions at high school athletic events. Circumstances have a bearing on the actions or services that are required to correct a problem and are therefore useful inclusions in statements of program outcome objectives.

There are other guidelines for deciding when program objectives are concrete enough. When program outcome objectives are developed for categories or groups of service beneficiaries, it is inevitable that the objectives will be more broadly conceived and less concrete than outcome statements formulated for particular service beneficiaries. The most concrete formulations for particular recipients are typically the responsibility of those who provide the service. Planners must provide examples of some indicators and the range of outcomes that should be pursued. However, staff should be given some latitude in defining specific outcomes for particular individuals depending on what is encountered at the point that services are delivered.

Some planners develop a catalogue of objectives with indicators. For example, community-based programs for emotionally impaired adults have developed indicators for aggression, safety, transportation, personal grooming, decision making, and many other behaviors. For this population, the indicators for improved skill in decision making include seeking information, examining and weighing alternatives, setting priorities, consulting with others, setting personal goals, and developing plans and taking steps to carry them out (Garwick and Brintnall, 1977, pp. 59–68).

If it is essential to identify behavior or conditions that need to cease, then the objective to achieve the absence or disappearance of something should be accompanied by a statement about what should take the place of that behavior or condition. For example, it is not sufficient to say that a community relations program is intended to eliminate racial conflict. It is more helpful to specify the behavior that should replace racial conflict or at least the kinds of conflict behavior that should be reduced—for example, "After participating in six conflict mediation sessions, teen members of racial groups involved in conflicts will work together on three community service projects."

Planners have to learn to be "comfortable" with being uncomfortable about their initial formulations. They can rarely formulate program objectives with a high level of precision on the first try. It is advisable to draft program objectives incrementally, with appropriate intervals. This process usually helps the team overcome the group delusion that its final statements are final.

State the Standards of Performance

Standards of performance refer to the measures intended to assess the achievement of particular outcome, process, or output objectives. These measures may include the time or interval required to achieve the objective or the frequency with which something is to occur. For example, in the PRCC examples, there are references to monthly intervals, percentage of parents that are expected to show improvements, and the average number of respite hours received and given. In the CAC example, victims will be interviewed as soon as possible but within twenty-four hours.

In addition, standards may specify outcomes such as the length of time for which the changes in the recipients are to be sustained or the preferred qualities of the condition or the behavior. For example, fathers in a parenting class will learn and will use age-appropriate disciplinary measures and will maintain their composure when dealing with their children's tantrums. Planners would have to further specify age-appropriate composure and inappropriate disciplinary measures. Adverbs are useful in specifying standards of performance because they express time, manner, or degree (for example, "implement time-outs immediately," "discipline a child consistently and appropriately," "exercise moderately," "behave tolerably," "perform passably").

Standards help figure out whether objectives are too low (no challenge) or too high (cannot be achieved or are unrealistic). By including standards of performance in objectives, it helps specify the intended outcomes, processes, or outputs. For example, the community relations program may strive to eliminate racial conflict at high school athletic events immediately, but racial harmony as evidenced by multiracial social groups sitting in the stands could take several months to a year.

Standards of performance may be stated in terms of changing or sustaining certain behavior or conditions. For example, a program change objective may address the need for the parents of children with developmental disabilities to decrease inappropriate protective behavior that blocks development of independent-living skills (for example, refusing permission to attend a special resident camp). Sometimes a change for the better is not possible, and objectives focus on sustaining a condition or behavior (for example, the level of functioning of a person who is physically challenged, or of an elder in an assisted-living situation). If the objective focuses on change, it should state the direction of change, for example, increase or decrease, positive or negative, or whatever criterion of direction is appropriate to the particular program goal.

Desired behavior or social conditions may be specified as quantitative or qualitative statements. For example, quantitative objectives may address the frequency, percentage, or distribution of an outcome or output of a service program. These are examples of quantitative objectives: as a consequence of the school retention program, 75 percent of the students who have been identified as at risk of dropping out will earn a high school diploma; one hundred meals will be home delivered to frail elderly persons three times per week. Qualitative objectives may address parents' self-reported improvements in life satisfaction because of their participation in a respite program for families with a member who is developmentally disabled.

Organize, Check, Document, and Display Program Goals and Objectives

In completing this stage of the planning process, the team should at least have produced rough drafts of its program goals and objectives. The team should pull together the drafts of these formulations and sort them hierarchically according to program goals and related outcome objectives and then array process and output objectives according to their related outcome objectives. Some attention should be given to the ordering of program objectives under a program goal (for example, juxtapose those that must be achieved sequentially). Once the program goals and objectives have been organized and arrayed, the team should check the formulations according to the following suggested guidelines:

1. Does every program goal have program outcome objectives? If every goal yields too many objectives, it should be restated as two or more goals with corollary objectives. If a goal yields only one objective, it may be too narrowly formulated.
2. Do the program outcome objectives have related process and output objectives?
3. Is there such an imbalance among program outcome objectives that five of them cover 30 percent of the problem and one covers 70 percent of the problem? Such an imbalance suggests that the team may be having difficulty formulating program outcome objectives in the area where there is an imbalance.
4. Is there a hierarchy or a priority among objectives? If so, is that evident in the sequencing and arrangement of objectives, or by another sign?
5. Is there congruence among the objectives? Can some objectives be achieved only at the expense of others? For example, children's protective services programs often struggle over the congruence between such objectives as

maintaining the family unit and protecting the neglected or abused child. Will the former be achieved at the expense of the latter? This situation should be flagged for attention in the design stage. Among other reasons to do so, funders expect the proposal to address such matters.

6. Are the program goals and objectives arrayed with attention to logical and instrumental relatedness among the outcomes.
7. Have so many program outcome objectives been formulated that their attainment is beyond any program's fulfillment?
8. Can the program objectives be feasibly attained in light of organizational and program resources, capabilities, and competencies?
9. Are the program objectives set so low that they are not challenging?
10. Are the program objectives stated in measurable terms?

The answers to these questions may reveal modifications that are needed in the statements and that can be made immediately, whereas others must be addressed later in the planning process. After making the adjustments, the team should prepare a working document of program outcome, process, and output objectives that can be used to guide the design of the service program. The working document must also be used as the basis for writing the final program goal and objective statements for the funding proposal (see Exhibit 3.1, Chapter Three, requisite item number 6, and see Chapter Eight).

There are many resources available to planners and service providers as they formulate program goals and objectives, and it is not necessary to start afresh. A Google search on the Internet using the key words "program goals and objectives in human service organizations" yielded over nine hundred thousand sites. As in any search, many are unrelated to the specific domains of interest. However, many sites are within the domains of nonprofit and governmental human service organizations. Their mission statements and program goals and objectives range from those that are exceedingly well formulated to those that are skimpy and in need of further development. Even when the program goal and objective statements are not well formulated, planners can use them as points of departure to formulate their own. Of the sites found through the Google search, more often than not, process objectives dominated the presentation of program goals and objectives. A more focused search on particular types of human service organizations (for example, youth-serving organizations, corrections, employment training) yielded more focused results. One site in particular (www.mygoal.com) is entirely devoted to goals, including goal plans—premade or customized—that pertain to many subjects germane to human service organizations of all sorts. Some publishers specialize in curricula that concentrate on goals and objectives, such as curricula on life skills pertaining to child development, education, and disabilities (see www.brookespublishing.com). In any case, with a few focused searches, and within a short time, the Internet is likely to yield several sites that planners will find useful as they develop program goals and objectives.

◆ ◆ ◆

Chapter Six outlines the initial tasks and decisions of the design stage of planning: reviewing the guidelines for designing new programs or changing existing ones and then deciding what the new service will be or how the existing program will be changed.

LAYING THE FOUNDATION FOR A SUCCESSFUL DESIGN

This is a good time to review what planners have accomplished and what they have in hand up to this point in the planning process. The problem analysis and needs assessment have been completed, and the findings have been written in a preliminary draft of the problem statement. Planners have some understanding of the nature of the problem, including its features, consequences, causes, magnitude, and the characteristics of the persons affected by the problem. The factors, needs, and segments of the population that will be the targets of the service program have been determined and documented. Those targets have been translated into working written statements of program goals and objectives. All of these write-ups must now be used as a reference to guide the planners' work during the design stage. Now the planning group can begin designing program changes or the new service program—the activities that will be directed toward the program goals and objectives that pertain to specified recipients with a particular condition and needs. The term *design* refers to the creative and technical process of deciding the features of a new or changed service program. The process involves translating the program goals and objectives, as well as the understandings of the problem, needs, and the target population, into a new or changed service plan. The term *design* also refers to the particular configuration of the essential components of the service program in the plan document. (See Chapter Seven.)

Figure 6.1 depicts what has been accomplished to this point in the planning process and what has to be addressed next.

FIGURE 6.1. SEQUENTIAL STEPS IN THE PLANNING PROCESS.

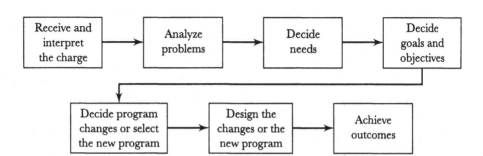

This chapter focuses on the initial tasks and decisions of the design stage of planning:

1. Review the boundaries and guidelines for selecting and designing program changes or a new service program.
2. Decide on the new service program or the programmatic changes in the existing service.

Keep these two things in mind: the ongoing revision and development of the work plan and the writing of the final program plan document. As the team enters the design stage, members must again decide what has to be done next, who needs to do it, and how it will be done. Eventually, the team must produce a program plan document and submit it for approval to the officials who issued the charge. (See the sections that discuss requisites for a program plan document in Chapters Three and Eight.) As the design stage unfolds and each design decision is made, it is advisable for planners to develop a work plan that includes note taking. This will ease the preparation of the narrative description of the service program to be included in the program plan document, which will also serve as the blueprints for the implementers, who must "build and install" the new or changed program.

Review Guidelines for Selecting and Designing Program Changes or a New Service Program

Chapter Three, Initiating a Planning Project, discussed how planners must review the charge, the mandates, and the organizational policies and commitments.

One reason for doing so is to find out the directives and constraints on various aspects of the planning process. Those reviews may have identified directives and constraints on the design of the service program. When they are found, the team must retrieve them at the beginning of this stage to figure out their significance for selecting and designing particular program changes or a new service program. If the team does not or cannot look into this matter at the outset, then it should do so at this stage. This can be accomplished by addressing the following questions:

1. Does the planning charge state or imply directives about the selection and design of the program changes or the new service program? For example, in the CAC case study in Chapter Four, the executive charged the work group to develop budget-neutral solutions to the waiting list problem. In the Parents' Respite Care Cooperative (PRCC) case example in Chapter Five, the planning committee knew from the outset that it would be developing a co-op based on a model program in another city.

2. Do mandates that have been given to the organization have stated or implied directives or constraints about the selection and design of program changes or the new service program? Some funders have design specifications for the problems, conditions, needs, or service programs earmarked for funding. These specifications must be incorporated into the design of the service program, or else the proposal will be rejected, or at best, planners will be asked to revise and resubmit it. Funders have different expectations about which elements of the service program must be documented and about the detail required. For example, one funder simply stated that the services proposed should be fully and clearly described. Another funder instructed applicants to document methods of recruiting recipients, measures for ensuring accessibility to minorities, procedures for reducing stigma and for maintaining confidentiality of records, program schedules and time lines, and more.

Some regulatory and accrediting agencies also have stipulations about particular service programs. For example, licensed day-care programs have required staffing ratios; nursing homes and assisted-living programs for the elderly must have a medication management program that conforms to state regulations; the number of patrons that can visit a museum at any one time is set by fire marshals.

3. Do the organization's policies have directives about the selection and design of program changes or a new service program? Are there organizational commitments to and sunk costs in facilities, particular programs, service delivery designs, beliefs, or staff qualifications that either preclude the pursuit of particular programs or designs or show preference for them?

Chapter Three discussed how important it is for planners to maintain an open, exploratory approach, because statutory, regulatory, and funding requirements change as the planning effort is being carried out. In addition, all relevant mandates and policies will not be discovered at the outset (despite the conscientious efforts of the planners), and some will inevitably be discovered while planning, or even during implementation. So during earlier stages, the team may have discovered additional directives and constraints or modifications of the initial ones, which must now be considered (for example, in one situation, changes in nursing home standards required a planning team to revise its staffing assumptions). Planners have an obligation to design programs that meet formal requirements and to develop discretionary features of the program that are congruent with required features. Designing programs with prohibited features is a fruitless exercise, unless planners believe that funders or officials can be persuaded to waive certain requirements, make exceptions, or allow a variance.

The planning group would be wise to list the design requirements and limitations from all of these sources so that the directives and constraints that it must face are known, as it moves into this stage of planning. After the boundaries of decision making have been established, the planning team can take the next step.

Decide on the New Service Program or Changes to the Existing One

In some ventures, planners do not have to concern themselves with these tasks because the decisions about them were made by officials at the outset of the planning effort. Sometimes officials issue a charge to develop a particular new service program or one based on an innovation or model developed elsewhere. In such cases, the planning group does not have to address alternative service programs. Instead it has to work on converting the program to the local situation. In planning a change in a current program, officials may issue a charge to develop a particular modification in response to new regulations, policies, funder's requirements, changes in the composition of the recipients, or the development of an improved practice. In this case, the group has to work on customizing the modification to the unique circumstances of the organization and the program.

Sometimes planners are given the freedom to select among alternative service programs or changes in an existing program. They must generate a limited set of options (congruent with directives and constraints) that have the promise of achieving program objectives, then screen and select one or more alternatives, and then develop and document the ones selected (Mayer, 1985, pp. 152–156).

A few cautionary remarks are in order here. During the initiation and analysis stages, ideas about program design will inevitably churn in the minds of the planners as they learn about the problem. They cannot resist zooming ahead to program design matters to entertain their hunches about what might or might not work. This generates some early sifting and sorting of solutions or program features, and the ones perceived as promising simmer while the team completes the tasks of the early stages of planning. It is understood that professional experience, keen insight, and intuition might enable a planner to come up with the right solution early in the planning process. Nevertheless planners should not short-circuit the design process. Their design work must be directed by their conception of the problem and the needs, and by the working statements of program goals and objectives.

Generate Alternative Solutions

The team can generate a limited set of alternative solutions by reviewing the notes in its working folder or by recalling ideas that emerged during earlier stages of the planning process. The range of individual and group techniques used to generate alternative solutions (for example, focus groups and structured group interviews) is well documented (Krueger, 2000; Johnson and Johnson, 1997; Van Gundy, 1981, pp. 75–146; and Delbecq and Van de Ven, 1977). These techniques often enable the planning team, the service recipients, the experts, the volunteers, or the other staff to contribute to the development or modification of the service program in a structured way.

It is advisable to scan specialized professional journals and the publications and research reports of the agencies of the U.S. government for descriptions and evaluations of service programs (to avoid "reinventing the wheel"). They are available in libraries that serve as repositories of government documents. These repositories contain publications that have a wealth of information about human service programs that is underused. (If you are not already doing this, you will be amazed when you discover the helpful documentation on those shelves. Examine the tabs on the inside back page to see how often the publications were borrowed.) In the professional literature, there are syntheses of studies, descriptions of best practices, and state-of-the-art or knowledge reviews on specialized interventions and service programs (for example, Manela and Moxley, 2002; Biegel and Blum, 1999; Crane, 1998; Hunt, 1997; Guttmann and Sussman, 1995; Schorr, 1988, 1997). Planners may conduct manual or computer searches. They can either do it alone or rely on librarians (information specialists) in university, hospital, court, or public libraries. These specialists can direct planners to indexes and databases if help is needed (Hayes, 1994, pp. 109–116). Depending on the time and the resources available, planners' explorations can range from "dipping into the literature" to sophisticated, systematic, and comprehensive analyses of particular interventions or service programs (Forness and Kavale, 1994; Rothman, Damron-Rodriguez, and Shenassa, 1994). The Internet can also be explored for Web sites that are relevant to the planners' work. (See Resources for Planning Service Programs.) All of these independent sources of information about the efficacy of interventions and service programs can be used to screen and select the most promising alternative.

Planners can also seek program documentation from officials in other programs, visit other program sites to confer with staff and service recipients, or scan service descriptions that have been published on the Internet or in compendiums. (See Resources for Planning Service Programs for a selected list of Web sites, and United Way of America, 1976). Any of these efforts are likely to yield an existing service program or ideas about service designs that have promise in achieving program objectives and that can be modified for application to a particular target population and organization.

The level of effort devoted to identifying and exploring options depends on the available time and resources, and also on whether officials or funders want a review of alternative solutions to be incorporated into the funding proposal. Planners rarely engage in a comprehensive scanning of alternative solutions, make an evaluation of the utility of each alternative, and then select the one with the most utility. The scale and complexity of such an approach would overwhelm planners, and most human service organizations could not afford it. Planners' decisions about new or changed programs are made in a context of bounded rationality in which there is limited scanning of alternatives (York, 1982, pp. 14–20; Etzioni, 1977, pp. 87–97), and decisions are typically made in a disjointed and incremental way (Lindblom, 1977, pp. 98–112). Some consultants or researchers with specialized expertise who have cumulative experience with a problem or a program may be able to engage in a more comprehensive and thorough decision process than the planners.

Screen Alternative Solutions and Select One or More of Them

After generating a list of alternative solutions, planners must screen them and select one or a combination of them. Several criteria must be considered in selecting a solution.

Alternative's Promise of Success. Does the alternative show promise of alleviating problems, meeting needs, and achieving program objectives (Thomas, 1984, p. 160)? Planners must entertain program hypotheses or theories about the likelihood of a particular solution affecting a change in a specific problem as it is experienced by a particular group of people (Kettner, Moroney, and Martin, 1999, pp. 73–88). Theories influence how one conceptualizes the problem and how a program is designed to deal with it. For example, if delinquency is attributed to a lack of opportunity for legitimate access to consumer goods and resources, then education, job training, and employment are services that are congruent with the conception of the problem. If delinquency is attributed to strained parental relations or emotional problems, then counseling services are congruent with the conception of the problem. Planners must determine that there is an influential relationship between the elements of the program and the factors that contribute to the problem. Is the alternative likely to solve the problem and meet needs as previously determined?

The PRCC case example from the previous chapter illustrates this point. The committee might have formulated the following program hypothesis: if parents have sufficient relief from caregiving duties provided by persons trained to meet their children's unique care requirements, and if parents can constructively unburden their frustrations and get support for in-home caregiving, then they are likely to sustain their in-home care for their children with disabilities and to improve family relationships. These hypothetical means-ends should be analyzed by planners to assess whether they can reasonably conclude that there can be an influential relationship between program goals and objectives in the respite care co-op. This analysis tests the logical adequacy of the planners' judgment about the efficacy of the service program.

Alternative's Goodness of Fit. Is there a goodness of fit between the alternative solution and the characteristics of those in need? Is the alternative solution responsive and sensitive to the characteristics of the target population? In the CAC case example, the work group was considering a change in staffing arrangements to deal with the waiting list problem. Instead of having all of the counselors provide all of the services, the work group was contemplating the assignment of one staff member as a specialized crisis counselor who would provide timely assistance to all incest cases. After completing the crisis counseling process, the victim would then be transferred to the long-term treatment counselor. Such a transfer would result in a discontinuity of care that would be troubling to some victims, especially those who had difficulty revealing the abusive incidents from the outset. So it turned out that the initial proposed modification was not sensitive to the needs of some victims, and it had to be amended accordingly.

In another situation, planners wanted to develop a new vocational program for high-functioning adults with mental retardation. In scanning alternative service programs, those that kept trainees in the workshop were rejected in favor of competitive community employment and enclaved workshops (for example, a cluster of trainees in a fast-food service under supervision of a job coach). Community-based vocational programs were believed to provide the developmental challenges essential to the growth of these high-functioning adults, whereas the sheltered workshop approaches were not. Furthermore, the sheltered workshop's need for reliable, high-functioning production workers led to their retention in the program beyond what was necessary to meet their vocational needs.

Alternative's Adequacy. Is the alternative solution adequate, suitable, sufficient, or commensurate with a particular condition (Flynn, 1992, pp. 78–79)? In the PRCC case example, the program provides at least twelve hours of respite care per month to emotionally and physically exhausted parents. However, it also requires these parents to contribute at least twelve hours of respite care per month for other members' children. This arrangement does not appear to be a solution commensurate with the parents' condition. However, in the cooperative model adopted by the PRCC, nearly all respite is provided in the homes of caregiving parents while they care for their own children. As a result, there is a net gain of relief most of the time, and the service is adequate.

Alternative's Compatibility. Is the alternative compatible (Thomas, 1984, p. 160)? In deciding changes in a current program, the planning team must assess whether the changes are compatible with the other components of the program. For example, one adult education program experienced a decline in enrollment when a firm hired many students for low-skill jobs. In order to boost enrollments, and in response to requests for educational services for mental health patients living in the community, school officials admitted them into the program. The new students required so much individual attention that the educational needs of the other adult learners were neglected. Clearly this change was not compatible with the goals and objectives of the program.

In selecting a new program, planners must decide if it is compatible with other programs in the organization. For example, officials in a community education program had developed a successful and well-subscribed educational day-care program for children whose parents were employed. Administrators declined an offer of funds to develop an educational program for people on public assistance that included some ex-offenders. The two programs could not coexist in the same building because some ex-offenders might pose safety and security problems for the children, and the fee-paying parents of children in day care would object to the arrangement.

Alternative's Possibility of Being Implemented. Can the alternative be implemented? Are the technical and structural aspects or processes of the program so complex that they cannot be carried out? Does the staff have the competence to institute and provide the service or carry out the change, and if not, can they be trained or given the necessary assistance, or can new staff be hired? What is the impact on implementation if other programs or organizations are to be involved? For example, in one situation, a suggestion for an intergenerational friendship program between an elementary school and an assisted-living center for the elderly was enthusiastically supported by officials from both organizations. After closer examination, it turned out that the program presented several operational problems that made it impractical. Teachers would have to obtain the parents' signed permission for their children's participation. Alternative plans would have to be developed for children whose parents refused or forgot to grant permission. From the standpoint of the elderly residents of the center, some probably prefer not to spend time with children. That being the case, officials would have to make alternative plans for them. The variations in the elders' level of functioning would require inordinate amounts of time to prepare highly individualized activities between elders and their student friends. Some programs require onerous interagency collaboration and accountability arrangements that cannot be feasibly implemented.

Alternative's Financial Feasibility. Does the organization have the financial and other resources to carry out the alternative? Is it financially feasible? What kind of space, facilities, and other capital costs are required? What operational or administrative support is necessary? What kind of staff support is necessary? Is it efficient? For example, a residential program for troubled youth wanted to buy and install a ropes course in a wooded area on its campus. The course is an elaborate structure of cargo nets, climbing and swinging ropes, and other equipment that provide unique challenges and require cooperation among users. The initial plan to purchase the course was sent back to the drawing board when a few staffing and storage questions were asked: Who is going to maintain the ropes course? What kinds of staff resources are required to put it up and take it down? What is the ratio of staff to residents that is essential for safe use of the course? Is it essential to build a fence to prevent unauthorized and unsupervised use of the course? Where will the equipment be stored during the winter months?

Systematic Comparison of Alternatives

To facilitate selection, planners can develop a table that summarizes the trade-offs among the alternatives and facilitates comparison of them. The PRCC case example demonstrates how a table might be constructed. For purposes of this illustration, the PRCC planners have now identified four different programmatic alternatives of respite care. See Table 6.1. Again, the example is illustrative, not definitive.

In this table, the PRCC committee relied on program-specific dimensions and judgments as contained within the Advantages and Disadvantages columns of Table 6.1 (for example, preparation of qualified caregivers, affordable respite care, parental involvement in respite, hours or length of respite). As the committee compared

TABLE 6.1. TRADE-OFFS OF RESPITE OPTIONS.

Respite Options	Advantages	Disadvantages
Co-op	Variable amounts of respite possible—at least an average of twelve hours per month, days, overnight, and weekends; affordable; compatible with current agency programs; up and running in one year; pool of qualified, trained caregivers; mutual support; likely to provide relief.	Parents must provide reciprocal hours of respite service; dependent on volunteers; co-op cannot deal with a large pool of parents.
Professional	Parents would not have to provide in-home care and reciprocate respite; qualified assistant caregivers; duration of care flexible; likely to provide respite; implementable within six months; could serve many parents.	Costly, therefore would be used infrequently; qualified caregivers have to be recruited, trained, and supervised; high turnover of caregivers.
Group home (weekend respite)	Long period of respite; no reciprocity of respite; qualified caregivers; could serve large pool of parents.	Very costly; capital expenditures required for a residence and furniture; staffing costs; high fees for parents even if subsidized; up to one year to implement; would be used infrequently; insufficient use of home—four days per week.
Group home (respite vacations)	Same as above.	Same as above. Also, high competition for respite during summer months; inefficient use of the home during the rest of the year.

Source: Adapted from Jansson, 1999, p. 213. Copyright © 1999. Reprinted with permission of Wadsworth, a division of Thomson Learning: www:thomsonrights.com, fax: 800-730-2215.

the advantages and disadvantages, it could have used these criteria to assess the four respite care options and select one of them. In addition, or instead, the committee might have synthesized its assessments by qualitatively ranking them (for example, high, medium, low, varies) to judge the relative merits of the respite options according to each criterion. See Table 6.2. Although planners may differ about the relative importance of the criteria and the assumptions on which the rankings are based, their compilation and presentation in a tangible form can facilitate discussion and resolution of differences and the selection of an alternative.

Examination of the comparative rankings in Table 6.2 indicates that overall the Co-op was given the most favorable assessment, but Professional In-Home Care Assistant received higher rankings on the first two criteria. The term *Varies*, in some of the cells, was used when committee members could not make a definitive judgment, because their rankings varied as they thought about caregiving situations in particular families. For example, Professional In-Home Care Assistants would provide the most relief (the first criterion), but it would be too costly and would therefore be used infrequently by many families. Therefore the criterion Congruence with the Characteristics of Those in Need was assessed as *Varies*. Plan-

TABLE 6.2. COMPARATIVE RANKINGS OF RESPITE OPTIONS.

| | *Respite Options* | | | |
Criteria	Co-op	Professional In-Home Care Assistant	Group Home Respite (weekends)	Group Home Respite (vacation)
Influential relationship between factors, needs, and service	Varies	High	Low	Low
Adequacy	Varies	High	Low	Low
Congruence with characteristics of those in need	High	Varies	Low	Low
Compatible with other organization programs	High	Low	Low	Low
Implementable	High	Low	Low	Low
Financial and other resources	Low cost	Medium	High	High

Source: Adapted from Jansson, 1999, p. 215. Copyright © 1999. Reprinted with permission of Wadsworth, a division of Thomson Learning: www:thomsonrights.com, fax: 800-730-2215.

ners also gave more weight to this criterion as they decided on the Co-op, which illustrates yet another way that planners can use the rankings in Table 6.2.

After the service is selected or the program change is decided, planners can proceed to develop the new or changed service program. At this stage of the planning project, if not earlier, team members are often confronted by the sober realization that their decisions have the potential to benefit—or fail to benefit—many persons. Occasionally, members voice their strong sense of responsibility and the team's obligation to make program design decisions that are in the best interests of recipients (notwithstanding that members may have different interpretations of what that means). Team members are concerned that failure to solve problems, meet needs, or improve community conditions will lead to a blaming of the victim: failure might be attributed to unresponsive recipients or intractable problems, when the failure might in fact be due to a flawed design. At times, these values and concerns can be invoked to overcome differences, mobilize consensus, and reach a sound design decision.

Before we discuss the key tasks that planners must complete to develop the elements of a service program, we introduce a case example that will illustrate our points in this and the next chapter.

◆ ◆ ◆

People and Pets Together Case Example: Outreach to the Elderly

Officials in a rural community look for a way to reach out to elderly residents.

Introduction

The County Council on Aging (CCOA) is located in Rural County, which is known for its farms and light industry. The county has several small towns that serve farming communities and three small cities, with the largest having a population of seven thousand people. The CCOA staff conducted telephone interviews with elderly persons in the county to understand their problems and assess their needs. The findings were reported to the CCOA board, whose members were troubled by what they heard. Almost 80 percent of the respondents had ten or fewer hours per week of contact with friends or relatives. Almost half of the two hundred respondents who were sixty-five years of age or older and lived alone reported age-related crises evolving from losses—children and relatives who have moved, the deaths of a spouse and friends, unemployment, diminished status, and reductions in meaningful activities. A high percentage of elders also reported one or more emotional troubles—loneliness, depression, restlessness, fear, vulnerability, feelings of emptiness, and a sense of hopelessness and uselessness.

Two CCOA staff members and two board members were charged to look further into the problem and recommend a program to deal with it. The group examined the study's findings, reviewed some literature (Zisselman, Rovner, Shmuely, and Ferrie, 1996; Cole and Gawlinski, 1995; Netting, Wilson, and New, 1987; and Beck and Katcher, 1983), explored some Internet sites (Washington State University, 2003), and conferred with staff from other programs. The group learned that companion pets can often help elders cope with some of the emotional reactions stemming from age-related crises. Pets provide elders with something to care for. Dogs and cats have to be fed, bathed, brushed, and otherwise engaged on a daily basis. They are responsive to their owners and provide an outward focus for their attention. Pets have helped elders improve their well-being and promote healthy living (for example, while walking their dogs, elders exercise and have social encounters). Dogs can increase the owner's sense of security, which can allay some fears, anxieties, and feelings of vulnerability. Pets can have a positive influence on an elder's reality orientation, because daily responsibility for pet care requires pet owners to be task oriented.

The group recommended and the CCOA Board approved the development of a cooperative program with the Humane Society called People and Pets Together (PPT). A representative from the Humane Society was added to the planning group. PPT would enable interested elders who live alone to adopt a dog or cat that would serve as a pet companion. Planners believed that PPT would also increase the elders' social network—staff from the Humane Society, other participants in PPT, other pet owners, veterinarians, and neighbors.

The next chapter will explore the essential components of service programs: participant activities, sequential order and phases of service activities, accessibility, duration or time span of activities, the amount of contact between staff and recipients, and different pathways through the program that recipients can travel. It also discusses key tasks in the design stage of planning.

CHAPTER SEVEN

DEVELOPING THE ESSENTIAL PROGRAM COMPONENTS

Once the planners have decided on the program changes or the new service program, work can begin on developing the *essential components:*

- Participant activities—staff participant activities and recipient participant activities
- Sequential order and phases of service activities
- Accessibility, including location and service hours
- Duration or time span of service activities
- Length and frequency of contacts with recipients
- Recipient pathways through the program

These are the critical universal building blocks of any service program and the main focus of this chapter. The discussion includes an explanation of each component and its related design tasks. The chapter also addresses other tasks of the design stage that planners must accomplish:

- Organize clusters of participant activities into service roles.
- Conduct an equal opportunity and diversity audit.
- Decide on the program's linkages to the host organization and the persons, groups, associations, and organizations in the community.
- Determine resource requirements.

In planning a new program, all of these basic components and tasks must be addressed. In planning a program change, one or more components, or *sub-components,* might be the focus of modification, but many or all others might then require derivative adjustments. Planners should be vigilant about this possibility. For example, think about the changes required in a summer resident camp program when the board members have changed admission policies to include children with physical disabilities during a special session at the end of the season.

This chapter begins by explaining the participant activities and the sequential order and phases, followed by a continuation of the People and Pets Together (PPT) case example from last chapter, which illustrates how planners can develop these two components. Then each of the remaining components is discussed. In real situations, these components are not developed in the serial fashion in which they must be presented here. They are usually developed concurrently or in a back-and-forth fashion, as some segments of the case example will illustrate, although some elements within a component might be addressed sequentially. Sometimes a component will be introduced in the chapter in advance of its explanation because it is embedded in the discussion of another component. For example, in the discussion on design tasks related to participant activities and sequential order, some aspects of accessibility, duration, and length and frequency of contact are introduced, even though these components have not yet been explained.

As indicated throughout this book, planners would be well advised to develop write-ups as their design work progresses. This cumulative record will be helpful in satisfying the documentation requirements of officials and funders. (See Chapter Three, Exhibit 3.1, requisite item numbers 8, 9, and 10, and see Chapter Eight.)

Participant Activities

The design of service programs requires attention to *program activity sequences,* generally concentrating on two types of participants: *service providers* and *service recipients.* Service providers necessarily include those persons who are in immediate contact with recipients—that is, those whose activities or interventions constitute the key process by which service is given. These service providers are sometimes referred to as *line staff, contact staff,* or *direct-service staff.* The perspective taken here requires inclusion of *all* personnel who have contact with recipients, regardless of their titles. For example, receptionists (who are sometimes volunteer greeters) perform key duties in explaining available services to prospective recipients, helping them complete initial forms, and so on. Bus or van drivers, patient accounts representatives, food service and maintenance staff (particularly in residential settings), and security personnel are examples of other participants whose activities ought to be considered in designing service programs.

Current recipients who are in contact with direct-service staff and prospective recipients who will be must also be considered in designing service programs. Likewise attention must be directed to secondary or indirect recipients, such as family members and significant others, who may participate in some aspect of the program process or otherwise need to be considered as the service program is designed.

The participant activities of the staff and the recipients must be addressed as planners develop program changes or the new service program. The required or expected behaviors of staff persons within activity sequences are generally known as *tasks* or *procedures*, which are sometimes specified in extensive detail regarding who should do what, when they should do it, and how they should do it. Other terms, such as *practices* and *standard operating procedures* (SOPs), are also used to refer to the customary or required patterns of staff activities (including their decisions). The words *method, technique,* and *best practices* are also used in the professional literature to refer to the required or expected behavior of staff. Note, however, that each of these terms is usually applied only to staff activities, so they tend to ignore or deemphasize recipient behaviors and decisions, which are also relevant to the design and functioning of service programs.

Recipient participant activities must be given at least the same attention as *staff participant activities,* because recipients are the reasons for the existence of service programs. In addition, recipients "are self-activating entities" (Hasenfeld, 1983, p. 9) with high degrees of complexity and variability, including levels of voluntariness and motivation, all of which must be addressed as the service program is designed. The recipients' involvement and cooperation are as critical to the program's effectiveness as anything the staff will do.

Activities refer to publicly observable behaviors, patterns, and decisions that guide actions and are documented (or that can be inferred from behaviors). Decisions must be taken into account because various choices and judgments are essential elements in all programs. For example, prospective recipients must decide whether to apply for services, and staff must decide whether they qualify. Staff must decide the service program that is appropriate, and prospective recipients must decide whether or not they want to participate in it. Actual program sequences include not only participant activities that are planned and required but also behaviors that are discretionary, evoked, and sometimes even forbidden. Although the concentration here is on the expected activities, other probable recipient and staff behaviors need to be identified (for example, in a school service program, classroom misconduct and absences of pupils or irritable conduct by harried administrative or frontline personnel).

Certain kinds of events must also be included in a full conception of activity sequences: predictable or likely occurrences (for example, national holidays, severe weather conditions that interrupt normal program operations); contingencies, which refer to events that may occur, but are not predictable, yet require anticipatory management (for example, staff absences due to illness, a camper sustaining an injury, elders in PPT becoming too ill to care for their pets); and milestones, which are occurrences that mark significant points in the service program (for example, an elementary school student with a learning disability completed an educational program, and he and his parents have been scheduled for a conference with school officials to decide his educational placement). Clearly, these kinds of events significantly affect participant decisions and behaviors and must be addressed by planners.

Sequential Order and Phases

Programs are composed of participant activities within particular periods or cycles. Unless these activities are carried out in some orderly way, there cannot be a program process, and recipients cannot receive service, or at least not as intended and expected. For this reason, this component of programs deserves special attention. Whether baking a cake, changing a tire, recycling household waste, conducting a parent education class, counseling spouses, or helping elders adopt a companion pet, there is some orderly way of proceeding, one step at a time. There are differences in the steps or their progression—as with various types of cakes and models of automobiles and jacks—and their idiosyncratic patterns, but some order must be followed if the desired results are to be gained. Wide variations are evident among programs, yet each adheres to a more or less appropriate progression of steps to reach its objectives, starting at the beginning and moving along until the end is reached.

In addition, within almost every activity sequence, subsets or segments of steps that are closely related to one another can be identified, each segment occurring at a typical period during the usual program cycle. Here these are designated as *phases* of activity sequences in order to focus attention on important subsets of activities and decisions within the total service process.

Within each phase, then, there is usually a prescribed or preferred (or at least typical) order of activities and a definite (preferred) order of phases within the cycle of the service program as a whole. Certain linked sets of activities and decisions within a phase must be completed sufficiently before the next phase can begin, proceeding in order through subsequent phases of the entire cycle. For example, in academic programs each term or semester is composed of characteristic subsets of activities (class sessions, tests, and the like), and the end of each year marks an important phase.

Cardiac and physical therapy programs also follow a predetermined schedule of rehabilitation sessions. For these and other kinds of programs, there are alternative phases that provide particular services for some recipients—depending on their characteristics or on developments occurring at an earlier phase. In educational programs, tracks and majors are well-known examples of planned alternative program sequences that occur at predefined points, with some students following one route while others follow a different route. And differential diagnosis can lead to differential services only when they are specifically planned within the larger cycle of the service program. In the PPT program, elders who have experience with pets will follow a different service path than those who have never had a pet. (This will become clearer in the discussion of the flowcharting of activity sequences or program processes through diagrams and charts that will be presented as the chapter continues.)

Most direct-service programs should have at least four major phases, referred to here as the *admission phase,* the *assessment phase,* the *intervention phase,* and the *termination phase.*

The admission phase is also known as application, registration, or intake. This phase includes all activities directed at securing each individual's participation in the program and culminates in decisions by the staff to offer or refuse service and by the prospective recipient to accept or decline recipient status and involvement. In some situations, refusal of service is followed by referral to another service program in the same or another organization and by the prospective recipient to accept or decline the referral.

The assessment phase is also referred to as screening, testing, investigation, diagnosis, social study, or evaluation, depending on the particular program and organization. Assessment includes a set of procedures to evaluate the attributes, behavior, status, condition, or situation of recipients, which leads to classification. Classification determines recipients' service status, the benefits to which they are entitled, and how they will be processed or served (Hasenfeld, 1983, p. 113). The assessment phase consists of all activities having to do with developing and confirming a service plan for each recipient, including recipient choices and decisions.

The intervention phase is also referred to as service, instruction, training, counseling, mediation, or treatment. This phase includes staff-recipient interactions directed at the achievement of service goals and objectives.

The final phase, termination, is also known as completion, graduation, discharge, case closing, release, dismissal, expulsion, or eviction, depending on the particular program or organization. This phase encompasses the steps needed to reach and implement a decision to end service to the recipient, including follow-up activities when they are part of the sequence.

The following sections discuss the elements of each phase to provide guidance to planners with the design of service programs. As stated earlier, the extent to which each element must be addressed depends on the focus of the planning effort—a new program or program change—the unique aspects of the planning venture, and the requirements of officials and funders. Planners can decide which elements to include in their design activities. For example, in some planning projects, the work group might only be required to rough out the application and assessment phases of the service program. The detail work would be carried out by the implementers.

Design the Elements of the Admission Phase

As planners decide the admission activities of a new or changed program, several matters usually require attention: dissemination and marketing of information about services, the criteria that will enable members of the target population to qualify for the program, and the admission process.

Dissemination and Marketing of Information.   Securing participation in the program begins with getting positive and cogent information about the service directly (or indirectly) to prospective recipients and sources of referral. Such information can be disseminated prior to admission (for example, to a residence for frail elderly persons), at the time of admission (for example, to a juvenile detention facility or runaway shelter), or under some circumstances not until after the service is provided (for example, hospital emergency services).

Some segments of the target population are capable of using services once they have been informed about them. Others know about a service, need it, but are reluctant to use it. Variations in motivation and capability are due to any number of factors, such as illiteracy, negative perceptions of service providers or negative experiences with them, denial that one has a problem, fears about revealing one's troubles, stigma, language differences, and alienation. In a study of family resource centers (FRCs), the researchers learned that there were significant differences in how respondents from different ethnic groups, and from urban and rural areas, first heard about the FRC. The findings also suggest that information dissemination and marketing strategies must address potential recipients' reasons for not using services (O'Donnell and Giovannoni, 2000). Often several methods of marketing and disseminating information have to be planned to enable prospective recipients to use it (for example, program pamphlets, the media, Web sites, phone calls, home visits, contacts with leaders in the target population or representatives of churches or schools, reliance on former recipients or bilingual staff and volunteers, direct contact by a representative of the program, or financial or in-kind incentives to encourage participation) (Boehm, 2003).

◆ ◆ ◆

People and Pets Together Case Example: First Design Stage Meeting

At the first meeting of the design stage, the chairperson directed the planning group's attention to the ways that PPT should disseminate information about the program in order to recruit elders with age-related problems who live alone. The group decided that a targeted information dissemination and case-finding approach was preferred. That being the case, the chairperson posed this question: "Who is likely to know these elders?" Several suggestions were offered: staff from other CCOA programs, volunteers who deliver hot meals to elders, visiting nurses, and clergy from local churches. The group decided that these were good suggestions, and the chairperson recorded them for eventual inclusion in the program proposal that has to be submitted to CCOA officials. The members also recognized that some sources of referral might be put off by the notion of companion pets for lonely elders. To counter this, they recommended the development of a pamphlet for skeptics that would explain the successful use of pet companions with patients in veterans' and children's hospitals, residents in nursing homes, and others. In addition, the members recommended that PPT staff should make a personal contact with the sources of referral outside the CCOA to explain the opportunities for participants in the program.

◆ ◆ ◆

Criteria for Qualifying for the Program. In addition to the criteria that prospective recipients have the interests, problems, conditions, or needs that are the focus of the planning effort, other qualifying criteria might include some personal and social characteristics: age, gender, educational achievement, residence, ability to pay for services, marital or family status, prior service record, motivation, willingness of significant others to participate, or others. The criteria may be few or numerous, simple or complex, universal or particular. Criteria to qualify for public assistance are numerous, complex, and particular (for example, income, value of assets, number of dependents, residence, ability to work, and work skills). In contrast, the criteria for membership in a neighborhood youth center are often few, simple, and universal (for example, applicants must live within a designated geographical area and be between the ages of six and eighteen). Universal criteria are inclusive within broad categories, whereas particular criteria are selective or restrictive (for example, a juvenile court can develop a probation program for all first offenders, or it can restrict it to first offenders from low-income families with single parents).

◆ ◆ ◆

People and Pets Together Case Example: Continuation of the First Design Stage Meeting

Later, during the first meeting of the design stage, the chairperson reminded the group that it was charged to develop the PPT program for county elders sixty-five years of age and older, who lived alone, who were lonely, or who had other emotional problems stemming from age-related crises. He suggested that these general criteria would be sufficient to provide guidelines to those making referrals to PPT. Elders would be admitted to the PPT program if they were interested in adopting a pet, if they had no physical or health barriers to caring for a pet, and if their residence and outside area were deemed appropriate for a pet. The group realized that some elders are on low fixed incomes and could not afford the $100 to $125 for veterinary and license fees, and for pet equipment. Planners agreed that low income should not be a barrier to participation in the program, and that funds should be sought to subsidize some adoptions. The chairperson took notes, which he would later develop for incorporation in the program proposal.

◆ ◆ ◆

Admission Process. The major elements that are usually included in the development and documentation of the admission process are discussed next.

1. *Initiation of the admission process.* Planners must decide who should initiate the admission process (for example, the prospective recipient, a parent in the case of minors, a staff member, a volunteer, or a representative from another program or agency). The decision about the initiator of service might be dictated by law or regulation (for example, as in the case of child protective services) or influenced by the needs and characteristics of the recipients (for example, staff may have to reach out to prospective recipients who are mistrustful of service providers).

2. *Information to be sought in processing admissions.* Some basic identifying information is required in any admission process in order to document the identity and characteristics of the individual recipient (for example, name, address, telephone number, age, composition of household, marital status, education, income, occupation, gender, and race). Specific information varies among service programs and is fundamentally dependent on the program's conception of the problem and the needs to be addressed (for example, in a homeless families' shelter, mothers seeking admission for themselves and their children are asked about domestic violence and current use of illegal substances). Whatever is included in the admission application form, the rationale for the information that is sought and how it will be

used should be thoughtfully decided and in some instances must be documented. For example, funders that support health or legal services often have dedicated sections in their grant application that require such documentation, including the need-to-know safeguards against the misuse of information and privacy and confidentiality issues. Prospective recipients may also want to know why particular information is being gathered and how the program intends to use it. Planners must consider these matters and develop explanations for them.

In developing new programs, sometimes planners and implementers can use or adapt existing admission forms and protocols developed by the organization. When this is not possible, decisions about the information to be obtained at admission may constitute a substantial undertaking. For this reason, sometimes planners do not invest themselves in this work, and officials defer it to the implementers if and when the program plan is approved or funded. Conversely, planners must detail the admission information and include it in the proposal when officials or funders have preferences or requirements for inclusion of particular segments of a target population in the service program. Such documentation provides officials or funders with a measure of assurance that the service program intends to be responsive to their preferences or requirements.

3. *Management of admission information.* The development of a new or revised system to manage admission information may include the admission application, the way admission information must be stored (for example, on a card or form, in a case record or computer file), retrieved (for example, manually, computer assisted), and distributed (for example, to other departments or personnel, to the recipient, to significant others, to referral or funding reimbursement agents). Rules governing access to the information and confidentiality of it also may have to be developed and documented.

4. *Sources of information about the applicant.* Typically, the prospective recipient is the source of the information. However, others may have to be involved either in addition to or instead of the recipient, because they are legally required to participate (for example, in the case of minors), because the recipient is not reliable (for example, an offender) or is unable to provide information (for example, a stroke patient), or because the perspectives of others are essential to initiate the service process (for example, crime victims, referral agents, recommendations of teachers concerning students in academic difficulty and in need of special services).

5. *Management of the admission process and decisions.* Planners must decide who will manage the admission process and who can or must make the admission decision. In some service programs, the qualifications for managing the admission process are not high, and virtually any staff member can guide the completion and submission of an application (for example, an application for membership in a

community center). In other service programs, the admission process and decision are complex and require staff with professional or technical skill, team reviews, or the approval of regulatory agents (for example, preapproval of hospitalization in some managed-care situations).

In designing the management of the admission process, planners may also have to consider the merits of a centralized versus a decentralized admission process. Centralization refers to the degree to which an organizational or program process is consolidated in one unit or role. Decentralization refers to the degree to which the process is dispersed in the organization. Hospital admission, for example, is often centralized, so that a patient can be assigned to a room and gain access to several departments and services in one process with one admissions official. Universities have both centralized and decentralized admission processes. Students are first admitted by a centralized graduate college office of admissions, but then they must seek entrance to a program and apply for a parking permit, housing, financial aid, and athletic tickets, all from different units within the university.

The size and complexity of the nonprofit organization and the service program, and the scale of program operations, must be considered by planners as they configure the management of admissions. For example, the admission process might be centralized and carried out by specialized personnel in large nonprofit organizations. However, in small nonprofit organizations or service programs, admissions might be assigned to several staff members who also perform other roles in the organization. Staff members who have sole responsibility for admission are likely to develop proficiency in processing and admitting recipients. However, a lone admission specialist in a small program or nonprofit organization might have difficulty coping with surges in applications. If the specialist resigns, goes on vacation, or takes sick leave, the organization might be temporarily incapacitated, because admission competencies were not developed among other staff members.

The work group would be mistaken if it addressed admission only as a bureaucratic event that must be planned for in a mechanically efficient and effective manner. Sometimes members of the target population do not want to apply for services due to the behavior of staff members who are inattentive to applicants and treat them in a perfunctory or brusque manner, whether the application procedures are bureaucratic or not. For recipients, admission is often imbued with meanings that planners must consider as the admission process is designed. For example, imagine the range of feelings and reactions of persons being admitted to a hospital, a correctional facility, a hospice, a domestic-assault shelter, or a foster home. Imagine the feelings of ambivalence when adult children seek admission of a parent to an assisted-living facility or nursing home. Even the application for services that appear to be emotionally neutral may be emotionally charged for some prospective recipients (for example, registration for a water aerobics class by a person who has recovered from a heart attack). Appropriate staff behavior during the application process is more likely if planners give careful attention to recipient behaviors that might be evoked by the admission process. The management of all of these feelings must be planned for as well as the qualifications of the person doing the managing.

6. *Site of admission process.* Ordinarily, admission is completed at the site where services are provided. However, the characteristics and conditions of recipients, or other factors, might suggest that other, or a combination of, locations are necessary or desirable (for example, an elder with diminished skills in independent living who might need home health care; an outreach worker who might initially meet gang members at the police precinct and later complete their admission to a youth service program in their neighborhood and residences). Sometimes admission has to be conducted off the program site and in the recipient's setting or in a neutral setting if the *prospective* recipients are to become *actual* recipients. Issues related to location are discussed more fully in the section on Accessibility.

7. *When admission is to be completed.* In many organizations, admission is completed prior to assessment and intervention, or admission and assessment are completed concurrently. However, in some programs, admission is completed after assessment (for example, patients in a mental health hospital evaluated for admission to a community residential program). In other programs, admission is concurrent with assessment and intervention (for example, a child taken into custody by protective services).

8. *Admission procedures.* All staff procedures, tasks, and decisions and all recipient steps and decisions must be decided and documented, and both sets can be more or less standardized. Standardization refers to the degree of uniformity of the admission process. Some procedures are highly standardized due to the nature of the benefits or services. For example, all persons applying for financial assistance from a government agency are required to complete a lengthy, complex, standardized application regardless of their characteristics and the nature of their indigence. Other admission procedures have little standardization and are determined by the characteristics of the recipients or their presenting problem and the discretion of the staff. For example, some churches sponsor open-door, no-questions-asked food programs in which recipients show up at noon and are provided with a meal.

Application procedures can facilitate or impede requests for admission, membership, services, or benefits. Sometimes such procedures take the form of highly ritualized, inflexible, and tedious application practices that are incongruent with the behavioral styles and self-perceptions of some recipients. For example, some "in-your-face-type" male gang members with poor reading skills, who are seeking employment services, have been unable to get through the application forms, have been intolerant of waiting in reception areas, and have failed to follow through with their appointments. It is important for application practices to be adapted to unique or eccentric recipients.

Difficulties with application procedures are not confined solely to such extreme cases. Many application practices are unnecessarily burdensome, inappropriate, or even offensive to intelligent, high-functioning individuals. For example, one adoption agency required prospective adoptive parents to complete lengthy, self-disclosing application forms prior to the first interview. Prospective adoptive parents reported their skepticism about such a tedious and intrusive first step. They found it more acceptable to go to another organization that conducted informational group meetings first, followed by private conferences, and then the formal application.

9. *Completion of the admission process.* Planners also have responsibility for documenting the completion of the admission process, including how staff should manage individuals who are rejected for admission and how staff should inform applicants about admission. In addition, planners make suggestions for managing the recipient's transition to the next phase of the service program.

Design the Elements of the Assessment Phase

In some service programs, admission and assessment are carried out concurrently. In others, they are carried out sequentially. Although there are common elements in both phases, the assessment phase has some unique elements that warrant separate attention. The major elements that are usually considered in designing and documenting the assessment process are discussed in this section (adapted from Thomas, 1984, pp. 44–45).

Again, the degree to which these components are detailed during the planning process varies from one planning venture to another. A complete assessment design is required if the planning effort is focused on a change in the existing assessment process or if the funder wants a detailed assessment protocol in the proposal for a new program. Under other circumstances, the planning team might rough out the assessment process and leave the finished work to the implementers.

Purpose and Focus of Assessment. Purposes necessarily vary from one service program to another, and planners must decide and document what is to be accomplished through the assessment process:

- Determine whether the recipient qualifies for services, benefits, or resources
- Describe the recipient's interests, goals, problems, conditions, needs, strengths, motivations, behavior, relationships, attitudes, values, background, history, or resources
- Ascertain causes of problems, needs, conditions, or relevant behavior
- Classify or label the recipient's condition, status, or situation
- Determine whether the recipient can benefit from the service
- Predict performance or outcomes

The focus of the assessment varies among service programs. In some service programs, there is no assessment activity for individuals, but needs and problems are assumed or understood for all members of a class (for example, new parents and family education classes, prospective retirees and retirement-planning workshops, library patrons and library services). In counseling programs, the personal and social characteristics of recipients and their problems are of interest. The assessment might address the recipients' strengths, the causes and consequences of their problems, family and developmental history, personality, and other factors. In some youth-serving agencies, the staff have to certify an applicant's age, residence, and parental permission for membership, and each applicant must pass a physical exam to qualify for participation in gym and swim activities.

Sources of Assessment Information. Assessment may involve only the service beneficiary, or it may include family members, referral agents (for example, teachers), or representatives of other organizations (for example, consumer credit counselors may have to contact credit departments of businesses). Assessors may be the sources of information when they have opportunities to observe recipients (for example, counselors observe student classroom behavior). Records of the results of previous assessments or services may also provide sources of information for updating, redoing, or designing an assessment. (The previous discussion in this chapter about sources of admission information is also relevant here.)

Who Conducts the Assessment. Sometimes the assessor is mandated by law or regulation (for example, county protective services staff are required to assess allegations of neglect and abuse; insurance companies require that a diagnosis must be completed by professionals with particular credentials). When planners have discretion, and depending on the situation, one or more assessors may be appropriate:

- The staff member providing the service
- Assessment specialist internal or external to the organization
- The recipient
- The recipient's significant other or family members
- Representatives from another organization
- Volunteers

Means of Assessment. Assessment information can be obtained in individual or group interviews, through observation of the recipient, or by using forms, schedules, checklists, inventories, instruments, and tests and measurements that are manually completed or computer assisted.

Timing of the Assessment. The assessment may be carried out prior to or concurrent with admission, prior to or concurrent with service, after the provision of service, or before, during, and after provision of service (for example, emergency surgical patients) (Thomas, 1984, p. 45).

Site of the Assessment. The factors previously discussed in the section on site of admission also apply here, as well as the factors discussed later in the chapter in the section called Accessibility.

Analysis of Findings and Development of the Service Plan. The steps to be followed in analyzing and interpreting the findings of the assessment, and in developing the service plan, must be detailed. Here are two ways that these steps have been carried out: one assessor with or without the review of a supervisor, or a diagnostic or service team with or without the review and approval of an official or an authorizing agent (for example, physicians are required to sign off on assessments of care plans for persons in nursing homes; school principals must review teacher assessments of students and must approve recommendations for expulsion before the assessments are forwarded to central administration).

Management of Assessment Information. The methods for documenting, storing, retrieving, duplicating, and distributing assessment findings must be addressed, including the policies governing these activities. For example, planners have to detail the way assessment information must be recorded (according to standardized protocol), stored (in a case record or computer file), retrieved (manually or computer assisted), and distributed (other departments or personnel, recipient, significant others, referral or funding reimbursement agents). Rules governing access to and confidentiality of the information may have to be written (for example, patients' and students' rights to records, privacy rights, recipient permission to distribute information, controls regarding who has a right to retrieve information).

Completion of the Assessment Process. The management of the transition from assessment to intervention must also be documented, whether the assessors are the same as the intervenors or not. As with admissions, planners must address assessment as a process and a set of results imbued with meanings for recipients and others that must be anticipated and planned for. Again, imagine the feelings of patients who must have an intrusive diagnostic procedure, such as a heart catheterization or a biopsy. Imagine how they might feel while they are waiting for the findings and when they are informed about them. Appropriate behavior on the part of staff during and after the assessment is more likely if program planners give careful attention to recipient behaviors that might be evoked by the assessment process and its results.

Design the Elements of the Intervention Phase

This phase includes staff-recipient interactions to address conditions or problems, meet needs, provide benefits or resources, and transact services to achieve program goals and effect the desired changes. The specific activities vary from program to program and depend on the focus of the planning effort—that is, a new program or a change in an existing one. Again, planners are reminded that a change in any of the other phases of the service program may require derivative changes in the intervention phase. This section discusses the major elements in developing the intervention phase. It is up to planners to decide which ones must be included in their program designs.

Benefits and Intervention Services to Be Provided. The service plan must include a description of the benefits (for example, emergency heating assistance, clothing, shelter) and any services to be provided (for example, tour of historical sites, children's encounters with the arts, housekeeping assistance, training for independent living, day care, drug counseling). The description should include staff or volunteer participant activities, techniques, procedures, work methods or approaches to be followed, and decisions to be made. (Eventually, these elements must be transformed into the service roles that will be responsible for carrying them out. This is discussed further in the section called Organize Clusters of Staff

Participant Activities into Service Roles later in the chapter.) Recipient behaviors, steps, and decisions must also be included in the description. For example, in a proposal to combat school violence in high schools, planners might recommend the production of videotaped portrayals of critical incidents and instructions in coping with them through the use of role plays and problem-solving exercises. Each of these items must be developed and documented, including participant activities of staff and students. The ways that planners can develop both sets of participant activities are detailed in a later section entitled Carrying Out the Tasks of the Design Stage: An Illustration.

Again, as in the admissions and assessment phases, participation in service programs is imbued with meaning for recipients that must be anticipated and planned for. As an exercise, you might try selecting a few service programs and imagine the meanings or feelings that might be evoked for recipients who participate in the programs. You might want to consider the attitudes, motivations, values, expectations, and perceptions that recipients might bring to the programs. For example, imagine persons convicted of driving under the influence who are sentenced to attendance at sobriety classes, and imagine spouses who are enrolled in a prenatal course. Then think about the reciprocal staff behaviors, tasks, or steps that might be necessary or appropriate.

Location. The location where services will be provided must be thought through to ensure their ongoing accessibility to recipients. Because the intervention phase is usually of longer duration than the other phases, recipients may not be able to sustain their service-seeking efforts "over the long haul" if there are locational or accessibility barriers that cannot be easily surmounted. (This is discussed more fully in the Accessibility section.)

Duration, Time Span, and Length and Frequency of Contacts. These related essential components must be addressed within all the phases of the service program and the program as a whole. However, in most service programs, the intervention phase is usually the longest and the one in which the recipient has the most frequent contact with service providers. These components are mentioned here because they are more conspicuous as planners design the intervention phase. (They are discussed in detail later in the chapter.)

Procedures for Recording Services, Interventions, Transactions, and Benefits. This element is not always addressed by planners. Sometimes it is left to the implementers to decide after the planners' overall proposal has been reviewed, perhaps modified, and approved by officials. If planners are asked to develop a preliminary information system about the intervention phase, they must decide what kind of information is needed and for what purpose, who will record it, when they will record it, and how they will do it. Some information requirements may be based on the organization's existing information system, but others may be based on funders' or organizational officials' requirements for the evaluation of outcome, process, and output objectives.

Design the Elements of the Termination Phase

In many service programs, providers prepare, and some recipients expect, acknowledgment for completion of all sorts of activities. Even in ordinary service programs that have simple or routine endings, termination often occurs with a great to-do. With or without ceremony, recipients receive certificates, badges, pins, ribbons, plaques, trophies, tickets, newspaper publicity, or they participate in recognition banquets or picnics. One or more of these acknowledgments have been used to commemorate completion of a basketball camp, adult education, scouting programs, preschool, a summer library reading program, a course on water safety and cardiopulmonary resuscitation, parenting classes, and physical-fitness programs.

In some service programs, the termination phase encompasses complex steps to reach and implement a decision to end service to recipients. The major elements that are usually considered in developing the termination process are presented next. Again, there is variation among planning ventures as to which of these elements must be developed and the extent to which they must be detailed. Complete development is required if officials or funders want a detailed termination component in the proposal for a new program. Revisions of termination in an existing program may focus on one or two elements, but it is wise to examine the effect of a change in one element on others.

Termination Policies and Procedures. The development of termination policies and procedures must include criteria for termination, methods of evaluating whether the criteria have been met, methods of communicating the findings of the evaluation to recipients and others, and in some programs, opportunities to challenge, appeal, or grieve termination decisions. Criteria for termination may be based on several factors:

- Success or failure in achieving service objectives
- Regulations of funders (for example, diagnostic related groups—DRGs—influencing hospital discharge practices of patients on Medicare)
- Change in status (for example, retired, employed, financially independent of parents)

- Noncompliance with program requirements (for example, failure to return over-due library books, missed appointments with parole officer)
- Unacceptable behavior (for example, bullying kids at the youth center, bringing drugs into a homeless shelter)
- Satisfaction of agreed-upon duration of service (for example, one week of summer day camp)
- Inability to maintain membership requirements (for example, pay dues)

Policies and procedures must also be developed concerning final write-ups: What should be included in the final report? Who gets it? Where should the recipient's record be stored? and Who has the right to access the record?

Termination may be imbued with meaning for recipients and their significant others. It may be an emotionally charged process that requires the attention of planners (for example, the transfer of a child from foster care back to her natural parents). Due to the nature of some human service programs and the conditions they address (for example, health and well-being), recipients and significant others are likely to have strong negative feelings about termination of services, particularly involuntary terminations (for example, exclusion from a homeless shelter for selling drugs while a resident, disqualification for disability benefits). Planners are advised to develop procedures for examining and managing recipients' feelings about termination of services.

Participants in the Termination Process. Participants in the termination process may include the recipient, significant others, staff, officials or representatives of other organizations, legal counsel, or recipient advocates. In some instances, participants are mandated by law or regulation (for example, the composition of child abuse teams that review decisions to return neglected children to their natural parents).

Timing of Termination. The timing of termination may be predetermined or uncertain (for example, courses end at a prearranged time, whereas the termination of foster care for a neglected child might be indeterminate). Time spans of the termination phase also vary among service programs (Fortune, 1985). Some are gradual and lengthy by necessity and are imbued with meanings for recipients. They may have invested themselves in the program and may have strong feelings about termination. The transition may involve a significant change in status (for example, the discharge of a patient from a rehabilitation hospital). That is why in some service programs, the experience of recipients during the time span of the termination phase merits special attention.

Termination may be initiated by recipients, and sometimes it is consequential for them and the service program. Steps must be planned—for example, to deal with unauthorized termination of services that are legally prescribed (for example, abusive parents who flee the state to avoid protective services). Some recipients who drop out of programs must be followed up to determine the reasons for their premature termination or to be advised of the consequences of their actions (for example, disqualification from benefits, health hazards for failure to complete a detoxification program). Sometimes premature terminations make it difficult for the program to comply with contractual requirements to serve a prescribed number of recipients, which usually leads to lower reimbursements from the funder.

Location of Termination. In most circumstances, termination takes place where services have been provided, and location may not merit special attention. However, safety and security of location may have to be addressed in some instances of involuntary or stressful terminations.

Strive for Continuity Within and Among Phases

As planners design the sequential order and phases, they must strive for *continuity in their service plan.* Continuity refers to the smooth transition and integration of activities, staff, and recipients from one phase of a program to another, from one program to another in the same organization, or from one organization to another. Planners must envision how the recipients will experience the various phases of the program. (See the section on flowcharting later in the chapter.) As a general rule, the number of handoffs should be limited (Cohen, 2002, p. 35). Attention to the groupings of program elements and work flow should facilitate continuity.

The importance of continuity and the consequences of discontinuity are more significant in some situations than in others (for example, when an educational aptitude assessment results in a recommendation for the transfer of a student to a special education program, or when an elder's level of functioning results in a recommendation for assisted-living arrangements). Many recipients are capable of self-managing continuities and discontinuities in service programs, and they do. Nevertheless some programs plan and implement ways of facilitating continuity to enhance recipients' experiences in the service program (for example, buddy systems for new members at a high school–band camp). Some ways that continuity may be facilitated and discontinuity may be prevented or minimized are discussed next.

Formalization. Standardized forms or prescriptive operating and governing procedures are formulated to facilitate continuity (for example, such forms and practices are used in nursing homes at admission and during shift changes to ensure proper management of patient medication).

The Liaison Role. Staff members or volunteers are assigned a linking role to ensure concerted action among units to facilitate a recipient's smooth transition from one phase of service to another (for example, when a patient is being admitted for outpatient surgery, some hospitals have specialized volunteers or aides who transport or accompany patients to all preoperative stations).

Case Management. A staff member is assigned to manage the transition from admission through termination in most if not all service provision (for example, in some cardiology practices, nurse practitioners are assigned to patients to manage office visits, diagnostic and some treatment procedures, and follow-ups).

Coordination by Plan. Two or more components of a program that are sequentially dependent on one another maintain continuity by developing an agreement as to what will be done after the others have made contact or completed their work (Thompson, 1967). For example, in some jurisdictions that have child trauma assessment centers, a coordination protocol is followed by health care, law enforcement, and child protective services personnel to spare the victim from duplicate interviews about the abuse.

Coordination by Mutual Adjustment. Two or more components of a program that are dependent on one another maintain continuity by frequent and extensive communication with one another under particular conditions (Thompson, 1967). For example, a manager of a group home for community mental health patients discovered that a patient had not taken his medication prior to getting in the agency van that was headed for the work activity center. He immediately called the supervisor of the work program to inform him about the patient's behavior when he fails to take his medication. After the medications were taken to the activity center and were administered to the patient, the supervisor later called the group home staff to report on the patient's adjustment.

Interagency Coalitions. A coalition is an interorganizational structure designed to foster cooperation and integration in the provision of services. Coalition building is a challenging, lengthy process that requires a respected leader, resources to support the planning effort, and a planning committee with a vision and a primary orientation to the recipients. A coalition is one approach in coping with competitive relationships among agencies, as well as the fragmentation and discontinuities in service delivery among providers that have a shared client population (Libby and Austin, 2002).

Recap

Up to this point, the discussion has focused on two of the components of service programs—participant activities and sequential order and phases. Participant activities include both staff and recipient behaviors and decisions. The four phases in service programs are admissions, assessment, intervention, and termination. The elements that must be considered in designing each phase have also been examined. This section concluded with a discussion of continuity of recipient experiences. Now the PPT example will be used in an extended illustration of an approach that planners can take in developing these first two essential components of a service program.

Carrying Out the Tasks of the Design Stage: An Illustration

This section examines the essential tasks that planners must complete in the design stage: identifying and listing the participants' activities, clustering, and sequential ordering.

Identify and List Participant Activities

The most rudimentary steps in planning activity sequences are to identify and jot down initial rough listings of participant activities, including required staff tasks, procedures, and decisions. These jottings can be made on large newsprint work sheets taped to the wall, or they can be keyed into a computer and projected on an electronic screen. These listings should be guided by the elements of the four phases of service programs. Table 7.1, Master Chart for Monitoring Development of Elements of the Four Phases of Service Programs, can assist planners in making sure the elements are addressed. Planners will not necessarily develop each element in the sequence listed. Experience shows that planners do not work that way at the outset of designing the essential components of service programs. As planners engage in their initial brainstorming session, they are anxious to propose as many ideas as possible. Based on their interest, knowledge, or what evolves from the creative process, or any number of reasons, planners may approach the development of the elements from many starting points—for example, they may start with an element in the Intervention Phase and then make backward and forward passes throughout the four phases. After completing the initial listing, planners may then wish to approach their development work in a more systematic way.

TABLE 7.1. MASTER CHART FOR MONITORING DEVELOPMENT OF ELEMENTS OF THE FOUR PHASES OF SERVICE PROGRAMS.

Admissions Phase

Elements of Service Programs	ElementNeeds Development (Yes/No/DNA)	Element Finished (Yes)	Diversity Addressed (Yes/No/DNA)
A. Dissemination of information about services			
B. Qualifying criteria for admission			
C. Admission process			
1. Initiation of the admission process			
2. Information to be sought in processing admissions			
3. Management of admission information			
4. Sources of information about applicants			
5. Management of the admission process and decision			
6. Site of the admission process/accessibility			
7. Duration of admission process			
8. Frequency of contacts			
9. Admission procedures			
10. Completion of admission			

Assessment Phase

Elements of Service Programs	ElementNeeds Development (Yes/No/DNA)	Element Finished (Yes)	Diversity Addressed (Yes/No/DNA)
A. Purpose and focus of assessment			
B. Sources of assessment information			
C. Who conducts assessments?			
D. Means of assessment			
E. Duration of assessment process and frequency of contact			
F. Timing of the assessment			
G. Site of the assessment/accessibility			
H. Analysis of findings and development of service plan			
I. Management of assessment information			
J. Completion of the assessmen process			

Intervention Phase

Elements of Service Programs	ElementNeeds Development (Yes/No/DNA)	Element Finished (Yes)	Diversity Addressed (Yes/No/DNA)
A. Staff participant activities in the provision of services/ interventions/benefits			
B. Recipient/significant others participant activities in the service program			
C. Service roles			
D. Duration or time span of service delivery			
E. Length of contact with recipients			
F. Frequency of contact with recipients			
G. Location of service provision/ accessibility			
H. Timing of the intervention/ service provision			
I. Procedures for recording benefits, interventions, and transactions			

Termination Phase

Elements of Service Programs	ElementNeeds Development (Yes/No/DNA)	Element Finished (Yes)	Diversity Addressed (Yes/No/DNA)
A. Termination policies and procedures			
B. Participants in the termination process			
C. Staff/recipient/significant others participant activities			
D. Duration of termination phase			
E. Frequency of contact between staff, recipients, and others during termination			
F. Timing of termination			
G. Location of termination process			

The chart can be used to guide the planners' development of the service program to make sure essential elements are addressed. The chart can also be used to evaluate the completeness of the written draft of the program design. Depending on the nature of the planning project, some elements may not have to be addressed. In that case, planners can write in DNA (does not apply) in the second column next to the particular element. If the element must be developed, planners can write in Yes. When the element has been adequately developed, planners can place a check mark or write in Yes in the third column next to the particular element. Obviously, planners can also develop their own symbols, and can use highlighters and colorful pens to develop their own coding schemes.

The chart can also be used to assess whether diversity issues are germane to the planning of program changes or the new program in a particular planning project. Diversity is an umbrella concept and includes gender, race, ethnicity, social class, age, and sexual orientation. If diversity is not germane to a particular element, planners can write in DNA. If diversity is germane to the program design, planners can flag the relevant elements with a highlighter. If diversity issues are germane to the program design but have not been addressed or have not been addressed adequately, planners can write in No in the fourth column next to the particular element. If diversity issues are adequately addressed, planners can write in Yes.

As the group is running out of suggestions, it can start listing and identifying required recipient behaviors and decisions, also according to the four phases. One easy way to start this second list is to examine the staff tasks listed and then identify the corresponding recipient behavior or decision. For example, the staff participant list might include "determine elder's ability to care for a pet" and "inform elder about what needs to be in place when the pet is taken home." The corresponding recipient behavior might be "elders must be willing and able to express what they think about having a pet" and "elders must understand and make necessary preparations to bring pets home." Some staff activities do not have corresponding recipient activities (for example, working out linkages with the Humane Society).

There are also staff activities corresponding to recipients' behavior and decisions. Elders might overestimate their ability to care for and afford a pet. The assessment process could end with the elder wanting a pet and the staff member recommending against it. Then what? Perhaps a referral to another CCOA program is in order. The listing of recipient behaviors stimulates planners into identifying situations that were not thought about during the listing of staff activities. The development of equivalent lists of recipient expected and desired behaviors forces planners to identify corresponding staff tasks, procedures, and decisions. There are recipient activities that do not have corresponding staff activities. For example, some elders may be lonely and living alone, but they function independently. After receiving the information about the PPT program at the first interview, they may decide to adopt a pet without getting involved with the PPT.

In summary, activity sequences comprise the whole series of staff and recipient actions and decisions—and other major events—that occur over time and are linked together in orderly patterns. Especially important within service programs are those that involve direct interactions between staff and recipients. The full series of these constitute a service program's repetitive cycle. The PPT case example illustrates how a group might initially identify and list participant activities according to phases in the PPT program.

◆ ◆ ◆

People and Pets Together Case Example: Continuation of the First Design Stage Meeting

The chairperson taped several large sheets of paper on the wall. One sheet was labeled Staff Tasks, Procedures, and Decisions, and the other was labeled Recipient Behaviors and Decisions. The sheets were divided into categories according to the sequential phases of a service program—Admission, Assessment, Intervention, and Termination. With the aid of an outline of the elements of the essential components of a service program, the group informally identified and listed participant activities of the PPT program—first the staff's and then the recipient's activities. At the end of the session, the work sheets contained the information contained in Exhibit 7.1.

After completing this initial rough listing, the group has accomplished a composite of ideas and concerns about many matters and issues that go into planning and conducting the PPT program—reflected as a series of jottings on the work sheets. The initial list almost never results in a complete enumeration of participant activities. Additional passes are required that will result in the identification of other tasks, behaviors, and decisions (for example, find out if the elder has allergies), further detailing of those already listed (for example, make it possible for the elder to return the pet if the adoption doesn't work out), and merging of items (for example, merge "downside of pet ownership" with "problems that could occur" and specify further).

Once they examine the rough list, planners will discover that it consists of various tasks, decisions, steps, ideas, assignments, time points, perhaps questions and

EXHIBIT 7.1. INITIAL ROUGH LIST OF STAFF TASKS, PROCEDURES, AND DECISIONS, AND RECIPIENT BEHAVIORS AND DECISIONS.

Staff Tasks, Procedures, Decisions	Recipient Behaviors and Decisions
Admission	
Inform elder about program.	Elder asks questions about the program.
Complete forms.	Elder completes forms.
Accept referrals.	How did you get my name?
Assessment	
Assess comfort with and ability to care for a pet.	Elder provides personal information and expresses feelings about pet ownership. Elder discusses ability/comfort with cleanups.
Develop assessment form.	Elder states preferences for kind of pet.
Determine pet preferences.	
Is residence appropriate for a pet?	
If there's a lease/rental—any pet restrictions?	Rental/lease agreement is reviewed.
Inform about the upside/downside of pet ownership.	Elder assesses whether he or she can afford a pet.
Inform about expenses associated with pet ownership.	
Assess need for financial assistance.	
Inform elder about problems that could occur.	What if elder wants a pet, but PPT decides elder can't handle it?
Intervention	
Help elder select pet.	Elder selects pet.
Arrange for elder to visit Humane Society (HS).	Elder drives self to HS, makes arrangements, or needs staff help.
Help elder prepare for pet's arrival.	Elder buys pet food, collar, leash, and so forth.
Coach elder in animal care—HS staff.	Elder learns to bathe, feed, groom, recognize pet illness.
Elder visit to HS.	Elder visits the HS.
Provide transportation for elder who doesn't drive.	
Can CCOA or HS vans be used?	
Is there an adequate supply of pets?	Elder wants more than one pet. Elder neglects the pet.
Termination	
Provide temporary postadoption assistance with volunteers or staff.	Elder may change his or her mind after the adoption. Elder doesn't want a volunteer visitor. Elder is able to care for pet. Elder is unable to care for pet.

uncertainties, all noted in different terms and arrangements on the work sheets. The list is likely to include some items that do not pertain to participant activities, but to other aspects of the proposed service program, so the list might include identification of who will be doing what (for example, Humane Society staff will train elders in pet care), needed resources (for example, transportation and pet supplies), implementation notes (for example, work out arrangements with a veterinarian), and major difficulties or constraints that must be faced as the planning effort moves forward (for example, adequate supply of pets). The team leader should not discourage these contributions but should flag them as other matters that the group must address later. The process of preparing rough notational listings is a very helpful way to stimulate a preliminary thinking through of the design and other work to be done, as well as the order in which it should proceed. All of these and still other components discussed later in the chapter need to be included in planning new or changed program activity sequences of even modest complexity.

These notes seem like a jumble of ideas and concerns, yet they are probably an accurate reflection of how the initial open-ended design session goes. The group will have to make several more passes through the list to develop a thorough and more refined list, and then they will have to cluster and sequentially order the participant activities.

Clustering

After further development of the list, the next sensible step is to sort through and note patterns, interrelatedness and dependencies, and similar kinds of steps, tasks, activities, and decisions and to cluster them in some commonsense way. Labeling the items as they are being sorted facilitates clustering. Several passes usually have to be made through the listing, and initial clusters have to be merged or subdivided before clustering is complete.

Rather than trying to think about all the different items on the staff list at once, planners are advised to proceed by identifying all of the steps that must be taken or all of the tasks that must be performed within one phase and then move on to the other phases. (The terms *step* and *task* are often used interchangeably and with little precision. The distinction made here is that only staff can be assigned tasks within programs, whereas both staff and recipients can engage in the activities necessary to achieve program goals.) The clustering of staff activities is perhaps easier than the clustering of recipient activities. However, a careful review of the listing and clustering of the staff activities already accomplished should enable the planning team to prepare corresponding clusters of the activities and decisions that are either expected or desired of recipients as they proceed through the sequence. For example, staff must find out whether elders have disabilities or health conditions that would limit their ability to care for a pet; correspondingly, elders must share this information, but they might withhold it, or "shave the truth." With both staff and recipient clusters in hand, planners should examine them in a back-and-forth fashion to check for corresponding activities, and they should strive for a thorough list of clustered activities.

Sequential Ordering

After completing the clustering, planners can turn to the sequential ordering of the main activities of a program. Some sequential ordering of participant activities is likely to have been accomplished intuitively, but incompletely, while planners clustered the list of participant activities. But sequential ordering requires attention in and of itself.

As planners scan the clusters, some clear patterns are usually seen. Some clusters can be ordered within the time-framed boundaries of the program or phases, perhaps only roughly as being toward the beginning, toward the end, or in the middle. For example, in Exhibit 7.2, Clustered and Sequentially Ordered Staff Participant Activities in the PPT Program, orientation activities precede assessment activities. Clusters may also appear as dependent sets, segments, or routines that constitute distinct periods within the entire activity sequence. For example, in Exhibit 7.2, assistance in preparing for the pet's homecoming depends on the kind of pet that is available and selected. Sometimes activities within a phase are not progressive, and sequential ordering is a matter of preference (for example, during the Assessment Phase, the order in which the PPT staff member finds out about the elder's financial resources and about the elder's physical ability to care for a pet). However, planners must figure out which activities within the phases must be demarcated and progressively ordered.

In fitting the refined list of activities and clusters into sequential order, some planners prefer to start at the beginning and list steps forward in some progressive sequence, and some prefer to work backward from the last step or event to the start. These are called *forward passes* and *backward passes*. Other planners prefer to note both the start and the end points or events and then work at filling in the intermediate steps, alternately working between start and end. Whatever the approach, planners can use the Master Chart depicted in Table 7.1 to help elicit a comprehensive listing of all steps and tasks and then a determination of the sequential order in which these steps and tasks occur, with clear definition of the start and end points. (Once familiarity with flowcharting methods has been gained, planners can use any composite approach that suits them.)

The characteristics of typical time durations, distinctive phases, and repetitive sets of activities (perhaps with major alternatives) are found even among service

EXHIBIT 7.2. CLUSTERED AND SEQUENTIALLY ORDERED STAFF PARTICIPANT ACTIVITIES IN THE PPT PROGRAM.

Application Phase
Receive Referral and Initiate Process

(a) If self-referral (phone or walk-in), orient elder to PPT, and if interested, arrange for home visit and assessment.

(b) If not a self-referral, phone elder for an appointment to conduct initial interview and home visit; inform elder about source of referral if he or she inquires about it.

Conduct Orientation (if elder was not oriented to PPT during an earlier contact)

(c) Inform elder about source of referral if he or she asks.

(d) Inform about goals and how the program operates.

(e) Find out if elder ever had a pet and what kind.

(f) If elder never had a pet, inform about the benefits, costs, and requirements of pet ownership.

(g) Inform about the assessment process that helps elders decide whether they want to participate in PPT and whether staff can recommend their participation.

Assessment Phase
Make Home Visit

(a) Find out reasons for interest in a pet.

(b) Determine whether elder is interested in a dog or a cat, what kind (breed, size, active, quiet), and what kinds of animals are not wanted.

(c) Determine whether elder has the financial resources to care for a pet (food, vet fees, dog bed, cat litter, medicines, and so forth).

(d) Find out if the elder is allergic to animals or if he or she has an allergic condition that might be affected by particular animals.

(e) Determine whether elder has any disabilities or health conditions that would limit his or her ability to care for a pet.

(f) If elder's residence is being leased or rented, find out if there are any restrictions regarding pets.

(g) Assess whether residence and outside area are adequate for the kind of pet the elder wants (size, fenced yard, basement, garage, and so forth).

(h) Assess whether elder is willing to contend with some problems that his or her particular pet might have or cause.

(i) Find out if elder has any worries or concerns about caring for a pet.

(j) Decide if elder is able to adopt a pet through PPT.

Intervention Phase
Plan Visit to Humane Society (HS)

(a) Find out when elder can visit HS.

(b) Arrange appointment with HS.

(c) Find out if elder needs a ride to and from HS.

Help Elder Select a Pet

(d) Provide guidance in selecting a particular pet based on assessment.

(e) Provide literature on type of pet of interest to elder.

(f) Elder selects pet.

Facilitate Pet Adoption

(g) Complete HS application, pay fees, and receive pet.

(h) Arrange for pet inoculations, spaying or neutering.

(i) Register pet with animal control and pay license fee.

Assist in Preparation for Pet's Homecoming

(j) Make sure pet supplies have been purchased or assist elder in doing so—for example, food, bowl, leash, collar, bed, and litter box.

(k) Coach elder in caring for the pet if needed—for example, feeding, bathing, brushing, exercising, housebreaking pups and kittens, dealing with fleas.

(l) Encourage elder to choose a place for the pet in the residence.

Conduct Postplacement

(m) Conduct home visit within one week after placement to assess how things are going and if assistance is needed.

(n) Arrange for dog obedience training or other pet care classes if elder is interested and able, or provide on-site coaching as needed.

(o) Follow up at least one more time—timing depends on each situation.

(p) Staff is available on call to help with pet care problems, transportation to vet, and so forth.

Termination Phase

(a) Terminate PPT involvement.

programs that appear highly unpatterned, constantly varying, and reactive to rapidly changing circumstances. Among programs that are widely believed to function in unpredictable modes are hospital emergency rooms (ERs), disaster relief organizations, and crisis help lines. Yet even for these, there is much evidence of consistency—or of efforts to function in patterned ways, with emphasis on converting the unpredictable as far as possible to the routine. Hospital emergency rooms appear to be disorderly only to the uninitiated: the use of triage is clearly a method of imposing order on seeming disorder. ER staff function with a very high level of expert planning, attempt to employ well-practiced and systematic procedures during and after the treatment of each new case, and follow up with disciplined case-by-case post hoc peer reviews. Modern disaster relief services energetically struggle to prepare—as much as possible—for calculable kinds of contingencies and to train personnel in semi-standardized practices or routines. Crisis help lines have protocols for dealing with the varying profiles of callers and their problems.

The phases of program cycles—admissions, assessment, intervention, and termination—need not be linear, in the sense that they always follow one after another in a fixed, unvarying order of progression. Programs vary in the sequencing of their phases. For example, aspects of admission and assessment often occur concurrently, as in the PPT case example, or when homeless individuals seek admission to an overnight shelter. ER patients with life-threatening injuries who are brought to an emergency room will be assessed and treated before they are processed through admissions. Sometimes transactions with recipients are terminated right after screening when they fail to qualify for a service, as in the case of some homeless family shelters that exclude parents who currently use illegal substances. But diversity in the ordering of program phases should not be misleading: every program manifests distinctive phases (with their typical activities) that are linked together in some planned order of relationships. More complex programs are likely to offer more alternatives for various subgroups of recipients, wider ranges of activities (and therefore of services), perhaps of longer duration, and so on. However, even simple programs such as PPT must offer alternatives for elders who have experience with pets and for those who do not; elders who want to return the pet, and those who want to keep it; elders who are having problems, and those who are not having problems with the pet; and elders whose poor health prevents them from taking proper care of their pets. Nevertheless almost all program cycles show high degrees of consistency, order, and patterning in their phases.

Examining the work of the PPT planners illustrates these matters. They took the initial rough listing (Exhibit 7.1) and ran with it. They sifted and sorted through the list, further developed staff and recipient participant activities, and clustered and sequentially ordered them within new phase names appropriate to the PPT Program (Exhibits 7.2 and 7.3).

EXHIBIT 7.3. CLUSTERED AND SEQUENTIALLY ORDERED LIST OF ACTIVITIES AND DECISIONS OF RECIPIENTS.

Elder Initiates Contact with PPT

(a) Makes phone inquiry.

(b) Makes inquiry at CCOA office.

(c) Decides for or against participation.

Elder Responds to CCOA Invitation to Consider Participation in PPT

(a) Rejects invitation during initial phone conversation.

(b) Asks questions about referral and program during initial phone conversation.

(c) Wants to explore further at CCOA office or wants to think about it.

(d) Accepts referral and makes appointment for initial interview and home visit.

Orientation of Elders to PPT Is Conducted

(a) Decides to work through PPT or go it alone.

Assessment Is Conducted

(a) Discuss reasons for wanting a pet.

(b) Explore the benefits and limitations of having a pet—realistic and unrealistic.

(c) Check with the landlord or leasing agent about pet restrictions.

(d) Make an honest assessment of physical and health conditions and ability to care for a pet.

(e) Assess whether a pet is affordable.

(f) Discuss preferences for a particular kind of pet—preference may be appropriate or inappropriate considering the type and size of the residence, the characteristics of the outside area.

(g) Discuss worries or concerns about caring for a pet (for example, barking dog, reactions of neighbors).

(h) Explore whether the residence and outside area are adequate for the pet that is preferred.

(i) Determine whether elder is unrealistic in his or her assessment of ability to care for a pet.

(j) See whether elder feels let down if he or she wants a pet but PPT can't recommend adoption.

Adoption Is Facilitated

(a) Completes Humane Society application for a pet or asks PPT staff for assistance in doing so.

(b) Pays application fees, pet registration and license fees, or asks PPT for subsidy.

(c) Makes sure Humane Society has given the pet all essential shots.

Follow-up and Termination Are Completed

(a) Elder is able to care for pet.

(b) Elder is unable to care for pet.

(c) Elder is able but doesn't want or like pet.

(d) Elder accepts or doesn't accept volunteer.

(e) Elder attends dog obedience/pet care classes.

Consider what the planning group has accomplished through these considerably revised two listings, clusterings, and sequential orderings. The experience of reviewing notes from the rough listing, and from using the Master Chart depicted in Table 7.1, obviously stimulated the inclusion of other related and important matters, which is a typical response in such a process. For example, Exhibit 7.2 has two clusters, Receive Referrals and Initiate Process and Conduct Orientation, that had not been posted in the rough listing in Exhibit 7.1. Exhibit 7.3 also has two clusters that had not been posted in the rough listing in Exhibit 7.1, Elder Initiates Contact with PPT and Elder Responds to CCOA Invitation to Consider Participation in PPT. Even more important is the grouping of the most previously cited matters, plus new items, into clustered and sequentially ordered sets of major topics, each of which contains specific points raised in the planning session. The clusters and their labels were used to decide whether some tasks and steps within clusters had to be added to the list (for example, see the Assessment cluster in Exhibit 7.2 and compare that with the Assessment items in the rough listing in Exhibit 7.1). Clustering and sequential ordering are accomplishments: they demonstrate an ability to identify dependencies and interrelated matters and to impose a reasonable organization on them. Further, the insertion of cluster headings shows an additional ability to facilitate communication in group planning—itself an elementary form of program documentation.

When the planning effort is directed at making some change in an ongoing program, the same methods are applicable, but with attention to certain complexities. Listing, clustering, and sequential ordering must address the modified activities, the assignments, the time frames that will be introduced, the features of the existing program for which there will be substitutions (or enhancements), as well as the several points at which these changes will impinge on still other aspects of the program. Planners should not simply yank one segment of a program and plug in a revised segment without considering how it can fit in. Otherwise the results will be flawed. Planning groups must undertake—in the same terms discussed here—a careful analysis of all parts of the current program likely to be affected directly or indirectly by the change and then formulate a new listing of the intended improvements and related adjustments. The clustering and sequential ordering are especially important at this point, because the aim is to achieve a careful meshing of the new and the old, paying attention to the implications for changes in staff duties, time intervals, differing resource requirements, and the like.

Planners have now produced a listing of the steps to be taken in a definite order of progression and some that are a matter of preference. Each of these methods for designing activity sequences—listing, clustering, and ordering—helps clarify the nature of the entire service program and reveal gaps where steps have been left out and need to be inserted. The listings and schedules of activities and decisions must invariably go through several modifications as the planning advances and becomes more fully detailed, settled, and documented.

Numerous other matters will come to mind during the design process, and each of these should be noted to avoid overlooking them entirely: those involving decisions about personnel or about program recipients; those having to do with needed resources and their limitations; those concerning operational linkages between the program and the host organization; and those requiring clearances or authorizations, communications and reports, rechecking regulations and mandatory forms, and so on, until all of the major features of an entire program have been fully identified, determined, and documented. A great deal of reviewing and rechecking is necessary to ensure that any program is adequately and completely developed and that omissions have been remedied before the final plan is ready for submission to officials.

After completing the clustering and sequential ordering just described, but later in the planning process, another scanning, clustering, and sequential ordering effort must be undertaken. Activities that are to be performed by particular personnel or other participants within the sequence must be identified, clustered, and sequentially ordered. Specific tasks must be assigned to particular persons as duties (or behaviors, or roles) that they are expected to perform. Eventually, each of these clusters must be listed on separate rosters or other summaries for each group or category of participants, so that concrete task assignments can then be prepared—with specific time points or deadlines for each activity or step and each person (for example, the division of labor between the PPT staff and the Humane Society). This aspect of program design will be explored later in the chapter.

Accessibility

Accessibility refers to the ease of access to available services for recipients. Fulfillment of program goals calls for optimizing accessibility, which can be approached by facilitating ease of use or by minimizing barriers to accessibility. Conceivably, some barriers could be universally constraining, but they are more likely to be limiting under specific circumstances and only for one or more segments of a target population (for example, some prospects for the PPT program may lack transportation or may have physical impairments that limit mobility). Accessibility must be addressed in planning and documenting each phase of the service program—admission, assessment, intervention, and termination—because barriers to accessibility may vary among phases of the service program for segments of the target population (for example, the proposed location for applying for admission to an employment training program might be accessible, but the proposed location of the training program may not be, or not for some minority or low-income groups).

Planners should be alert to the planning and documentation requirements of officials and funders for whom accessibility is a special issue. They often want accessibility explicitly addressed in a separate section of the proposal, because they want assurances that the program has a plan to connect with hard-to-serve or underserved segments of the target population. Compliance with this requirement does not mean that planners must strip mentions of accessibility from other sections of the program design narrative. Rather, planners must supplement their embedded discussion of accessibility with a dedicated discussion.

During earlier stages of planning, the team probably addressed accessibility incidentally or intuitively for at least some segments of the target population. For example, after completing a needs assessment of inner-city youth, staff who were planning a summer resident camp discovered that many single parents could not transport their children to camp, nor could they afford physical examinations and appropriate clothing. Planners probably thought about ways of overcoming those barriers to a camp experience and perhaps even jotted some notes as soon as the discovery was made. However, during the design stage, planners must address accessibility purposefully. Experience and observation suggest that planners think about accessibility early during the design stage, while they list, sift and sort, and cluster participant activities. However, the task for planners at this point is to determine whether some features of the program are hampering for some segments of the target population and to remedy or minimize the lack of fit by modifying the feature or giving special assistance to members of the segment.

The following discussion is intended to help planners make decisions about accessibility and facilitate its eventual documentation. The focus here is on factors related to accessibility, hindrances to service use, and ways of minimizing them and facilitating access. The most commonly observed hindrances are discussed.

Location

Decisions about the location where services will be provided may appear to be straightforward ones—services will be sited in one or more of the organization's existing facilities. Program planners may have little or no discretion as to where services are provided to beneficiaries, because an organization's investment in a building, its lease agreement, or its occupancy budget do not allow for flexibility. However, even if the location is fixed, planners should assess whether the proposed location is physically and socially accessible to all segments of the target population, and if not, they should strive to modify hindering conditions or assist segments of the target population to surmount locational barriers.

Although program services exist and are ready for use, they may be inaccessible due to the location of the program in relation to the location of the residences of segments of the target population. Examples include the distance between the program site and the residences of prospective recipients, lack of transportation, problems with public transportation, travel time, road and weather conditions, and topographical barriers.

An organization may be physically but not socially accessible to some prospective recipients due to their perception of the locale of the program site. For example, the location of a youth employment office in a white community known for its racial intolerance conveys a strong psychological message that "minority youth need not apply." Sometimes the perceived risk of traveling to a program located in a blighted or high-crime area makes the service virtually inaccessible (for example, fear of encounters with street people or the homeless persons who frequent the area). Others resent the affront to their self-esteem or social status that they think is implied in a referral to an organization located in a district perceived as undesirable. Residents of urban communities that are rife with drug dealing and violence cannot easily get away from home and face real dilemmas as they try to access services. These examples suggest that the social accessibility of the program merits consideration in program planning and that some apparent locational barriers may also be community or ethnic barriers.

Locational barriers to accessibility are not trifling program planning matters. No-shows, canceled appointments, or premature termination of services due to locational problems have consequences, such as losses of revenue, inefficient use of staff resources, or failure to comply with obligations made in contracts or other grants. Location can facilitate or impede the achievement of program objectives. Situating youth correctional facilities at great distances from the families of offenders does not facilitate maintenance of family ties and support. Group homes for former psychiatric patients cannot be located in the country if the program goal focuses on their integration into the community and acquisition of independent-living skills. The site of service provision is also important when limited visibility of recipients is essential to protect them, to minimize stigma, or to safeguard anonymity (for example, shelters for abused women and treatment centers for sexually assaulted children and youth).

Service Hours

The hours of 8 A.M. to 5 P.M. from Monday through Friday constitute the typical service hours of many programs, and such scheduling is convenient for many users of their services. However, this scheduling creates serious problems for important segments of the target population (for example, people who are employed during the day may not be able to leave their jobs for two hours per week to keep a weekly counseling appointment). Some organizations have recognized such barriers and have adjusted their service hours and days to include evening and Saturday appointments. Many leisure-time or other service agencies recognize that their services must be made available when most of the target population is not working or in school. As a result, such agencies often have extended service hours every day or are open on weekends (for example, libraries, YMCA and YWCA, Boys and Girls Clubs). Other agencies recognize that some problems and needs do not manifest themselves neatly within the structure of a typical work-week. Consequently, services are available twenty-four hours a day, as in protective services, help lines, homeless shelters, assertive community treatment programs, and residential programs. In any case, program planners must schedule service hours during the times and the days that provide opportunities for ease of access for the target population. At the same time, planners must recognize that there are some constraints on the scheduling of service hours and days. For example, some facilities do not open on weekends or during the evening unless essential support, maintenance, or security personnel are in the building; or if the costs of running the heating or air-conditioning plant prohibit an extension of service hours (this example demonstrates how planners "have to think of everything" and anticipate the feasibility of implementation while the service program is being designed).

Other Hindrances

The physical impairments of recipients are not necessarily handicapping, but social and organizational responses to them often are. Planners should explore ways in which the organization can accommodate recipients. Structural designs of buildings and facilities impede accessibility for those who are frail or physically disabled. Examples of such barriers include the lack of preferred parking spaces on the ground floor of parking structures or near building entrances; the absence of curb cuts; unstable, uneven, or hazardous pathways (wood chips, stones, wooden decks); stairways leading to building entrances; narrow doorways, halls, and toilet stalls; and inappropriate chairs or seats and seating arrangements in offices, meeting rooms, and auditoriums.

For many services, lack of money is a barrier to participation in the service program. Some people who need or want a service or a benefit cannot afford admission, user or service fees, membership dues, or deposits. Lack of money is often associated with other limiting conditions of target populations. For example, children from low-income families referred to a summer resident camp, whose fees were subsidized, could not afford to pay for the required physical examination; did not have some of the essential clothing, bedding, and luggage; and did not have the means to get to and from the camp. A full-time staff member was assigned to attend to all of these limitations to enable the children to attend camp. Having a low income does not necessarily preclude access to services, but program planners need to remain sensitive to the relationship between income and use of services. Sliding fee scales, fee waivers, "camperships" (like scholarships), compensating the program for fees or services by contributing to the work of the organization, vouchers, cooperatives, and mutual support groups are some of the strategies that are used to overcome income barriers to the use of services.

There are any number of other factors, singly or in combination, that might hinder access to services: visual, hearing, or intellectual impairments; community norms and attitudes toward particular organizations or services; cultural, ethnic, or religious factors; educational achievement; and language proficiency. Planners must be vigilant about the unique service barriers to current or prospective recipients and strive to minimize them or facilitate access.

Facilitating Access and Minimizing Hindrances

The following is a list of some approaches used by planners to facilitate access and minimize hindrances:

- *Branch units.* Branch, extension, or satellite units are established to overcome barriers such as distance, transportation, and elapsed time required to reach the program or to surmount cultural, racial, ethnic, or other social barriers.
- *Co-location.* Organizations that have complementary programs or common recipients may provide services in the same location to facilitate accessibility and collaboration.
- *Host settings.* Organizations provide services in a host setting (for example, a public health organization might provide children's health services in schools because virtually all of the target population is accessible there).
- *Mobile offices.* Some agencies have customized recreational vehicles or trailers that are driven to remote locations on a regular basis. Mobile offices are also used in metropolitan areas in mall, school, and church parking lots to conduct health promotion and health screenings. Libraries in urban areas rely on bookmobiles to make library materials accessible to elders or to encourage certain target populations to use the library's resources.
- *Specialized transportation.* Specialized transportation services such as Dial-a-Ride or Care-a-Van meet the unique transportation problems of persons with low income or disabilities, compensate for the absence of a public transportation system, and reach recipients in remote areas.

- *Volunteer facilitators.* Volunteers drive recipients to program sites, coparticipate in activities, or provide support and encouragement to enable use of community resources and services (for example, church members coparticipate with visually impaired persons in long-distance races or skiing).

Although accessibility can be enhanced in the aforementioned ways, it is not ensured. Occasionally, hindering features of the program are unwittingly embedded in its design or arise in the course of program implementation or operation (that is, introduced by staff or brought about by regulatory changes, conflicts with other organizations, or funding cutbacks). Consequently, programs have to be examined while they are in operation to determine which features appear to be reducing use of services to a meaningful extent and which segments of the target population are experiencing the barriers. Accessibility can also be promoted through the design of service roles that include methods of reaching out to the target population. These matters are discussed later in the chapter in the section on service roles.

Duration or Time Span, Length of Contact, and Frequency of Contact

Duration or *time span, length of contact,* and *frequency of contact* with recipients are essential components of a service program. In this section, they are defined, ways of estimating them are discussed, and the case example is used to illustrate some methods of estimation.

Duration and time span. The activity sequences of programs take place over more or less definite time periods. The durations of service programs tend to be of three types. The first type conforms to predetermined calendar dates and is exemplified by school programs that last a school year of about nine months, and by summer outdoor camping sessions.

The second type consists of set time spans that are repeated on a regular schedule, as in museum tours with a docent, thirty-day detoxification programs, and some overnight shelter programs that require the homeless to be in by 9 P.M. and out by 8 A.M. Programs of both types of duration often provide services to groups of recipients who are admitted and proceed through the sequence as a cohort—such as children in school grades—although in other kinds of programs, called *constant flow,* recipients enter singly and may have little contact with one another (emergency rooms, departments of public welfare, counseling agencies).

The third type of program duration is defined in terms of the differing periods required to reach a certain level of achievement or result (for example, lengths of stay in a hospital, duration of mental health counseling, offender probation periods, number of respite hours a family needs to experience relief from providing in-home care to a child with a disability). This kind of program tends to admit and proceed with service recipients singly, but some do so in small groups. The time spans of these programs vary or are indeterminate, because they depend on the course of events in the process of providing the service: some interventions work more effectively for some recipients than others; some techniques don't work and others have to be tried; occasionally, service providers give up (for example, school suspensions and expulsions); the problems of some recipients worsen; some recipients move in and out of the program, drop out, move, or otherwise discontinue participation in the program). In addition, some problems are intractable and the length of time to ameliorate a condition is uncertain. However, arbitrary (but not irrational) durations are often imposed on these programs by funders, regulatory agencies, or organizational policies. For example, DRGs in Medicare specify limits on reimbursable lengths of stay in hospitals by types of illness, health insurance policies govern reimbursable lengths of stay in psychiatric hospitals, judges decide a child's duration of care in a foster home, and some domestic crisis centers give assaulted spouses and their children a maximum of thirty days of shelter care to stabilize their situations. However, even in these cases, recipients are not always automatically ejected if their time runs out, regardless of the ways their exits come about.

There are quite different logistical implications between programs of determinate and indeterminate duration. Scheduling for the indeterminate type is much harder to do, especially when expert personnel must be available, as predictions are difficult concerning just how long or when this or that staffer or other resources will be needed. This type can also be more demanding of staff decision making, because they often have to make judgments about what to do next, when to do it, and when enough is enough. However, determinate duration cohort programs may require a broader range of necessary resources marshaled and ready right on time, if not through the cycle, or the whole cohort sequence falters. As an example, compare the scheduling of a three-day blood drive (determinate) with the scheduling of evening and weekend on-call and back-up duty for residential care staff in a runaway shelter (indeterminate).

Length of contact. The length of each encounter or session with the service recipient also has to be planned or estimated so that planners can calculate how many recipients can receive a particular service during a particular period of time. For example, in driver education programs the amount of time that each student can drive on the training course is prescribed to enable instructors to schedule optimal use of the vehicles and facilities during each day, week, and month of the semester. For some programs, the length of the encounter with recipients can be predetermined (for example, a one-hour class session); for others, it may vary (for example, phone conferences on a help line between a person in crisis and a counselor); or it may be indeterminate (for example, some home intervention or protective services encounters are unpredictable due to the complexity of the family crisis or the seriousness of the abuse or neglect discovered at the time of investigation). When the exact length of a session cannot be figured out—or cannot easily be figured out—planners tend to rely on averages or assumptions about averages of sessions or encounters.

Frequency of contact. Planners must also decide the frequency of contact that is wanted between staff and recipients. Frequency of contacts may be high (daily contacts with intellectually challenged adults who are training for independent living), moderate (once a week for a teen in conflict with his parents), or low (once a month to monitor the medication regimen of a patient). Contacts may be regular, intermittent, or irregular. In some service programs, variable frequencies of contact may be required to address variations in the needs and characteristics of recipients.

These components—duration or time span, length of contact, and frequency of contact—should be considered concurrently to assess the implications of a decision about each on the others. For example, in dealing with child neglect, some programs have shortened the duration of service and have increased the length and frequency of home visiting to stabilize families quickly while parents are motivated to avoid the placement of their children in foster homes.

Having defined the meaning of duration or time span, and length and frequency of contact, we now turn to the estimation of the actual time points, intervals, or time frames that must be inserted in the ordered listing. When should the program start and end? For some programs, the specific end time is known in advance, and one can figure backward from that time to the start time—which might be the present. Under other conditions, the final event can occur whenever all the necessary steps have been taken, so it is the start time that has to be set. Determining the start point and the end point sets the temporal boundaries of the program, at least approximately or tentatively, which is vital for figuring time intervals for the steps and tasks within these limits. Keep in mind that for many programs, there are no preset calendar dates marking their start and end points, but the maximum duration or length of time for the service has been fixed. For still other service programs, the duration, and eventually the particular times or dates, will be determined only after the entire effort has been planned, but time is a scarce resource and plans must often be revised to shorten the duration.

Now planning can proceed by assigning a definite time interval or point for each activity and step on the listing. For example, the first step marks the start, and the second should occur so many minutes, hours, or days later. Some tasks require known lengths of time, and they should be noted (for example, advance notice for reserving facility space, length of time to conduct an interview or administer a diagnostic test). The time needed for other steps may be unknown or may be estimated only roughly. And many tasks cannot be undertaken until others have been completed, so their periods are defined by the time points when these other tasks are expected to be finished. Deadlines and fixed calendar dates are commonly set for many programs, whereas others are defined in terms of how many minutes, hours, days, weeks, or months (or even sessions) are required for their completion, independent of calendar dates.

The following portion of the PPT case example illustrates how the group approached some of these matters. Only a few clusters that were discussed by the group are included here, but the group's estimates for each phase of the PPT program are depicted in Exhibit 7.4. Although PPT participants will enter the program with varying levels of functioning and independence, the estimates are based on elders who would need moderate staff assistance. Later in the planning process, the team will have to estimate the number of elders who need different levels of assistance and then adjust the time requirements, as well as the estimate of the number of elders to be served and the staffing requirements.

EXHIBIT 7.4. ESTIMATES OF TIME REQUIREMENTS AND FREQUENCY OF CONTACTS IN THE PPT PROGRAM.

Application Phase—includes receiving referral, orientation, and application (½ hour)
Assessment Phase—includes one home visit and assessment (2½ hours)
Intervention Phase—includes home visit, trip to Humane Society and pet store, coaching in pet care (3 hours)
Termination Phase—includes two home visits (1 to 2 hours)

———

Estimated total staff time to process one applicant: 7 to 8 hours
Estimated span of time to complete assessment and a pet placement: 2 weeks
Estimated number of face-to-face contacts per elder: 4 to 7
Estimated number of group contacts with others in PPT program: 1 pet care class
Estimated duration of service program: 4 weeks

◆ ◆ ◆

People and Pets Together Case Example: Estimating Length and Frequency of Contact

The chairperson directed the group's attention to estimating the length of the home visit and the span of time required to complete the application and assessment.

Home Visit and Orientation

One of the senior reps on the team suggested that orientation to the PPT program would take at least fifteen minutes and up to thirty minutes by the time the staff member explained the program, answered questions, and engaged in small talk. The assessment, and the inevitable social aspects of the first visit, could take another thirty minutes, considering the many areas that needed to be explored (for example, ability to care for a pet, adequate indoor and outdoor space, financial resources, and lease restrictions if applicable). Another member advised that travel time should be added to the estimate. If the elder lived in the same town as the location of the CCOA office, travel time would be no more than thirty minutes for a round trip. However, round-trip travel to other towns could take up to one hour. The chairperson suggested that home visits to elders in outlying towns could be clustered in one day. The group discussed whether a pilot program should be established in the CCOA's home location to concentrate developmental efforts and minimize travel time and expenses. The group decided to recommend that other communities should be phased in. For estimation purposes, it was decided to conservatively allocate a half hour for travel for a home visit.

Another senior rep from the CCOA board suggested that a decision to adopt a pet and join PPT should not be made right after the orientation and assessment. She suggested that the elder should be given a week "to think on it." Furthermore, the PPT staff member should also take some time to think about the interview. Callbacks might be necessary to check pet restrictions in lease or rental agreements or other matters that might come up. In the end, the group estimated that approximately two to two and a half hours would be needed to make the home visit and conduct an assessment, and there would be at least one week between assessment and adoption.

Postplacement Follow-Up Visits

The chairperson directed the group to a discussion of the frequency, length, and timing of postplacement follow-up visits. A member started the discussion with, "It all depends. If the person owned a pet once before, she may not need any help. If the pet is a pup or a kitten, that's one thing. If it's an older pet that's housebroken, that's another." Another member responded that one objective of the program was to promote socialization and to reduce loneliness. That being the case, previous pet ownership and the pet's stage of development were not the decisive factors. "Furthermore, we shouldn't make this too complicated. Otherwise it will be too difficult to manage. Everyone who adopts a pet should be visited within the first week of adoption and at least one other time to find out if the elder needs any assistance with the pet (for example, drive the elder to the vet or a course on animal care; the pet is doing some things the elder doesn't want it to do). If a staff member made the visits, she might be able to complete the follow-up in fifteen minutes, if no complications were discovered. If a volunteer made the visit, perhaps more time could be spent, in keeping with the social opportunity goals of the program. The decision concerning who would make the postplacement visits was postponed, but at the end of the meeting the group had the initial estimates in hand.

◆ ◆ ◆

Exhibit 7.4 depicts the group's initial estimates.

This kind of detailing is important because it helps planners figure out the level of effort required to provide the service and whether their estimates seem sensible. Several passes through the clustered and sequentially ordered lists typically reveal oversights in some estimations (for example, one member reminded the group that its travel time estimates would have to be increased when the PPT program was extended to elders in other cities and townships in the county). The group's discussion illustrates how recipients' needs and program objectives influence decisions about the duration of the program cycle and the length and frequency of contacts. The elders' level of functioning and independence, and their need for socialization opportunities, will also influence postplacement visitation patterns.

A little further down the line in the planning process, time requirements will also help planners (and implementers) figure out how to organize the clusters of participant activities into service roles. However, before focusing on that, it is important to discuss recipient paths within and through service programs and charting of activity sequences. After examining these matters, planners often gain additional insights into the exigencies of providing the service, including service roles and time requirements.

Recipient Paths Through Service Programs

When focusing on developing a person-centered sequence of activities, it is important to understand another key concept. As already discussed, each program's cycle is intended to provide an orderly progression of activities and decisions through its several phases. Recipients, then, can be considered to have various *service paths* as they proceed through these events, including interactions with program personnel. Ideally, program staff hope that most persons who become recipients will follow the paths intended for them as they receive effective program service. Some recipients will wend their ways through designated alternative phases or segments, as cited in earlier examples, but others will drop out or service will be terminated before they complete the program. Such departures are not necessarily failures, as in the case of elders who decide against adopting a pet after looking into the program.

Each of these routes or pathways within the boundaries of the program has integrity and important meanings for the recipients as individuals and for the program as a whole. For example, in many school districts, individual educational planning committees strive to mainstream physically or intellectually challenged students into as much of the conventional instructional program as their abilities allow; different sets of these students follow somewhat different educational paths. Libraries have different processing pathways and experiences depending on what is borrowed (best-sellers, reference works, videos), who the patron is (resident versus nonresident, child or adult, one who is applying for a loan card versus one who has a card), and the status of the patron (one with delinquent fines, overdue books, or a lost library card). The concept of a recipient path generally pertains to a single program but may include experiences among linked programs in the same or different organizations (for example, in the case of the PPT, some elders might enroll in a pet care class sponsored by the Humane Society or a dog obedience class offered by a community education program; a runaway might be taken into custody by a city police officer, detained in a youth shelter run by a church agency, and adjudicated in a county juvenile court).

Use of the recipient path concept facilitates the examination and formulation of series of decisions and activities and their results in terms that acknowledge the primacy of the *recipient-as-person,* while also offering graphic means for planning, monitoring, and documenting program operations (Cohen, 2002). Pathways-through-service programs are of fundamental importance to program results, and issues of a program's intended effectiveness, efficiency, attrition, and retention need to be fully addressed. Although narrative descriptions of recipient paths can be readily developed, such documentation can be burdensome. However, flow-charting methods can be adapted to plan for recipients' differing paths, particularly where they are intended, well known, or especially problematic. This is the subject of the following discussion.

Charting the Sequences of Activities and Recipient Paths

Charts, diagrams, and other schematics have proven to be useful across a wide variety of fields. The reasons for general reliance on these graphics underlie our interest in them: they summarize complex information in ways that allow one to comprehend it, they show procedures in a step-by-step manner that is easier to grasp than from narrative instructions alone, and they allow both rapid modification of draft designs and alternative perspectives on selected components of the whole enterprise.

Flowcharts are widely used in the analysis, description and documentation, planning, and management of programs and projects. In graphic form, they display bounded sequences of activities and events and their relationships in terms of time and function. Flowcharts differ in terms of the major aspects of the activity and event sequence being displayed, the purposes of the chart, and the persons who will use it. For example, direct-service program flowcharts are sometimes organized around the typical recipient's path in, through, and out of the program. Sometimes they display a program's case-processing operations and emphasize the progression of staff tasks performed through several phases of the program. In this case, flowcharts are also used to assess the amount of time from the beginning to the end of a program or service cycle to decide whether some activities or the time it takes to complete them can be compacted (Ng, Kent, and Egbert, 2000). Occasionally, charts are also developed to display a program's interconnections with other programs within or outside the host organization. In keeping with the recipient-as-person approach in designing service programs, a combined approach is recommended, one that emphasizes the interactions between staff and recipients. (See Figure 7.1, and note the abbreviations of activities in rectangles 1.4, 1.6, and 2.0, for example. See also the explanations in the Flowchart Narrative.) The flowchart will be discussed in detail in a later section of the chapter.

A flowchart is a powerful means of accomplishing all of these purposes with a minimum of technical knowledge and no artistic ability whatsoever. Plastic templates with various shapes, lines, and arrows are available and can be used by a novice to draw flowcharts. Flowcharts can also be drawn with specialized computer software programs or software embedded in word-processing applications in home or office computers. Readers who are interested in exploring computer-assisted charting, including temporary free trials, may search www.shareware.com. Here the elements of a flowchart are presented in a simplified format with instructions for its preparation and an explanation and illustration of its relevant uses.

In this section, using a flowchart is discussed for the purpose at hand: planning and documenting a simple program. Whatever the kind or format, charting is used interactively with the other planning methods discussed to achieve the analysis and formulation of a sequence of activities. Through the following discussion, including an example of charting, readers will see that it can be carried out concurrently with listing, clustering, and sequential ordering. Flowcharts can be used to display an existing program for purposes of description, reporting,

FIGURE 7.1. INITIAL FLOWCHART OF A SEQUENCE OF ACTIVITIES IN THE PPT PROGRAM AND FLOWCHART NARRATIVE.

Application and Assessment Phase

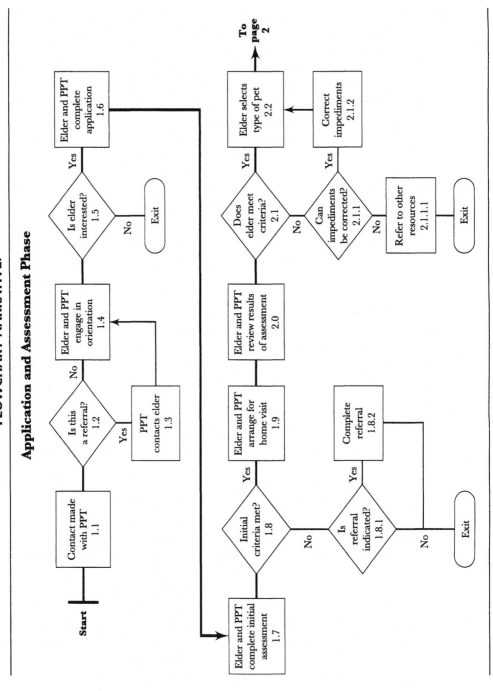

Note: PPT = staff member.

FIGURE 7.1. INITIAL FLOWCHART OF A SEQUENCE OF ACTIVITIES IN THE PPT PROGRAM AND FLOWCHART NARRATIVE. *(continued)*

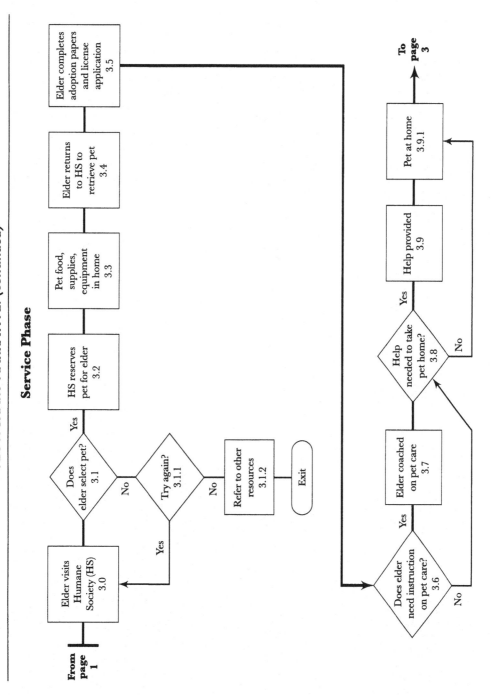

Service Phase

FIGURE 7.1. INITIAL FLOWCHART OF A SEQUENCE OF ACTIVITIES IN THE PPT PROGRAM AND FLOWCHART NARRATIVE. *(continued)*

Termination Phase

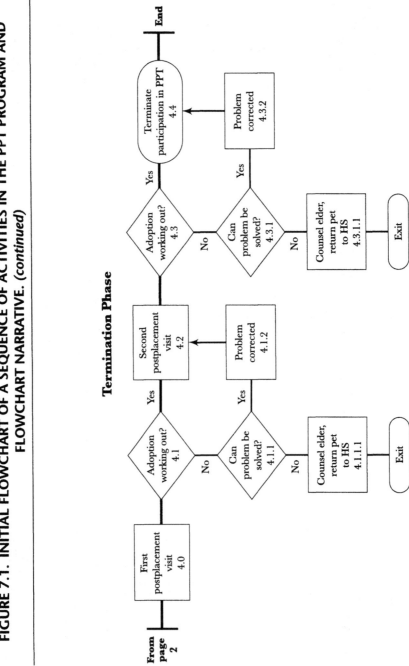

FIGURE 7.1. INITIAL FLOWCHART OF A SEQUENCE OF ACTIVITIES IN THE PPT PROGRAM AND FLOWCHART NARRATIVE. *(continued)*

Application and Assessment Phase

1.1 A person from the community initiates contact with a representative of the PPT program.

1.2 Representative finds out if the person is making a referral and if so collects information about the elder.

1.3 A PPT staff member contacts the elder to invite him or her to consider participation in the program.

1.4 Elder is informed about the goals and services of the PPT program and is given an opportunity to ask questions.

1.5 Upon gaining an understanding of PPT, elder decides whether or not he or she is interested in applying for the program.

1.6 Elder and a PPT staff member complete the application.

1.7 Elder and PPT staff member complete initial assessment of ability to care for a pet.

1.8 In consultation with the elder, PPT staff member decides whether initial criteria for participation are met.

1.8.1 If criteria are not met, elder and PPT staff member discuss whether a referral to other programs within or outside the CCOA should be considered.

1.8.2 If elder is interested in another program, complete the referral in the elder's behalf or provide information so he or she can apply for the program.

1.9 Elder and the PPT staff member arrange an appointment for a home visit to complete an on-site assessment.

2.0 Elder and the PPT staff member complete the on-site assessment and review results.

2.1 In consultation with the elder, the staff member decides whether all criteria for participation have been satisfied.

2.1.1 If the elder fails to meet one or more criteria, elder and the PPT member decide whether impediments to participation can be corrected.

2.1.1.1 If barriers cannot be corrected, refer elder to other resources if he or she is interested.

2.1.2 Elder and the PPT staff member, independently or cooperatively, correct the impediments to participation.

2.2 Elder expresses preference for type of pet he or she is interested in and capable of caring for.

FIGURE 7.1. INITIAL FLOWCHART OF A SEQUENCE OF ACTIVITIES IN THE PPT PROGRAM AND FLOWCHART NARRATIVE. *(continued)*

Service Phase

3.0   Elder visits the Humane Society by him- or herself, or with a PPT staff member, to find out what kinds of pets are available.

3.1   Elder decides whether preferred type of pet is available.

3.1.1   Preferred pet is not available, and elder has to decide whether to return to the Humane Society to try again or to terminate.

3.1.2   Elder decides to terminate, and elder and PPT staff member discuss whether referral to another resource is desired by the elder.

3.2   Elder selects pet and Humane Society reserves pet for elder until preparations for homecoming can be completed.

3.3   Pet food, supplies, and equipment are in the home either through purchase by the elder, financial assistance, or in-kind contribution.

3.4   Elder returns to the Humane Society by him- or herself, or with a PPT staff member, to retrieve pet.

3.5   Elder completes adoption papers and license application.

3.6   Elder and HS representative decide whether elder needs instruction on pet care.

3.7   Elder is coached on pet care.

3.8   Elder and PPT staff member decide whether elder needs help in transporting the pet home.

3.9   Help is provided by the PPT staff member, a friend, or a relative.

3.9.1   Pet is in the home.

Termination Phase

4.0   First postplacement home visit is made to assess how the adoption is working out.

4.1   Elder and PPT representative decide whether adoption is working out.

4.1.1   If the adoption is not working out, can the problem be solved?

4.1.1.1   If the problem cannot be corrected, counsel the elder, and return the pet to the Humane Society.

4.1.2   If the problem can be corrected by the elder, or with PPT staff assistance, then correct it.

4.2   Second postplacement home visit is made to assess how the adoption is working out.

4.3   Elder and PPT representative decide whether adoption is working out.

4.3.1   If the adoption is not working out, can the problem be solved?

4.3.1.1   If the problem cannot be corrected, counsel the elder, and return the pet to the Humane Society.

4.3.2   If the problem can be corrected by the elder, or with PPT staff assistance, then correct it.

4.4   Adoption of pet is complete. Terminate participation in the PPT Program.

review, or analysis. Charting may be done prospectively, as here, preparing a design for a new program or project with its key activities, decisions, events, and participants. Or charting may be used to portray some combination of existing and new program features, as when making plans to introduce changes in selected aspects of an ongoing program. An existing sequence of activities cannot be fully charted until it has been taken apart and its step-by-step operations meticulously analyzed. Conversely, the attempt to display a planned new (or changed) sequence in diagrammatic form requires formulating activities one at a time, and this method is a potent aid in the planning process.

Completed charts provide schematic representations of the activities, steps, and other components of service programs. Textual documentation of a program should accompany the charts or other diagrams to explain the sequence and to describe other features not set forth graphically (for example, see the Flowchart Narrative). Charts are only as good as the analysis or planning whose results they reflect. In analysis and such charting, as in planning and text documentation, choices must be made about the particular focus and about the kind and amount of detail that should be presented. Too little detail obscures a sequence and limits understanding, but too much detail may overwhelm and confuse the reader or user. Program designs and project plans are frequently developed with high degrees of detail that are available for certain users, but summary documentation that uses simplified charting is given to most readers. Returning to the PPT case example, the reader can see how the planning group might develop the initial chart of the sequence of activities and the recipient paths in the PPT program.

Charting the Sequences of Activities and Recipient Paths in the PPT Program

This is what the PPT planners have completed up to this point in the planning process: the work group has write-ups and lists that contain clustered and sequentially ordered staff participant activities that must be performed to carry out the service program. Some recipient participant activities, both expected and desired, have also been listed, clustered, and sequentially ordered. In addition, the group has made initial estimates of the duration of the program cycle and the length and frequency of contacts between the recipients and the staff. This indicates that much of the groundwork essential to the graphic portrayal of activity sequences and recipient paths has already been completed, but staff activities and recipient paths have not been adequately documented yet.

Planners should have these lists in hand and should refer to them as the flowchart is drawn. (Refer to Exhibits 7.2, 7.3, and 7.4.) Assume that the initial flowchart was drawn by the chairperson to be presented and discussed at a meeting of the group to help it confirm, revise, and document what had been designed up to that point. (See Figure 7.1.) When final plans are completed, a revised chart will be drawn. Again, the chart addresses only the tasks that must be performed to provide the service.

The flowchart (Figure 7.1) will be examined in two ways. There is discussion of the charting of a program cycle—that is, how charting helps the group to move the planning process along, and the PPT example is used to illustrate charting.

This initial version of the chart shows the dark thick main line along which there are shapes with brief labels, which are abbreviations of activities within each phase. These labels identify significant activities involving either staff or recipients or both and nine decisions along the main line, all in proper progression between the start and end points of the displayed sequence. Numbers may be placed within or next to the shapes, and these correspond to clarifications in the attached text documentation, which is the *flowchart narrative*. In all charting, lines without arrows are used to connect flow that moves from left to right or top to bottom. Lines with arrows are used to indicate flow from right to left or from bottom to top. Reliance on the main line of staff and recipient activities is the organizing basis for both the graphical structure of the chart and the selection of key steps to be displayed. (Other program processes that can result in different subpaths that depart from the main line are discussed later in the chapter.) The three main phases of this program are depicted in Figure 7.1. They are labeled Application and Assessment Phase, Service Phase, and Termination Phase (with vertical markers separating them). This combination of shapes and lines yields an uncluttered chart that enables planners to assess the merits of their initial program designs.

Only three basic shapes are used: *rectangles* indicate actions or steps (for example, contact made with PPT, orientation of elder, completion of application); *diamonds* indicate a decision (for example, after elders have been oriented to the program, they must decide whether they are interested in participating in the PPT Program); and *ovals* indicate an exit from or termination of the program cycle. Other shapes are also used in flowcharts (for example, circles to identify the staff and the other participants who are associated with each step and decision). In the interest of simplicity, these are not included here. (Later in the planning of the PPT program, staff and other participants' roles must be linked to activities and decisions. They probably include a program coordinator, a support staff member, a relative, a pastor, or a neighbor, among other participants.)

Shapes and lines below the main line are subpaths. They are used to document activities and decisions that represent likely departures from an expected or desired activity sequence for some elders. These represent contingencies that can reasonably be anticipated. Of course, endless others occur in serving recipients and in their lives (for example, the pet could get sick, or the elder could become too ill to care for the pet). Some subpaths represent a continuation of participation in the service program. Others indicate a program exit.

For all phases of the service program, an economy of design is gained by including in each activity rectangle the reciprocal actions to be taken by the staff and by the recipients. For example, in the activity Elder and PPT Arrange for Home Visit, if the participant's actions had been separated at each point, a prior rectangle would have shown staff arranging a home visit, another rectangle would have been needed to show recipient's agreement to a home visit, and so on. Diagramming these linked actions in single rectangles, however, avoided doubling their number along the main line. (Perhaps the most frequent uses for such combined shapes in program flowcharting occur for interview and test activities—in both instances, a staff member performs one role in the interaction, and a recipient performs another.)

Note that the second decision diamond—Is Elder Interested?—indicates a simple yes-or-no unilateral choice by persons being asked to decide whether they are interested in participation in the PPT Program. Those deciding no are exited. A positive choice continues the process along the main line. However, a negative choice at a later decision point may result in looping back to repeat one or more events, taking a special off-line path with eventual return to the main line, or exiting the process—sometimes with a follow-up step and sometimes with no follow-up steps.

One benefit of charting is that it forces planners to think about particular steps and decisions in a particular sequence. For example, in one segment of the chart, the elder travels to the Humane Society to shop for a pet, and the pet of interest may not be available. That being the case, another activity needs to be inserted in the chart: either the elder or a PPT staff member must call the Humane Society staff to find out if the pet of interest is available. Perhaps a form and a procedure should be developed with staff from the Humane Society so that they can be on the lookout for and reserve particular pets preferred by elders in the PPT Program.

The ordered clustering in Exhibits 7.2 and 7.3 document a much more detailed set of activities, but all of these are now condensed into very few rectangles and diamonds on the diagram. (The chart as developed at this point in the planning process has some limitations that are discussed later in the chapter.) The chart shows that some PPT participants will experience different paths. For example, some elders will need coaching about pet care and help in getting the pet home. Some elders may go to the Humane Society to select a pet, but after seeing what is available, they may not want to select a pet at that time. In that case, the process must loop back to a prior step. In the postplacement period, elders who are having difficulties with their pets will take a different path than those who are not having such difficulties. Some recipients will follow smooth paths in which they move uninterrupted from one step to another, and others will have some starts and stops and repetitions. However, some other paths have not been depicted. For example, nothing is shown about the timing of the pet care classes at the Humane Society or the local Community Education Center. Perhaps the work group had not thought about it, or perhaps some thought had been given to it, but the group could not figure out its placement in the sequence of activities at this point in the planning process.

Flowcharts facilitate the analysis of the sequencing of activities and steps. For example, the Service Phase of the chart has a diamond (3.8) that indicates a decision has to be made about whether the elder needs help in taking the pet home (for example, a pet cage, transportation). However, that decision should be made earlier in the service phase, most likely right after the elder selects the pet at the Humane Society (around 3.2). Adequate arrangements for helping the elder take the pet home must be made in advance of that activity.

Flowcharts often elicit ideas about alternative ways of providing the service. For example, up to this point, orientation has been discussed as a person-to-person activity, whereas a group orientation with an informative video would be more efficient and would also provide opportunities for socialization. In general, a flowchart that is developed in the course of planning should be designed for adaptation and later used to inform and guide the activities of other persons who will carry out the steps decided upon.

Having seen that there are some limitations in the initial chart, presume that it was prepared only to clarify the work group's initial design decisions at a quite early point in its work and that one or more additional, more-detailed charts will be drawn later. The reader could practice the development of a flowchart by revising the whole initial chart, or by taking one or two segments and detailing them more thoroughly. For example, how would you detail the charting of elders who initiate the inquiry about PPT via a phone call versus those who are walk-ins? How would you detail the management of referrals from other organizations or individuals? Sometimes planners develop separate flowcharts for different groups of recipients depending on their particular set of characteristics. Readers are invited to draw a chart for independent, high-functioning elders who can self-manage their way through aspects of the program (who nevertheless happen to be lonely and are living alone) and another chart for elders with physical disabilities who need assistance to participate in the program. Readers may also insert circles into the diagram and label them with the persons responsible for the activity.

Recap

At this point in the design stage, planners have a working version of the essential components of the proposed new or changed service program. All components are subject to further revision and refinement as the planning process moves toward a conclusion. Aspects of some components may need alteration as a consequence of the decisions that planners make as they carry out the remaining tasks of the design stage.

Organize the Clusters of Staff Participant Activities into Service Roles

Earlier in the design stage, the initial, rough lists of staff participant activities were further developed and then clustered based on their patterns, interrelatedness and dependencies, or similarity in activities, tasks, steps, and decisions. At this point, another clustering effort must be undertaken with these staff participant activities. They must now be assigned to particular persons as duties, behaviors, or roles that have to be performed. The criteria for developing the initial clusters can also be helpful in developing clusters of service roles, but additional criteria must be considered.

Some staff participant activities must be clustered together into particular service roles because requirements are set forth in statutes, regulations, or standards (for example, in some states, statutes require that interviews with alleged perpetrators and victims of child abuse must be completed by a protective services investigator within a designated period after its discovery; in nursing homes, a patient's medication dosage cannot be changed without authorization from the attending physician). Other participant activities must be clustered into a service role because particular professional or technical competencies are essential for its performance (for example, interviews with victims of sexual assault must be conducted by a person qualified to conduct the disclosure protocol; in nursing homes, only staff who have had special training in feeding patients can help those with eating or swallowing problems). Some service roles are predetermined, because the organization has an established or preferred way of carrying out particular tasks (for example, in some schools, advising is assigned to academic and career counselors, whereas in others it is assigned to homeroom teachers). So as planners begin to cluster staff participant activities into service roles, they must ascertain whether any clusters are required or preferred and which ones can be decided by the work group.

In deciding service roles, planners must reexamine their initial estimates of time requirements and frequency of contacts (for example, see Exhibit 7.4 in the PPT case example) in relation to the service roles that now must be developed. Some of these initial estimates are likely to change as the work group assigns particular tasks to particular service roles. A return to the PPT case example will illustrate how the group clustered some participant activities into service roles.

◆ ◆ ◆

People and Pets Together Case Example: Planners Cluster Activities into Service Roles

The chairperson asked the group to direct its attention to Exhibits 7.2, 7.3, and 7.4, the working draft of the flowchart, and its other relevant write-ups for the purpose of deciding service roles essential to the program.

The group started with the activity Receive Referral and Initiate Process at the top of Exhibit 7.2. The chair stated that elders might refer themselves or be referred by others. If they were self-referrals, they might initiate contact over the phone, or they might walk in to the CCOA's offices. In both cases, if the PPT staff member was not available, the secretary could take some basic information and orient the elder to the program. The group agreed that referrals by others should be handled by the PPT staffer. Those making the referral would have some information about the elder that would help the staff member prepare for the first contact. The group agreed that its original estimate of thirty minutes to complete these tasks was high. The phone contacts and walk-ins managed by the secretaries would take about five minutes. Furthermore, considering that they served other programs and could not tie up the phones, five minutes, more or less, was the limit. If more time was needed, the secretary should inform the interested elder that the PPT staffer would make a follow-up call. Similar activities by the PPT staffer that would include orientation to the program might average around fifteen minutes.

One member suggested that the PPT staffer should conduct group orientations for those elders who were capable and had the means to come to the CCOA facility. This approach would be more efficient and would provide a social opportunity for the elders, which was one of the goals of the program. If elders could not come to the facility, then a home visit would be conducted by the PPT staffer.

The chair expressed his belief that when the word about the program got around, some lonely but otherwise high-functioning elders might not want to participate in the program, but they might want to adopt a pet. The group concluded that these elders might want to self-manage a pet adoption with little or no assistance, but without participation in the PPT Program. In these cases, the elder would be referred to the Humane Society, either by a secretary or the PPT staff member. Eventually, they might even be recruited as volunteers to follow up with those who needed help.

After examining the next set of clusters in the exhibits, the group concluded that the PPT staffer should conduct the assessment, because that phase calls for someone who understands aging and elders. The original estimate of up to two and a half hours for travel to the homes and for completion of the assessment was deemed appropriate for the more challenging referrals. However, elders with high levels of functioning, who also had experience with pets, might only require an hour. The amount of time devoted to assessment would therefore vary depending on the characteristics of the applicants.

There was extended discussion about who should do what with respect to two clusters—deciding on a pet and adoption. The representative from the Humane Society suggested that its staff could provide information about different breeds of pets, assist the elder in selecting a pet, complete the paperwork, make arrangements for neutering or spaying, arrange for a staff member or volunteer to coach the elder on pet care, and enroll the elder in dog obedience or pet care classes.

To help the group with its decision making, the chairperson directed the group's attention back to the findings of the regional planning agency's needs assessment and the group's explorations into the problems of lonely elders. The chairperson reminded the group that some elders do not function well and independently, and they would need encouragement and assistance with the adoption process. "Some elders cannot be passed back and forth between different staff and volunteers. That would confuse them. They need continuity and someone who can work with them patiently." The group was persuaded by the chair's remarks and concluded that a dual approach should be developed: one for more self-sufficient elders and another for those who needed assistance.

Self-sufficient elders would be encouraged to self-manage the adoption process, including relations with the Humane Society staff and volunteers. This approach would provide more socialization opportunities for elders and would enable staff to make more effective use of their time with the elders who were less independent. A different approach was developed for elders who needed assistance:

1. The PPT staff member will be trained by the Humane Society just as it now trains its staff and volunteers.
2. The PPT staff member will be primarily responsible for most of the tasks in the three clusters, but Humane Society staff will assist in decision making on site if called upon.
3. The Humane Society will arrange for all inoculations and spaying or neutering.
4. The PPT staff member will provide initial coaching on pet care.

The original estimate of three hours for the intervention phase was deemed appropriate for the elders who would need the most assistance.

The group turned its attention to the postplacement visits. One CCOA board member remarked that the characteristics and problems of prospective participants and the objectives of the PPT program suggested that the staff member was not the best choice for all postplacement visits. She believed that volunteers from the CCOA, the Humane Society, and church groups could perform the postplacement tasks for many participants. "I believe the volunteers should be trained. They may want to continue visiting the participants even when their involvement in PPT is officially over. Maybe the volunteers and elders will connect and go out together. Some of the early graduates of the PPT program who are self-sufficient may even become volunteers or can be used to encourage others to sign up. I just think volunteers would make it more social. Besides, we don't need to tie up a staff member for many of those postplacement visits." The group was enthusiastic about the idea, but the question of continuity came up again. The group decided on a flexible approach: staff postplacement visits for those who absolutely needed it, and volunteers for those who could handle it.

The chairperson ended the discussion by offering to write up the group's decisions about who was going to do what.

◆ ◆ ◆

The clustering of staff roles and tasks has important consequences for the way services are provided and for program effectiveness. In the PPT case study, the involvement of volunteers with higher-functioning elders provides the elders with more socialization opportunities than could be provided by the staff member alone. The delegation of some postplacement visits to volunteers provides the staff member with opportunities to concentrate on elders who need a high level of expertise and proficiency. Conversely, the staff member must find time to recruit, screen, train, supervise, and reward volunteers. The staff member who performs multiple roles may find that one role demands an inordinate amount of time or competes with the time required to perform other roles, thereby diminishing the amount or quality of attention given to volunteers or elders. Planners must decide which aspects should be optimized and which consequences have to be tolerated.

In clustering tasks into service roles, planners are also drawn into thinking about the staffing plan (for example, the PPT staffer should understand aging and the elderly). Undertaking such concurrent consideration is fine, but staffing plans are rarely, if ever, developed without administrative officials who understand the organization's personnel policies and budget. In addition, planners must avoid the "we-need-a-full-time-staff-member-to-do-it-all" trap and must be open to several options in the assignment of service roles (for example, a part-time staff member, existing staff, a volunteer, a recipient, a representative from another agency, or others can perform a service role).

In deciding service roles, planners must give attention to staff initiative, which refers to an official, planned decision about the deployment of staff and a program's way of governing them, rather than to an individual staff member's motivations or styles of operation. Service roles may be carried out within a range from low to high initiative. In low-initiative modes, staff members perform their service roles in a passive or reactive way; services are provided only when the recipient initiates contact and requests service. In high-initiative modes, staff members are assertive and reach out to members of the target population, even when they do not request service or even express resistance when it is offered. High initiative may take several forms. Staff reach out to recipients in their own homes, neighborhoods, or associations, or they enlist opinion leaders or representatives from the target population to make contacts in behalf of the organization (see Litwak and Meyer, 1974, for a theoretical perspective; and Hatchett and Duran, 2002; O'Donnell and Giovannoni, 2000; Zippay, 1999; and Wuenschell, 1997, for studies of outreach methods). High frequencies of contact and contacts of long duration are other examples of high initiative. Many factors influence the design of staff initiative: the health and well-being of the prospective or current recipients; the degree of resistance, hostility, and alienation of the target population vis-à-vis the organization; voluntary versus involuntary status as a recipient; the motivation of prospective recipients; legal or administrative mandates (as in protective services); dropout or failure-to-keep-appointment rates; the desire to attract a particular market or increase market share; and the costs of high versus low initiative.

In some organizations, combinations of low and high staff initiative are common, and they take several forms. Sometimes high initiative is used in the early stages of intervention to overcome mistrust and resistance. As they diminish, staff members may then carry out service roles with low initiative. In some organizations, all staff members are assigned to some recipients who require low initiative and some who need high initiative. In other organizations, selected staff members are assigned to engage in high-initiative roles, because they have the temperament and competence to do so.

Following completion of the preliminary organization of service roles, planners have laid some ground work for their later collaboration with administrative officials in developing the staffing plan and in estimating the units of service that can be provided. However, before moving to those tasks, planners must consider nonservice roles that will reduce the staff time and organizational resources available for service roles. The total workweek of forty hours is never solely dedicated to service. The two main nonservice roles pertain to the service program's place in the administrative structure of the host organization and its relationship with other organizations.

Conduct an Equal Opportunity and Diversity Audit

Planners have an obligation to be sensitive and responsive to ethnic and cultural factors, including differences in language, customs, values, and attitudes. Planners must also be mindful of the insidious and institutionalized nature of discriminatory practices based on gender, age, race, ethnicity, social class, and sexual orientation. Ideally, equal opportunity and diversity issues are addressed as planners go through each stage of program planning. If work groups include representatives of diverse groups, or if they have access to key informants or stakeholders, then these issues are more likely to be addressed successfully. Nevertheless, at this juncture in the planning project, planners should pause and conduct an equal opportunity and diversity audit of the essential components of the proposed new program or program changes. The Master Chart depicted in Table 7.1 can be used to help planners conduct such an audit. (For examples of other assessment tools, see Flynn, 1992, pp. 90–91; and Ministry For Children and Families, 2004.) Readers who are interested in an insightful and poignant account of failures and successes in adaptations to cultural differences are encouraged to read *The Spirit Catches You and You Fall Down: A Hmong Child, Her American Doctors, and the Collision of Two Cultures* (Fadiman, 1997).

Decide on Linkages Between Service Program, Host Organization, and Other Organizations

Planners must decide where the new or changed service program might fit within the host organization and make recommendations about the linkages that will be established between the service program and other units in the host organization. Will the program "stand alone," or will it be a part of another program within the organization? In either case, what kind of support will the service program require from the organization or host program? The relationship of the new or changed service program to the administrative structure of the organization should be figured out. What kinds of organizational resources will be shared? What kind of operating and governing procedures must be established between the new or changed service program and other units in the organization? These and other questions must be addressed by the planners in the PPT case example. Who in the CCOA will supervise the staff member in the PPT program? What roles will the PPT staff member perform in the organization? Will the PPT staff member have some responsibility for organizational maintenance and development activities (for example, staff development and training, staff meetings)? Requirements for detailing these matters vary among funders and officials and vary depending on whether planners are changing an existing program or developing a new one.

Linkages with other organizations, associations, groups, or persons in the community must also be developed. These linkages may include referral arrangements, agreements regarding joint responsibility for assessment or the sharing of assessment information, cooperative arrangements essential to the provision of services, advisory committees, or resources that will be shared or contributed. Agreements may be highly formalized in contracts, less formalized in a letter of understanding, or not formalized but nevertheless binding as in agreements sealed with a handshake. In the PPT case example, a member of the Humane Society was a member of the planning group. She made a verbal commitment that Humane Society staff would assist elders with some aspects of pet adoption. That commitment has to be reported back to agency officials and approved, and the Humane Society representative has to work with the planning group to develop procedures regarding how that adoption assistance will in fact be provided. Linkages also have to be established with organizations that will be the sources of volunteers. At a minimum, letters of understanding must be written indicating that the organizations will assist in the recruitment of volunteers for the PPT program. In a case vignette in Chapter Eight, you will see that the PPT planning group decided to establish a steering committee composed of elders, a representative from the Humane Society, a veterinarian, and a representative from one of the main targets for recruitment of volunteers.

Linkages of the program to the organization and other organizations in the community will involve staff in nonservice roles, and both will have a bearing on the time that is available for service provision. These nonservice roles must be considered as planners develop a staffing plan and as they make estimates of the units of service that might be provided to recipients.

Determine Resource Requirements

The material resources to support the program changes or the new service program must also be determined by the work group (for example, facilities, supplies, equipment, transportation, and financial or in-kind assistance for recipients) (Schaefer, 1987, pp. 51–70). Planners can conduct a resource analysis by completing four steps and organizing the results into a summary table. The four steps are these: (1) decide the resources that are needed; (2) identify the resources that the organization already has; (3) if the organization does not have the needed resources, determine where they can be obtained; and (4) determine ways that the service program can make do without the resources that cannot be found (Schram, 1997, pp. 148–150). (These same steps will have to be repeated by the program's implementers, who may have to install an approved modified plan.) Table 7.2 is an example of how three of the four steps might have been completed by the PPT planners.

TABLE 7.2. RESOURCE ANALYSIS FOR THE PPT PROGRAM.

Resources Needed	Resources in Hand	Possible Sources
1. Pet cages		Humane Society (HS) or funders
2. Pet care supplies and equipment		Funders
3. Van	CCOA	
4. Financial aid/fees		Funder/Veterinarian/HS
5. Awards for volunteers	CCOA	
6. Office space	CCOA	
7. Audiovisual equipment	CCOA	
8. Videotapes, literature on pet care		HS/libraries
9. Office equipment	CCOA	
10. Cell phone	CCOA	
11. Satellite office space		Agencies/churches

Source: Adapted from Schram, 1997, pp. 148–149. Copyright © 1997 by Sage Publications, Inc. Reprinted by permission of Sage Publications, Inc.

The staffing plan and the human resource requirements in the design stage are not discussed here, because planners rarely, if ever, develop and document the staffing plan on their own. This work, and the program budget, are usually addressed toward the end of the planning process and always collaboratively with administrative officials, who understand organizational personnel policies and the budget. However, planners must first produce the penultimate documentation of the program changes or the new service program that enables officials to make an informed decision about the staffing and resource requirements.

Recap and a Look Ahead

Now take stock of what has been accomplished in the design stage. Planners have identified, listed, and clustered participant activities and have organized them in sequential order and phases. Accessibility has been addressed, and decisions have been made about the duration, length, and frequency of contacts. A flowchart has been drawn to graphically display activity sequences and recipient service pathways. Staff participant activities have been clustered into service roles. Linkages of the service program to the host organization and other persons, groups, associations, and organizations in the community have been addressed. The resources required to operate the program have been determined. All of these matters are subject to further revision and refinement as the design stage draws to a conclusion. The lists, working notes, and rough charts that have been developed so far must be transformed into a preliminary written narrative, charts, or other graphics. This preliminary documentation of the proposed new or changed service program must be written according to the requirements set forth by officials or funders.

This documentation is deemed preliminary because the work of the design stage and aspects of the previous stages are usually not completed until the next and final stage—the documentation stage. In that stage, planners must take a holistic approach in assessing the goodness of fit among all components of the emerging program plan document, including two components that have not yet been addressed—the staffing plan and the program budget. Final design decisions cannot be made until all of these have been developed and reviewed in relation to one another. Such a review may result in affirmation of the service plan, or in rectification of omissions and flawed design features. The staffing plan or an element of the proposed budget might necessitate changes in some aspects of the problem to be addressed, some program objectives, and some features of the service plan.

◆ ◆ ◆

Final documentation of the service plan in a project narrative is just one task of the next stage of planning. Some of the results and products of earlier stages of planning, and all other documentation requirements of officials and funders, must also be completed in final form. Chapter Eight is about wrapping it up and writing it up.

DOCUMENTING THE COMPLETED PROGRAM PLAN

Before addressing the tasks of the documentation stage, it would be useful to review the planning process, what the team should have accomplished so far, and what planners should have in hand at this stage of their work. Planning began with the issuance of a charge from organizational officials to the planning team. The charge authorized the team to develop a new service program or a change in an existing program. The team reviewed, interpreted, and clarified the charge; explored whether there were any relevant mandates; and developed a work plan to carry out the planning project. Planners knew from the outset that at the completion of their work, a written report or proposal would have to be prepared and submitted to officials for review and approval. Readers may recall the advice that planners should find out or decide the documentation requirements at the outset of the planning process. These requirements should have guided the team's ongoing documentation of the results of its efforts in each planning stage (and should now guide the preparation of the final report or proposal).

The team then proceeded to the analysis stage of planning. Team members explored what they already knew about the problem or condition and what more they needed to know. If they concluded that more must be learned, they then decided on the approaches to use to further understand the nature of the problems or conditions of concern. The findings from the problem analysis were used to determine needs and decide priorities. The team should have answered this question: Which aspects of which problem experienced by which persons should be the targets of the new or changed service program? The findings and conclusions should have been documented in a preliminary draft of the problem statement.

Planners turned next to the formulation of goals and objectives, including outcome, process, and output objectives. These formulations were recorded as working statements to be reconsidered in light of decisions that would be made in subsequent planning stages.

While mindful of the findings from the problem analysis and needs assessment, and of the working statements of goals and objectives, planners developed the essential components of the program changes or the new service program. These components were written up in a preliminary draft of the service plan.

So as planners begin the documentation stage of planning, they should have the preliminary draft of the problem statement, the working statement of goals and objectives, the written preliminary service plan, and perhaps some other write-ups, charts, and tables. All of these documented results of the team's work represent a cumulative record that now serves as the basis for the final report or proposal.

This chapter addresses the main components that should be included in a report of a completed program planning process. The report or proposal should present well-organized written documents—*the plan*—for official review and approval. As planners prepare to write the final proposal, they must again address the documentation requirements that they agreed on or those set forth by organizational officials who issued the charge to plan. If planners were charged to prepare their plan for ultimate submission to a funder, then its documentation requirements must also be addressed in the proposal submitted to officials. Organizational officials and funders are the most important readerships for whom the proposal must be written. Furthermore, officials must review and sign off first (incorporating any changes that they impose) before any other readers external to the agency get to read the plan.

As planners sort through their written work, they are likely to find components that are well developed as well as some loose ends and glitches. More often than not, components of the proposed program change or the new service program need further development, documentation in hand must be refined, and additional text must be composed. Planners must work back and forth among the sections to purposefully check the goodness of fit between the nature of the problem and needs, the program goals and objectives, and the program changes or the new service program. This fine-tuning of the proposal will necessitate rewrites. This can be vexing, but it will ensure that it is as complete as officials and funders want it to be. Don't forget the implementers who will have to put the program into place.

Planners might assume that reviewers or decision makers will not read every section of the document or will not read every section carefully, so planners might be inclined to omit some of the information that is cited in this chapter. This assumption might be correct, but it overlooks the possibility that reviewers will divide their joint task and assign all parts among themselves to ensure full coverage. Reviewers may have good reason to suspect that what is poorly written—or not presented—directly reflects the quality and extent of thinking that went into the report, and they may make their decisions accordingly. As important, missing information about critical features of the intended program changes or the new service program deprives the prospective implementers of the plan, and they must make up for these gaps.

In this chapter, the documentation tasks and the requisites of a program plan document are detailed. The chapter takes a comprehensive approach, while also recognizing that officials and funders have variable informational and documentation requirements. For example, large foundations and federal and state funders usually require extensive detailing that is guided by explicit instructions regarding how it should be done. These funders typically have forms that must be completed, line spacing and margin stipulations, and page limitations on narratives. Small foundations and local funders may only require a two-page to five-page proposal that outlines the general features of the plan. If the proposal is not intended for anyone outside the organization, officials of organizations may have their own in-house requirements and formats. Documentation also varies depending on whether it pertains to program change or a new program. For example, if the planning effort is focused on a change in the existing admission system of an organization, then a completely documented admission design is required. However, in documenting the components of a new program, a detailed admission component may not be required by the funder. Planners may have to outline the admission process but leave the finishing work to the implementers.

This chapter presents the requisites of a program plan document in the order in which they are typically requested by officials and in many funders' requests for proposals (RFPs). It is up to planners to decide the adaptation of these requisites to the particular preferences of officials and funders.

Requisites for Program Plan Documents

In this section, each of the requisites for program plan documents is listed along with details of everything that is required to be in it.

Title Page and Executive Summary

A title page is usually the first page of the entire document and typically includes the name of the proposed program change or the new program, the officials to whom the document is being presented, the group or unit submitting the plan, the date of submission, and the host organization's name.

An executive summary, typically located at the front of the document, is now in wide use, replacing shorter abstracts of the contents. The summary presents the document's main elements concisely, including recommendations for approval and any other action (see the last requisite). The executive summary is intended for organizational decision makers who will, presumably, review the entire document but can then return to this statement in addressing the main matters requiring decision and authorization for the next steps. In proposals to be submitted to funders, the summary identifies the applicant or bidder. It includes at least one sentence on problems, conditions, or needs and on goals, the service program, and the funds requested.

Citation of Authors, Contributors, and Sources of Plan Materials

The persons directly responsible for submission of the plan and its documentation—and others who made significant contributions to it—are customarily listed (even if they are not authors of the final text). When they are members of a work group, team, or committee, all of them are listed, beginning with the chair, coordinator, or person in charge. If the planning team includes representatives of other organizations as well as employees, all of them are properly identified (for example, an interagency advisory committee may have provided overall guidance, with most of the work being performed by staff). Occasionally, consultants have prepared and submitted all or parts of the plan, and they should be listed.

Table of Contents or Outline of the Plan Document

The main sections, appendixes, and attachments are listed in some standard form, each with title, page, and other identification. Charts, figures, and similar displays may be separately listed thereafter.

Statement of the Charge, Authorization, or Mandate

The plan has been prepared in response to some official charge or authorization, and wherever possible this should be reported in its original terms, with as little paraphrasing or summarizing as feasible. Persons reviewing the document need to be reminded or to learn about the original charge and the authorization for the work represented by the document. The charge may be based on internal communication, proceedings of a board of directors, a local government act, and the like. The charge may be derived from external mandates, as with federal or state government legislative or executive actions or funding-body initiatives, and each deserves citation. But because the planning work goes on within organizations, the document should specify the internal charge, sometimes appearing only as an executive's directive.

Introduction of the Submitting Agency

An Introduction is required if the proposal is intended for submission to external funders or to officials within a large organization that may not be sufficiently familiar with one of their branch units or programs (for example, state service programs administered and offered at the county level). The Introduction describes the organization, including its mission and goals, auspices, years of service, authority and governance structure, and number of staff and their qualifications. This section also briefly describes the organization's service programs, the recipients' characteristics, and the number of persons served. Statements about accomplishments, support, endorsements, awards, licenses, and accreditation are also included. The Introduction should address the legitimacy and credibility of the organization. Many organizations already have all of this documentation on file, but it usually needs updating and customizing to meet the requirements of particular funders. In addition, and in a separate section, some funders want to know about an organization's capability to host and conduct the particular program for which funding is being sought.

Statement of Problem or Condition Being Addressed and Summary of Analysis and Assessment Findings

This component documents the findings from the problem analysis and needs assessment, including the nature of the problem or condition, its features, its consequences, its magnitude, and its distribution. The narrative includes a description of the characteristics of those affected by the problem or condition and how they experience it. The factors that contribute to or sustain the problem or condition or the barriers to their modification are also discussed. All of these topics are usually followed by a discussion of needs: What is essential or desired to maintain well-being? What is necessary to relieve a state of deficiency? Sometimes officials or funders want this section to include a review of existing community services (if any) that address the needs that have been identified.

Officials or funders may also want tables and charts included in this section, with brief interpretive comments, but others prefer the tables and charts in an appendix. Some funders do not want such items in the plan document at all but expect data and findings to be incorporated in the narrative.

Officials and funders must come away from a reading of this section saying, "Planners have documented their understanding of the nature of the problem or condition. They have made a compelling case that intervention in the form of a new service program (or a program change) is desirable or essential."

Some funders and officials also want documentation concerning the methodologies that were used to obtain the information presented in the section on the problem statement. For this reason, this section should include information about the investigative methods used in the problem analysis and needs assessment, the sources of data, the number and characteristics of respondents or informants (if any), and the date the data were obtained or published.

Identification of the Target Population to Be Served

This section describes the members of the target population and the rationale for their selection as the proposed service recipients. Planners typically discover more problems and needs than a service program can meet, so priorities must be stated: Which aspects of the problems and needs experienced by persons with particular characteristics should be the targets of a new or changed program? The desired location of this information in the proposal varies among funders. Some want it in a separate section, others want it merged into the problem statement, and still others want it in the program narrative.

Statement of Program Goals and Objectives

The needs and priorities of the target population must be transformed into program goals and outcome, process, and output objectives. Officials and funders typically want all of these nested in hierarchical order. Planners must carefully formulate, distinguish, and cluster each type of objective. (Listing process and output objectives under the label "outcome objectives" will suggest to officials or funders that planners are not clear about ends and the relationship among the types of objectives.) Outcome objectives must address the specific, anticipated, and desired future results, as well as the accomplishments and changes in the behavior or conditions of the target population. Process objectives denote the means by which the outcome objectives are to be achieved. Output objectives pertain to the units of service to be provided during a given time.

When planners have been charged with responsibility for planning a change in the operations of an existing program, then changes in existing process objectives or formulations of new ones are likely. Such revisions may require concomitant modifications of outcome and output objectives.

Program Narrative or Description of Services

This component bears the main burden of the program description, but cross-references to other sections can minimize redundancy in the report and assist readers in understanding the program. The program narrative is perhaps the most difficult component to write succinctly, an important reason for using charts and other graphic displays to supplement the text. To ensure that readers understand what new or changed service will be provided, how it will be accomplished, at what points various tasks will occur, and who will be doing them, a full explication of the main participants and their key activities, decisions, and interactions is necessary. This includes basic information about the major phases of the service program, sequential order of participant activities, accessibility, durations or time periods of the program cycle, and frequency and length of contacts. When these elements are addressed, both the activities of staff and recipients should be documented, as emphasized in the previous chapter. When assurances can be given that the plan focuses only on change in a limited segment of an ongoing program, the documentation may deal only with that (but include its linkages to other, unchanged segments).

The essential components of the service program must be detailed sufficiently so that decision makers can comprehend what is being proposed. Much of this information will eventually find its way into a manual of standard operating procedures (SOPs) during implementation. The documentation requirements for each of the four program phases discussed in Chapter Seven are presented here and consolidated with the other requisites in this chapter to serve as a handy reference when readers are at work.

Documenting the Elements of the Admission Phase. As planners finally decide the admission activities of a new or changed program, several matters usually require documentation: a dissemination of information about services, the criteria that enable members of the target population to qualify for the program, recipients' access to services, and the admission process. Several major elements are usually included in the documentation of the admission process:

- Initiation of the admission process
- Information to be sought in processing admissions
- Management of admission information
- Source of information about applicants
- Who manages the admission process and makes the admission decision
- Site of the admission process
- Duration of the admission process and frequency of contact
- When admission is to be completed

- Admission procedures
- Completion of the admission process

Documenting the Elements of the Assessment Phase. Several major elements are usually considered in documenting the assessment process:

- Purpose and focus of assessment
- Source of assessment information
- Who will conduct the assessment
- Means of assessment
- Duration of the assessment process and frequency of contact
- When the assessment will be completed
- Where the assessment will be completed
- Who will analyze and interpret the findings and develop the service plan
- Management of assessment information
- Completion of the assessment process

Documenting the Elements of the Intervention Phase. The intervention phase includes all staff and recipient participant activities directed at transacting benefits and services to address conditions or problems, to meet needs, and to achieve program goals and objectives. The description should include the following elements:

- The services, techniques, interventions, work methods, procedures, and benefits to be provided, including staff and recipient participant activities in each phase of the program
- Service roles
- Duration or time span of service delivery, frequency, and length of contact between recipients and staff
- Accessibility
- Procedures for recording interventions, transactions, and benefits

Documenting the Elements of the Termination Phase. Several elements of the termination process require documentation:

- Termination policies and procedures
- Participants in the termination process
- Duration of the termination phase and frequency of contact
- Timing of termination
- Location of termination

Because of the difficulties of relying only on textual narratives, the text of this whole section is usually supplemented by flowcharts and other displays that present and synthesize details that are challenging to summarize in writing. The more important of these materials belong in this part of the report, whereas others can be located in appendixes or attachments. For example, a clear flowchart displaying the entire program cycle and its major phases, participants, and other key elements is best included here. Highly detailed or technical information, whether in text form or other form, may be developed and cited as backup materials, available if requested and ready for the implementation work, but not included in the main report document.

The rationale for the proposed new program or the changed program must be explained, including the extent to which the needs of the target population will be met and the program objectives will be achieved. Some officials and funders require this discussion to address several questions: Why is *this* new or changed program or *this* particular design being proposed? Are there studies that attest to the efficacy of the proposed new or changed program? Has the proposed new or changed program been implemented elsewhere, and has it been successful? Anticipated problems or obstacles for achieving expected results through the proposed new or changed program should be identified and discussed, with contingency or alternative plans and rationales included.

Some funders want assurances that planners have addressed the unique characteristics and problems of particular segments of the target population. Accordingly, they want documentation of the program features that have been designed or adjusted to be responsive to these segments.

Discussion of Accessibility

As stated in Chapter Seven, some funders want accessibility addressed in a dedicated section, and others are satisfied with a discussion within the project narrative. In any case, service locations and hours must be documented. Any variations in location and service hours among the different phases of the service program should be explained. If there are barriers to accessibility for some segments of the target population, they must be identified, and approaches to overcoming or minimizing them must be explained. Prospective recipients might encounter one or more barriers, such as distance between residence and service site, poor or no transportation, work hours that compete with service hours, as well as cultural, ethnic, religious, community, educational, or income factors, among others.

Linkages with the Host Organization

The nesting of the new service program among the host organization's other services must be described, as well as its location in the administrative structure, with concrete explanation of the person in charge and the lines of authority and accountability. Program changes also require such documentation if the proposed plan includes alterations in the program's existing location in the organization's structure. A diagram or organizational chart that displays the interconnections of the proposed new program or the changed program with existing units in the organization is desirable.

Calendars, Schedules, and Time Lines for Service Phases and Cycles

Summary information about a new program's basic cycle, the expected start date, annual or other schedule if appropriate, and major phases should be included in the plan document. Information about the basic cycle might include the proposed day-to-day program and program schedule, as well as a typical work hour, day, week, or other period of service for most recipients. Similar information is needed for a plan to change an existing program, with some emphasis on any proposed differences in its chronological aspects. Officials and funders sometimes want the calendars, time lines, and schedules organized according to start-up and operational phases. Funders increasingly require that this information be presented in some graphic format, often referring to time lines, flowcharts, and the like, because they greatly aid understanding of information also given in textual descriptions.

The foregoing refers to the operational aspects of the program. Other important dates or time frames known to the planners, such as key review and report schedules, should also be included. For example, the original planning charge may have incorporated a schedule for both planning and implementation, or there may be an intention to apply for outside funding within a fixed deadline or by the due date for a coordinating body's approval request, or cooperating organizations may have set dates for confirmation of joint plans—all of which represent essential information needed by decision makers.

Relationships to Other Service Programs

A new program's success may critically depend on exchanges with other services; change in an ongoing program may involve modifying some ties to another program in the same or in a separate organization. When a program is dependent on another program for referral of persons served, whether in or out, or for sharing of information, facilities, personnel, and the like, suitable arrangements should be worked out during the planning process, at least in general terms. These connections are then spelled out in the document so their feasibility can be weighed: decision makers need to know the cost, negotiations, approvals, interruptions, lead times, and other seemingly peripheral implications of a plan for a given program.

Beyond this, numerous programs function within larger networks of related services—sometimes called *systems,* as in the areas of criminal justice, environmental protection, children's services, and medical services. In most of these areas, various local, regional, or state-level coordinating or oversight bodies perform authoritative functions of service coordination, standard setting, regulation, and the like. In this context, the new or changed program plan may have to be submitted for another group's formal approval before it can be launched by the host organization. If collaboration with other organizations is necessary, agreement letters (or summaries of positive negotiations) should accompany the plan.

Officials reviewing program plans (new or changed) may not require formal determination of all of the matters at the time the plan report is submitted, but they invariably expect that each requirement has been concretely identified in the document and that they have assurances that the plan under review will merit all necessary approvals from both coordinate service organizations and oversight bodies. Any of these that have not been formally completed at the time of plan submission should be called to the attention of officials. (This can be done in a memorandum of transmittal, which is discussed in the last section of this chapter.)

The Staffing Plan

The staffing plan is rarely developed by the planning team itself. The team leader, and perhaps another team member, usually work out the staffing plan with the executive director or a member of the administration in charge of human resources. In a large organization, the team leader may have to work with several specialists from the human resources department. All of these officials are knowledgeable about matters that have a bearing on staffing and the design of staff positions in their organizations. These matters may include collective-bargaining agreements, staff position classifications, personnel policies, staffing patterns, workloads, compensation packages, affirmative action policies, as well as licensing, regulatory, and accreditation requirements pertaining to personnel. Furthermore, the staffing plan must be linked with the program budget. Because of this, officials who are knowledgeable about the organization's budget must also be involved in the development of the staffing plan. (Readers from small nonprofit organizations who find themselves in planning situations in which they must develop the staffing plan may find it helpful to consult Pynes, 1997; Sovereign, 1998; Pecora and Austin, 1987; and the Web sites for Aspen Publishers, 2004; and Grantsmanship Center, 2004.)

Some of the groundwork for the staffing plan has already been completed and documented, as planners developed and clustered their lists of participant activities, organized the clusters into service roles, and figured out linkages with the host organization and other organizations. These descriptions should be shared with officials. Now the team leader, and perhaps one or two other team representatives, and officials must cluster and assign service roles to persons in positions. A *position* is a cluster of related duties, roles, and tasks, officially recognized by the organization and performed on a full-time or part-time basis, with or without compensation. Staff positions refer to the persons who will be compensated to perform the activities of the program and provide the services, as well as to support and administrative staff who will be involved in a direct or indirect way.

Funders and officials vary in their requirements for a staffing plan. Most want a personnel roster that lists the number and types of staff and documentation on their roles, tasks, responsibilities, or assignments in the service program. All workers involved in the program—those who perform service and nonservice roles—should be included in the documentation (for example, paid supervisory, direct-service, and support staff, as well as volunteers, consultants, or providers of service from other organizations). The qualifications for the positions should include the knowledge, skill, qualities, education, training, and experience that are required or preferred. Résumés of known or proposed staff are included in an appendix. The staffing plan should address how the proposed personnel link up with the organization's job classification system and whether the positions are full-time or part-time. Some funders want a start-up staffing plan and one for ongoing operations. Some want detailed task analyses (see the case example that follows) and a staff deployment plan (for example, how child-care staff will be deployed in a weekend respite facility). The elements of the staffing plan will vary depending on what funders and officials want.

Under certain conditions or for some problems, planners may have to recommend that some, many, or all of the staff should have one or more of the key characteristics of the recipients (for example, same gender, race, ethnicity, or sexual orientation or similar age range, disabilities, or experiences). Matching characteristics may be necessary to overcome the barriers to trust experienced by some groups (Saulnier, 2002; Kruzich, Friesen, Williams-Murphy, and Longley, 2002; Shapiro, 1994; Shilts, 1987). For example, in a program to reduce infant mortality among low-income African American women, officials decided to recruit African American women who were raised in the inner city and who had entrée into the community to link with expectant mothers who needed prenatal health services. In planning a mental health program for veterans who were experiencing posttraumatic shock, staff recommended hiring a counselor who was a veteran. Representation conveys that kindred persons are employed in the program and are likely to understand the unique ways that a particular group experiences problems and needs.

Organizational declarations and professional values notwithstanding, age, gender, race and ethnicity, and sexual orientation are bases for discrimination, personal or institutional, that are likely to account for the small number of recipients from some segments of the target population. Program planners must be vigilant and sensitive to such barriers and must facilitate ease of access and utilization of services.

The People and Pets Together (PPT) case example is used here to examine the staffing plan developed by the chair of the planning team and the host organization's human resource specialist. Note how many components of the PPT coordinator's task analysis and job description are based on the clustering of participant activities displayed in Exhibit 7.2 in Chapter Seven. Some officials and funders require extensive detailing to validate that there is enough work to justify the staffing requests and related personnel costs. Note too that the tasks of the start-up phase provide some direction to the implementers (assuming the program plan is approved). The case example here focuses primarily on the position entitled PPT coordinator.

◆ ◆ ◆

People and Pets Together Case Example: Outline of the Staffing Plan

The following list represents the PPT proposed requirements for staffing:

1. One PPT coordinator: one full-time equivalent (FTE), year one (see task analysis).
2. One secretary: in-kind contribution of County Commission on Aging (CCOA), .15 FTE. Serves as project receptionist, orients walk-ins to the project in coordinator's absence, provides supportive services.
3. Thirty community volunteers to work with transportation assistance and post-adoption visits. Volunteers will serve one participant at a time, will have time-limited relationships, and will be asked to serve several participants per year.
4. Humane Society staff will provide assistance with pet selection, spaying and neutering, pet care instruction, and classes.

5. Selected vets to do occasional pro bono work or at a reduced fee in cooperation with the Humane Society.

Task Analysis of the Program Coordinator Position: Start-up Phase

The following list represents the PPT proposed set of tasks for the program coordinator:

1. Work with PPT steering committee: (a) recruit members, including elders, a Humane Society staff member, and representatives of organizations with access to prospective volunteers; (b) formalize purposes and functions of the steering committee, operating and governing procedures; (c) facilitate the work of the steering committee—schedule meetings, plan and prepare for meetings; and (d) develop a work plan with the steering committee.
2. Market the program: disseminate information to referral sources, organizations that are likely sources of volunteers, and the target population.
3. Develop working relationship with the Humane Society, Animal Control, veterinarians, churches, licensing agency, and dog obedience schools.
4. Implement the PPT Program: (a) identify and carry out implementation tasks and sequencing—for example, complete the design of the admission and assessment process, design admission and assessment forms, purchase equipment and supplies, develop working relationship with the host organization, decide on qualifications and characteristics of volunteers, decide targets and methods of recruitment, develop a plan to recruit, screen, select, train, and supervise volunteers to work with elders, develop criteria for subsidized adoptions for elders with limited incomes, develop protocol to match volunteers with elders, develop a plan of action for failed adoptions; (b) decide milestones and time lines; and (c) activate the program and make it operational.

Task Analysis of the Program Coordinator Position: Operational Phase

The task analysis of the position comprises delineation of program operations, program administration, and organizational duties.

Program Operations The analysis covered four areas of program operations:

1. Admissions: receive and process referrals and delegate to appropriate support staff; determine if elder qualifies for PPT; orient elder to PPT.
2. Assessment: reach out to elders in their homes and assess their financial, physical, and emotional ability to care for a pet; determine whether residence and environment are appropriate for the particular pet the elder wishes to adopt.
3. Facilitating the elder's adoption of the pet: assist elder in selecting and adopting a pet; arrange or provide transportation if necessary; assist in preparations for homecoming of pet, including purchases of supplies; match elder with a volunteer.

4. Follow-up and termination: conduct or delegate follow-up visits to determine if adoption is going well and if elder needs assistance; make arrangements for care of pet if adoption is not going well.

Program Administration The analysis covered nine areas of program administration:

1. Recruit, screen, select, match, train, supervise, evaluate, and reward volunteers.
2. Order and maintain necessary program supplies and equipment.
3. Develop and manage the program budget.
4. Collect service information and compile reports as required by the executive director.
5. Evaluate the effort and effectiveness of the program.
6. Seek additional sources of funding under the direction of the executive director.
7. Maintain working arrangements with collaborating agencies.
8. Staff the steering committee.
9. Continue to market the program to the target population and sources of referral as necessary.

Organizational Duties The analysis covered three primary organizational duties:

1. Report to the executive director of CCOA.
2. Serve as a member of the CCOA's Management Council.
3. Participate in CCOA staff meetings and staff development programs.

Description of the Program Coordinator Position

The PPT coordinator is responsible for implementing, managing, and carrying out a pet adoption program in Rural County for elders who are sixty-five years of age or older, who live alone, and who are experiencing age-related crises including loneliness. The coordinator is responsible for screening elders, matching elders and pets, developing and implementing a volunteer program, and maintaining relationships with collaborating organizations and associations. Knowledge of and experience in working with elders is required. Knowledge of the requirements of pet care and comfort with dogs and cats are required. Ability to conduct home visits with elders in small towns and rural areas is required. A bachelor's degree in a human service field is preferred.

If the program plan is approved, the task analysis, job description, and qualifications are essential as implementers try to figure out what the planners had in mind when they designed the program. Poorly designed or inadequately formalized staff positions can contribute to failure to achieve program goals, poor performance, and conflict. All of these may occur when people have different expectations as to how a person should perform the roles of a position. Staff who have too many roles or tasks may not be able to provide services effectively or efficiently, or staff may make decisions about role or task priorities that are personally desirable but programmatically undesirable. Sometimes conflict is inadvertently "built into" a position, because the consequences of the design were not given sufficient consideration. It is also true though that even when one considers such aspects of design, the consequences are not always predictable, and program planners have to rely on trial and error and the lessons of experience (Pecora and Austin, 1987, pp. 18–32).

Estimation of Units of Service

Now that planners have come this far in the design stage, they have enough information to figure out how many elders might be served in the PPT Program. A unit of service is a way of measuring and reporting production in terms of volume and quantity (for example, in business and industry—number of mattresses sold, air passengers served, tons of household waste recycled, and cars produced; in human service organizations—the number of library patrons served, days of child care provided, retirement-planning seminars offered, and children placed in foster care). In planning new service programs or changes in existing ones, funders or officials want an estimate of the units of service that would be provided if the plan were approved and implemented.

Planners have probably thought about (if not talked about) the units of service that might be provided to recipients at a few earlier points in the planning process. As indicated in Chapter Three in the discussion on the nature of planning, it is a back-and-forth process and requires a holistic perspective. As planners move through the stages of planning, they must be mindful of the relationship of one component to the other components of the plan. Estimates of units of service are a special case in point.

At the outset of planning, the charge, the mandates, or the stipulations of officials or funders about the new or changed program may have contained references bearing on units of service (for example, funding support may be tied to a minimum or maximum number of recipients; standards of licensing agencies set capacity limits on the number of children who can occupy a cabin at a resident camp based on square feet of space available per child). During the analysis stage, planners cannot help but think about units of service when they explore the nature of the problem and estimate its magnitude and distribution. During the goal and objective stage, when planners formulated preliminary output objectives, they had to give some consideration to units of service. In the case example in Chapter Five, the PRCC had to decide how many respite care cooperatives could be established in one year and what a cooperative wanted to accomplish each month. Now that the service program and staffing plan have been developed, the units of service and output objectives can be more reliably estimated. These estimates are usually made in collaboration with the executive of the host organization or the officials responsible for budget estimation, funding requests, or grants administration.

Five types of measures are often used to quantify units of service:

1. Time units, such as one hour of home health care or psychiatric consultation, one overnight of respite care
2. Episode or activity units, such as an individual or group counseling session, a class meeting, an admission, a referral
3. Material units, such as meals served, books lent, drugs prescribed
4. Output or service completion unit, such as pet adoptions completed, foster children or homeless families placed, volunteers recruited, lifeguards trained
5. Outcome units, such as the number of developmentally disabled adults who acquired such independent-living skills as housekeeping and use of public transportation, or the number of elders who improved their scores on a life satisfaction scale after two months of participation in the pet adoption program

Instructions on how to calculate these units of service can be found in Kettner, Moroney, and Martin (1999, pp. 119–128). Units of service do not necessarily reflect all aspects of staff direct-service activities, such as work with ineligible persons during the application phase, nor all aspects of administrative activities, such as record keeping, staff meetings, and training sessions.

Several factors must be taken into consideration when planners have discretion in defining units of service. Does the unit of service capture what the staff do? Can it be used to make projections about the scale of the program? Is the unit understandable and meaningful to staff and funders? Returning to the PPT case example will demonstrate how the chair of the planning team and an official estimated units of service.

◆ ◆ ◆

People and Pets Together Case Example: Estimating Units of Service

In preparation for making estimates on the units of service, the chair provided a hand-out based on the CCOA needs assessment:

- There were approximately twenty-eight hundred persons in the county who were sixty-five years old or older and who lived alone.
- Two hundred respondents from the random sample phone survey of elders in the county reported that they lived alone and were experiencing age-related crises, including loneliness.
- Almost 80 percent of the two hundred respondents had ten or fewer hours per week of contact with friends or relatives.

The chair suggested that even if some of those elders had a pet, didn't want one, or would not qualify for the program for one reason or another, there would still be a large enough pool of elders who might need and benefit from the PPT program.

They decided to begin the estimation process by figuring out how much time would be needed for ten nonservice activities essential to the start-up and ongoing operations of the service program. They worked from the task analysis and calculated the following estimates.

Nonservice Tasks	Hours per Year
Work with the steering committee	20
Recruit volunteers	30
Screen at least forty volunteers	40
Train at least thirty volunteers	30
Match and assign thirty volunteers to sixty elders	30
Supervise thirty volunteers (a half hour, four times per year)	60
Provide volunteer recognition	20
Administer start-up and ongoing program activities	640
Conduct organizational activities	95
Collaborate on tasks with other organizations	60
Total	1,025

These 1,025 nonservice hours were subtracted from 1,920 hours (the total number of work hours for one FTE staff member for one year—that is, 40 hours times forty-eight weeks), which resulted in a remainder of 895 possible service hours. The planners had estimated earlier that an elder in need of moderate staff assistance would require approximately 7.5 hours of service from the point of referral to the last post-placement adoption visit. A self-managed elder might require 1 to 3 hours. An elder in need of significant staff assistance would require approximately 10 hours. They agreed that the proportional distribution of these three groups could not be estimated, and they decided to stick with the estimate based on elders who needed moderate assistance. They divided 895 hours by 7.5 hours and calculated that approximately 120 elders could be served by the program.

◆ ◆ ◆

This kind of information enables planners and officials to figure out, compare, and evaluate costs per unit of service and to assess whether planners have carefully thought through the staffing plan and some aspects of implementation.

The Program Budget: Estimating Program Costs

Service programs require a variety of human and material resources to conduct their business, ranging from staff through space and equipment to supplies and special materials. Fundamental to every program, of course, is the need for support funds to acquire resources in the marketplace. Because a service organization (and its programs) is not different in this respect from a business, a manufacturing plant, a household, or a farm, officials rely on terms of reference that are shared throughout the profit and nonprofit sectors. Standardized ways of identifying almost all personnel and material resources are well codified, as are methods for presenting them. Following is a representative list of budget expense items used by many funders and agencies to estimate the costs of a new program or a changed service program.

Budget line items

Personnel salaries and wages

Health and retirement benefits

Payroll taxes

Professional fees (consultants)

Supplies

Telephone, fax, and Internet (communications)

Postage and shipping

Occupancy

Rental and maintenance of equipment

Print and publications

Travel

Conferences and conventions (often included in travel)

Special assistance to individuals and clients

Membership dues

Awards and grants

Equipment

Depreciation or amortization (for buildings and equipment)

The budget is a ubiquitous format for listing all resources that must be procured in the marketplace. It always uses ordinary monetary values (that is, market costs) for each resource, presenting the figures in clusters by types of resources (such as personnel, space and facilities, equipment, supplies). The outline of budget categories can be a helpful guide as planners begin to specify the resources required for a new or changed program, and it affords an orderly way to identify and present much of the information relevant to this component.

Depending on the expectations of officials or funders, the program budget may be as simple as a one-page form of projected expenses, or it may be a complex presentation of forms and narrative explanations that specify and justify each expense item. New expenses and the organization's contributions from its ongoing budget to the new or changed program must be included in some budget requests.

The development of the program budget is another matter that is developed jointly, usually with the chair of the planning team and a member of the administration—someone who "keeps the books." Organizations and funders usually have standard budget estimation forms that delineate the line items for which estimates must be made (Vinter and Kish, 1984, p. 363). Funders typically provide instructions for detailing the documentation that they want in the proposed budget. For readers who find themselves in planning situations in which they must develop the program budget, there are many helpful resources available, including books (Kettner, Moroney, and Martin, 1999, pp. 173–214; Maddox, 1999; Shim and Siegel, 1997; and Vinter and Kish, 1984), handbooks, forms, virtual seminars, and catalogues that are online or may be ordered online (Aspen Publishers, 2004; Foundation Center, 2004; and Grantsmanship Center, 2004).

Personnel who will manage the program and conduct its activities consist of employed staff, volunteers, decision makers, and occasionally consultants or other specialists. Organizations typically have established personnel classification systems that denote all existing types of jobs, their status, compensation rates, and other basic elements. These should be used to delineate who does what to conduct the program in the proposal, summarized in a standard personnel roster for the program. This includes details about their levels and periods of service (for example, part-time or full-time, on annual or seasonal bases, compiled in standard terms as FTEs), salary rates, and other essentials. If the plan calls for staff who are not presently within the organization's system, or for modifications in existing job descriptions, they are concretely noted. Similar information about volunteers that assist in providing program services is generally included.

Most other resources that are required to conduct the program are identified and listed in standard ways, particularly when they represent new or unusual demands on the host organization's available resources. Only the most inconsequential program change would require no shift in any resource.

Administrative officials with expertise in budgeting may not have the necessary practical understanding of a particular service program to be able to decide on essential program resources, such as equipment, appliances, supplies, and transportation services. For example, an official working on a budget for a new children's day treatment program is unlikely to know which vehicles are appropriate for the safe transport of children and which athletic, recreational, and craft supplies are appropriate for children with emotional troubles. Accordingly, planners must work with officials in formulating the program budget. In the PPT case study, planners must clue in the budget officer concerning the resources that are essential to the implementation of the program (for example, portable animal carriers that can be placed in a car or van, instructional video on animal care, mileage reimbursements, and the annual appreciation breakfast for volunteers).

Organization's Ability to Host and Conduct the Program

Outside funding and oversight bodies invariably want to know if the organization that is intending to launch a new program (or expand an ongoing one) has the assets, features, and capabilities necessary to perform all of the required associated tasks:

1. Legitimation and support as appropriate within the local community and by accrediting and licensing authorities
2. Congruence of the program's goals, objectives, and services with the mission of the host organization
3. Essential resources other than those included in the support budget request (for example, facilities, staff competencies)
4. The experience and managerial capacities to administer and account for the program

As noted previously, organizational decision makers are also concerned with all of these matters in reviewing proposals. Planners should inform officials about the additional burdens that a program change will place on administrative and support services, or about how a new program will be viewed by important constituencies.

Procedures for Monitoring Program Processes and Assessing Results

In this information age, there are obligations to record and report many facts and events in service programs, some essential for reasons internal to the program, others required of all services within the host organization, and some imposed by oversight, funding, and other bodies. Of obvious importance is information about service recipients, about service activities that were undertaken with regard to them, and about staff and volunteer decisions (including who made the decisions) as the program process unfolded. In addition to their use in responsible management of program operations, such service records and statistics are essential for assessment of service results or outputs. Plans for new or changed programs should include specific attention to monitoring and assessment procedures, which are then documented in this component.

Sometimes the program monitoring and accountability requirements are substantial, and a plan for the evaluation of outcomes or effectiveness is expected by officials as a condition of approval, or by funders as a condition of a funding award. In these situations, planners (or the implementation team) either hand off this part of the project to an evaluation team, an inside expert, or an outside consultant or work with them. However, there are evaluation questions and types of evaluations (for example, program monitoring or program effort evaluation) that planners or implementers can formulate and that program staff can carry out routinely and easily. Turning back to the PPT case example will illustrate the kinds of measures that do not require specialized expertise in evaluative research and information processing technology.

◆ ◆ ◆

People and Pets Together Case Example: Compiling Information for Program Monitoring

Officials from the County Council on Aging want to monitor program efforts and obtain some qualitative measures of outcomes, so the planning team compiled lists for each area.

Information About Participants

The planning team developed the following list:

- Age
- Sex
- Educational level
- Health status in relation to ability to care for a pet
- Sufficient financial resources to care for a pet
- Type of residence
- Residential property appropriate for a pet
- Ownership of a motor vehicle
- Ability to drive
- Source of referral
- Distance of residence from PPT offices and the Humane Society

Measures of Service Activities

The planning team developed the following list:

- Number of information disseminations about PPT
- Types of information disseminations and audience
- Number and type of volunteer recruitment appeals made
- Number and characteristics of volunteers recruited
- Number of volunteers trained
- Number of elder self-initiated inquiries about PPT
- Number and source of referrals to PPT
- Number of elders who were oriented to the program
- Number of elders who sought admission
- Number of elders screened
- Number of elders admitted to PPT
- Number of home visits
- Number of staff and volunteer visits to the Humane Society
- Number of pet adoptions completed
- Length of time required to find an acceptable pet
- Number and kinds of pets that were adopted
- Number and kinds of problems elders had with pets
- Number of elders who attended pet care and dog obedience classes
- Range and average number of postplacement visits by staff and volunteers
- Range and average number of volunteer hours served per elder
- Number of failed pet adoptions
- Number of elders satisfied with service activities

Outcomes

The planning team developed the following list (see also Delta Society, 2003):

- Measures of the satisfaction of pet companionship
- Self-reports of improved life satisfaction
- Increase in social opportunities
- New membership in groups or organizations
- Participants who became volunteers

◆ ◆ ◆

Information about recipients and service activities can be entered on forms and into a computer and easily retrieved for tallies. It's a worthy exercise to take a few of the items and examine the merits of measuring them. If the PPT program does not recruit enough volunteers, staff can look at the number and type of information disseminations and their audiences. If the number of elders interested in the program far exceeds the number who adopt a pet, then staff must figure out the reasons for the attrition and the barriers to success. If the number of failed adoptions is high, staff can look for the factors that contribute to failures. As part of the exercise, readers may want to examine the measures and think about their usefulness to officials, program staff, volunteers, and current and prospective recipients.

When program staff examine the results of such evaluations, they often learn that the results do not conform to their impressions of program recipients and service activities. Their impressions may be formed by a few dominant experiences with particular recipients, or their experiences may be skewed in comparison with those of other staff members. By aggregating the activities of individual staff members and the experiences of individual recipients, staff and administrators are able to discern patterns and monitor program operations. If programs are not functioning properly, program staff and officials can adjust them accordingly. Readers who want more information on program evaluation can consult the many specialized books on this subject (Posavac and Carey, 2003; Westerfelt and Dietz, 2001; Royse and Thyer, 2000; Martin and Kettner, 1996; and Gray, 1995).

Program Reporting and Accountability Requirements

Beyond using the information internally, the host organization cannot fulfill its legal and fiduciary obligations for all of its programs unless it systematically reports detailed information for review by others. For many programs, the organization is obligated to provide periodic summaries of information to outside regulatory, funding, and other authorities. The particular procedures, forms, time periods, and processing and reporting obligations for all necessary program information should be detailed in appropriate parts of the report (although final details about forms and so forth may be passed over to the implementation effort).

Statutory, Regulatory, Code, Certification, and Other Requirements

Human service organizations and their programs must adhere to numerous federal, state, and local government requirements. Some are applicable to all (for example, IRS, state corporation, and Office of Equal Opportunity requirements). Others apply only to certain programs (for example, state and local fire prevention requirements, health codes, zoning ordinances for residential services, certifications for several licensed providers). Funders of service programs impose other, diverse requirements (for example, service standards). Almost all of these requirements are stated in formal language contained in various official sources, and they must be fulfilled in standardized ways (for example, forms must be completed to document that substance abuse counselors have met training and certification requirements; long-term care and assisted-living facilities must meet certification requirements for medication management).

Again, completion of any or all of these requirements may not be necessary at the time a plan report is submitted for approval, but each should be cited somewhere in the document so that necessary action can be authorized for the implementation process. The planners may have identified some requirements that are expected to present special difficulties—perhaps obtaining a zoning ordinance offset or an interim approval by some regulatory body. These ought to be brought to attention during the review.

Plan Review and Approval Steps and Implementation Recommendations

The charge for planning may have included some directives about how and when the program plan document would be reviewed and then moved toward implementation or submission to a funding agency, if approved. As often happens during the typical back-and-forth planning process, officials may have begun to give attention to follow-up steps that they wish to be taken during the plan's review, or after its approval. The final plan document should cite all such steps at the time of the plan review (for example, advancing negotiations with another service organization, meeting some deadline for clearance with an oversight body).

Even if officials have not given attention to follow-up steps, the planners probably now know about a number of critical steps that should be taken, as part of the review and approval process, or later during implementation, and these must be clearly noted. Planners often list these steps in a memorandum of transmittal attached to the plan document that is submitted to officials. The memorandum may also include assurance that the plan has been shared with key staff (not necessarily for concurrence) and that major internal staff units (for example, financial, administrative, and human resources units, buildings and grounds, food service, or their equivalents in small organizations) have approved its provisions, and if they have not, why not. In addition, planners are obligated to bring forth any policy issues, internal or external, that they may see in the proposal. The memorandum should give officials and implementers a "heads up" about any problems, risks, or difficulties that might occur. Without such detailed guidance, the implementers of the approved plan—perhaps including one or two of the original planners—will flounder as they pursue the tasks of bringing an approved plan to fruition.

The plan document is usually distributed to officials prior to their review meeting to give them ample time to study it and prepare to discuss it at the meeting. Sometimes officials are asked by their presiding chair to submit written comments beforehand, which are then compiled for presentation and discussion at the review meeting. Other times, officials are asked to call in, or they are polled, to find out whether or not they support the proposal. Officials who have strong negative opinions (or who represent persons with such opinions) may call the presiding chair in advance of the meeting whether or not they are invited to do so. Others with such opinions may withhold comment, try to rally opposition to the proposal, and wait until the review meeting to express their views.

Prior to the meeting at which the proposal is to be reviewed, the leader of the planning team is usually informed about the officials' views of the proposal if they are known. If such notice is not offered, the team leader should try to find out the questions and leanings of officials. Whether team leaders get information beforehand or not, they should engage team members in anticipation management to envision best-case to worst-case scenarios and prepare for the review meeting accordingly. Even in a best-case scenario, the leader and other team members should be prepared for questions and challenges. Planners must be vigilant. Most meetings are positive and constructive. But on occasion, when one or two officials, or citizen representatives, or disgruntled staff members oppose the proposal, they can be harsh in expressing their views. Team members can immunize themselves against these reactions by anticipating and discussing worst-case scenarios and devising strategies to cope with them.

Typically, the leader, and one or two team members, attend and participate in the review meeting with officials. The presiding chair usually begins by informing officials of the charge to the team, and then the leader is asked to make a brief presentation on the team's efforts and the program plan document. Planners should not use all of their time "talking at" officials. It is advisable for planners to develop a PowerPoint presentation and rely on visual aids such as slides, transparencies and overhead projectors, or handouts that include graphics and outlines.

After the plan is reviewed, officials have several options. The plan may be approved as submitted. The plan may be rejected in whole or in part. Rejection may be followed by a directive to cease planning or to make changes and resubmit the plan. Officials may request the team leader to incorporate their directed changes into the program plan document, or they may want the planning team to be reconvened, work on the changes, and submit the revised proposal for review and approval. Planners should not be surprised or upset if officials alter the proposal or ask the team to reconvene to further develop the plan. Such decisions by officials are normal aspects of the planning process. When officials give final approval, they can submit the plan to funders, or if the plan pertains to an in-house proposal, officials can prepare it for implementation.

After officials approve the proposal at their review meeting, a considerate work group leader will inform the other members about the decision. Even if the proposal pertains to a small-scale program change, members are eager to hear what officials said and decided. For large-scale or significant projects, members who did not attend the meeting are probably watching the clock and waiting to hear the news. Work group members deserve to be informed, considering the time and effort they invested in the planning project.

The successful completion of some planning projects is just another workaday event without any whoop-de-do. The successful completion of other projects is an occasion for thanks and recognition. The type of expression is typically determined by the type and scale of the planning venture and the nature of its success (for example, letters of appreciation from senior officials, complimentary letters to the executive directors or department heads of team members from other organizations or departments, breakfast receptions to personally thank members for their efforts, awards, and accolades at public meetings, in newspaper accounts, and in television news reports). Whatever approach is used, planners deserve appreciation and recognition for their contributions, especially if officials want to appoint or ask them to serve again.

◆ ◆ ◆

Final approval of the plan document by officials represents the end of the planning project. However, as you will see in the Conclusion, there is more work to be done.

CONCLUSION

Even when final approval of the plan document has been received, there is more work to be done.

Managing Stakeholder Reactions to the Plan

Depending on the nature of the planning project, sometimes officials of the sponsoring organization arrange group meetings with different stakeholders to explain and interpret the approved plan (for example, staff meetings, interagency meetings with executives of nonprofit organizations, interdepartmental meetings with heads of governmental units, and public meetings with current or prospective recipients or their spokespersons). Officials also want to provide the opportunity for stakeholders to express their views about the plan and offer suggestions for how it should be implemented. Some stakeholders expect such meetings and demand them if they are not scheduled. The team leader may be asked to lead or assist in the interpretation of the approved plan and provide opportunities for stakeholders to ask questions and make statements. Occasionally, an influential member of the stakeholder community serves as spokesperson for the plan (for example, in one situation a board president and prominent attorney who was respected in the law enforcement community explained the program plan to judges, prosecutors, and police officials).

Experienced planners and officials have identified three types of reactions that stakeholders have when they learn about the features of the approved plan: they endorse and praise; they disapprove and criticize; or they are indifferent. The approval of a program change or a new program is likely to have its supporters and its critics, both within and outside the organization that sponsored the planning project.

After the plan has been approved, and the planning team has been discharged from its duties, technically it has no authority or official responsibility to receive and manage stakeholder reactions. Whether critical or concerned stakeholders know about this technicality or not, sometimes they contact the team leader or other members to complain, point out aspects of the plan in need of further development, "get the inside story," or otherwise hold the team accountable. No plan is perfect. Planning is a process with limits, compromises, trade-offs, and impositions, and planners may not even be responsible for what the critics do not like (for example, new laws or regulations, declines in revenue, or judicial decisions that require compromises or impose decisions on planners).

The team leader or other members may feel obligated or pressured to respond, due to an "informal system" of relationships or connections with stakeholders. There are many acceptable ways to handle concerns and criticisms from stakeholders, too numerous to detail here. Obviously, these situations must be sensitively and diplomatically managed. One team leader takes a judicious approach after being informed of dissatisfactions with the plan. She expresses gratitude for being alerted to matters that might require further attention and regrets that the plan did not meet stakeholder preferences. Depending on the stakeholder, she either assures the person that the information will be communicated to officials, or she urges a direct contact with them. She further explains that only officials have updated information about the status of the plan. ("It's out of our hands.") Officials may seek the leader's advice or the advice of other team members in deciding how to respond to stakeholders. However, one principle is clear: organizational officials, not the planners, have the responsibility to address stakeholder issues, because officials approved the plan and now they "own it." In addition, some stakeholders only want to talk to the person at the top.

Sometimes stakeholder criticism is understandable and justified. For example, in some low-income or minority communities, their experience with government and nonprofit organizations might incline them to be cynical and skeptical about the proposed plan. In some communities, residents believe that they have been "studied to death" and that officials made commitments, which in turn led to a rise in expectations, followed by disappointment when commitments were not kept. In another situation, persons with chronic mental health problems were facing another set of cutbacks and a restructuring of service programs that had enabled them to live independently in the community. They, and those who spoke in their behalf, opposed the revisions. The strong feelings of these individuals are reflected in the comment, "We are not going to be grateful when they throw us a bone." Although these recipients and their spokespersons will use the revised programs, they believe that acceptance of the program without complaint will lead to official acquiescence down the road.

Looking Back

When the planning project ends, sometimes a key official and the work group leader meet to discuss the review meeting and to look back and reflect on the planning experience. First and foremost, they are likely to discuss what occurred at the review meeting when officials made their decision about the proposed program plan. Such discussions often focus on the officials who supported and those who opposed (if any) all or some aspects of the proposal, the reasons for their support or opposition, and any alterations that officials might have made to the plan as submitted by the work group. The degree of support and criticism and the type of support and criticism among stakeholders within and outside the organization are also likely to receive attention. The key official and the leader might also explore some aspects of the planning experience, such as the composition of the work group and the contributions of its members, the methods used in the problem analysis and needs assessment, the adequacy of organizational support for the project, workloads, and the adequacy of recipient or citizen representation. The members of the work group probably discussed one or more of these matters at their last meeting or in the course of the planning project, and the team leader is likely to share their views with the official. All of these discussions are useful in identifying the lessons that were learned from the planning project and that might have a bearing on the organization's future planning ventures.

Appreciating Contributions and Mending Relationships

As team members look back at their planning experience (individually, in subgroups, or as a group), they recognize that some members contributed more than others; some brought unique knowledge, skill, or perspectives to the planning project; some were selected to the team because they represented key stakeholders; a few brought hidden or up-front agendas; and at least one person had an ax to grind. Some members were task leaders, and others were more skilled in interpersonal relations and group dynamics. After learning that officials have approved the proposal, planners usually feel good about themselves and most of their colleagues, even if team members occasionally experienced strained relations during the course of planning. When the planning project is lengthy and challenging, planners consider the successful completion of their work as quite a feat, especially if the project was the first time they had worked together.

Planning inevitably produces conflict, as members champion their perspectives and preferences in such matters as the problem analysis and needs assessment, the setting of priorities, and the features of the program changes or the new program. Some conflicts are considered minor and normal aspects of decision making in groups, and members do not give their conflicts a second thought. Other conflicts require group attention or meetings outside the group with the parties to the conflict to begin mending organizational or personal relationships. If conflicts are not settled when they occur, then the completion of the planning project might be the last appropriate opportunity to settle them and to mend strained relationships among persons and organizations that have to work together on the plan that was just approved. For example, in one planning project, a senior official of an advocacy organization bluntly criticized several government departments, represented by members on the planning team, for "neglecting my consumers." At the outset of another project, a representative of a community organization declared, "With some exceptions, the people sitting at this table are incapable of understanding the problems of my community." In both instances, a team member, respected by both the confronters and the confronted, mediated a session to reestablish a working relationship among the parties. Depending on the nature of the project and what is at stake in the conflict, the approval of the proposal often results in letting bygones be bygones (especially if the parties to the conflict share in external funding). Then again, there are exceptions, and the conflict may extend into the implementation process.

Looking Ahead: Implementation

After the planning project has been completed, planners are also inclined to look ahead: What's next for the plan? In some instances, the approved plan is handed off to the implementation team. In other instances, implementation of the approved plan is contingent on external funding, and the next step is an application for such support. Even if the application is timely submitted, and it results in a funding award, implementation might not be initiated for several months or up to a year after the program plan was approved by organizational officials. Funders have extended timetables for the submission and review of fund applications, and for the announcement and distribution of awards. Sometimes the funding request has to be divided into two proposals that must be submitted to two different funders (for example, one funder supports program operations but not capital improvements, whereas the other funder supports capital improvements but not program operations). Other times, initial applications for funds are rejected, and officials resubmit proposals with or without revisions to several funders, one after the other. Experience shows that some resubmissions of program funding requests result in success. Whatever the path to a funding award, the application process will delay the initiation of implementation. And some approved plans are never implemented, because fund applications are rejected. Funders may decide that the proposal is not worthy of support, or they may decide that it is worthy of support, but funds are limited, and other proposals are a better match with the funding organization's mission and priorities.

The *process* of implementation begins after organization officials have decided to authorize proceeding with initiation of a new program or changes in an existing program and when persons are designated and charged with responsibilities as members of an implementation team. The *work* of implementation commences with the implementation team's receipt and review of its charge, including the program plan document that has been approved (as amended and supplemented) by organizational officials (and perhaps by fund officials). The aim of implementation is to bring the program plan, its designs and decisions, into operational reality—that is, to specify, construct, and activate the requisite organizational arrangements and to mobilize and prepare the human resources and other resources so that new service can begin, or program changes can be instituted. Much work is often needed to launch or phase in the changed or new program, to embed it into the organization's larger structure and processes, and perhaps to monitor and debug operational difficulties that typically arise.

The Implementers

A considerable range of competencies is required to accomplish the diverse tasks of implementation. It is therefore usually undertaken by a team or work group of persons who, as in program planning, collaborate in playing various roles and making particular contributions to the work.

Many implementation tasks focus on intramural matters, so they typically are best performed by personnel within the organization. For example, fitting new program job specifications to existing staff position classifications, and perhaps selecting among current employees or volunteers to assume new duties, are seen as inside matters. Other intramural tasks include adaptation or new uses of space, reallocation of resources needed to conduct the new or changed program, and adjustment of its operations to mesh with those of other ongoing services.

Implementation proceeds effectively if there is detailed knowledge about all such matters in the organization and insight into how they can best be dealt with so that a viable service program can be achieved.

Implementation activities are often carried forward under the guidance of middle-management personnel, using teams composed of existing staff and working with a few others: peers, volunteers, current or prospective recipients, community representatives, consultants, or decision makers. The authority to charge, direct, and approve all aspects of this process, however, remains at the organization's executive and policymaking levels, as with program planning. And of course, outside persons or units with potent influence, needed funding, or regulatory authority exercise their interests in the implementation process.

The major elements of service programs that have been discussed in this book should be understood by those responsible for implementation, or there is a risk of doing unwitting damage in their work. That being the case, persons who have substantial knowledge of how service programs actually function can make significant contributions to the process of changing them or to the process of starting new ones. Experience in some program-related planning effort is also desirable before undertaking implementation, because there are many kinds of knowledge and skills that are directly transferable between these two major processes. And under most real-world circumstances, at least some of those who participated in the planning process are likely to continue working in the implementation process. This is generally advantageous, as they can assist in explaining sections of the documented plan, or in clarifying earlier intentions.

Continuities Between Planning, Implementation, and Service Operations

The planning process is essentially a search or creation endeavor. Particulars of the desired result (a program plan) are only sketchily known at the start. That is why the terms *design* or *development* are used here to denote its essential character. An analogy can be made to an architect who designs an entirely new structure from the ground up, for a specified purpose and on a particular site. The architect must frequently consult with clients, scrap early sketches, retrace steps to make changes, and gradually work toward a design that wins client approval. The result is, of course, an architectural plan with blueprints.

Because the approved plan is known at the start of implementation, the work now at hand is to take this design and move from it to the reality of service operations, where particular persons will be doing concrete things in real time. Here the analogy can be made to an engineering or construction firm: they must take the plans of others and build the actual structure, whether a bridge or a residence. The result must conform to the design specifications and be ready for use on completion. For them, and for those implementing program plans, the problem lies in how to achieve the desired (but known) results in a timely way.

The most elementary connection between the two processes is the dependency of the second process, implementation, on the first process, program planning results. Both the merits and the limitations or problems that are inherent in the program plan will be embedded in the service program if the implementation endeavor executes that design literally.

The approved plan document may present problems of either a substantive or a procedural nature. Substantive difficulties involve faulty conceptions of the problem or the needs to be met through the new or changed program, imperfect identification of the population to be served, unforeseen strains with the host organization's mission or its public acceptance, and the like. Procedural difficulties include service methods that are impractical or too costly, incorrect specification of the staff skills required to deliver the service as planned, and lack of reliable quality assurance measures and methods.

Knowledgeable implementation personnel may spot these design flaws in the course of their work and make alterations in the program's actual provisions—one reason for seeking participation of persons who have program knowledge. Implementers will inevitably encounter several places at which the plan has gaps or fails to specify some factor that is essential to a program's conduct. These flaws and limitations can be remedied before service commences, yet they complicate the work at hand. When they are not detected, the difficulties that ensue must be handled by the personnel and decision makers who are responsible for service delivery—or hamper the service process and results.

In sum, the implementation process is heavily dependent on—but not wholly governed by—the documented results in the program design and the charge. And, in turn, the actual service program is greatly influenced by both of the preceding processes—planning and implementation. Once the service program is operational, it is similarly dependent on (and influenced most directly by) the implementation that brought it into being. Prior decisions and actions can never entirely determine future courses of human events. The actual program—new or changed—may be better, it may be more efficient, it may be more effective, or it may suffer by comparison to the design. Yet the program always assumes a pattern of its own. Implementation steps are the intermediary means to improve as much as possible on original conceptions and plans.

A Final Word

We hope that our book has helped you understand how to approach and carry out the planning of human service programs and that you have detected our enthusiasm for planning projects. Involvement in program planning provides opportunities for personal and professional growth, as well as service to the community. You can study and understand conditions and problems and inform and interpret them to others. You can work on changing programs and developing new ones that have the potential to improve the human condition. You can learn about other disciplines, their perspectives and approaches, by working on a team with individuals who have knowledge and skills different from your own. You can meet individuals from diverse segments of the community and learn about their life experiences and how they cope with them. You have the opportunity to give them a voice if they need one and want one. Involvement in planning is an enriching experience. We hope that our book helps you plan human service programs effectively and that you will find the planning process as challenging and rewarding as we have.

RESOURCES FOR PLANNING SERVICE PROGRAMS

The Internet is an efficient means of accessing information that is useful in planning service programs, including how-to guides, planning tools, project management resources, group leadership information, program descriptions, study results, and data from nonprofit agencies and all levels of government. The sites with an asterisk are gateways or have outstanding links to many resources useful to planners.

Aging

Administration on Aging [www.aoa.dhhs.gov]
AARP's WebPlace [www.aarp.org]

America's Charities

Links to charitable organizations providing direct services in thousands of local communities [http://www.charities.org]*

Canadian Heritage Information Network

Links to Canadian museums and galleries, the Heritage Forum, and reference databases [http://www.chin.gc.ca]*

Children and Youth

Center for the Future of Children [www.childwelfare.com/kids/ewlinks.htm]
Child Welfare [www.futureofchildren.org]
National Center for Children in Poverty [www.nccp.org]
Safe Place [www.oseda.missouri.edu]
Sexual Abuse Statistics [www.prevent-abuse-now.com/stats.htm]
UNICEF [www.unicef.org/pon96/indust4.htm]
Youth Risk Behavior Surveillance System, Centers for Disease Control [www.cdc.gov/nccdphp/dash/yrbs/ov.htm]

Domestic Violence

Family Violence Prevention Fund [www.fvpf.org/facts]

Economic Statistics

The Conference Board is a private nonprofit organization that publishes a wide range of economic statistics [http://www.conference-board.org]

Education

National Center for Educational Statistics [www.nces.ed.gov]

Government Resources: General

Department of Health and Human Services [www.dhhs.gov]
Library of Congress [www.loc.gov]
Nonprofit Gateway is a network of links to federal government information and services [http://www.nonprofit.gov]*
U.S. Department of Labor, Bureau of Labor Statistics [www.bls.gov]
Social Statistics Briefing Room [www.whitehouse.gov/fsbr/ssbr.htm]
U.S. Census Bureau [www.census.gov]

Health

Centers for Disease Control and Prevention [www.cdc.gov/scientific.htm]
Indian Health Services [www.ihs.gov]
Office of Minority Health [www.omhrc.gov]
National Center for Health Statistics [www.cdc.gov/nchs/express.htm]
NIH Health Information Index [www.nih.gov/news]

University of Kansas, Work Group on Health Promotion and Community De-velopment. Community Tool Box [http://ctb.ku.edu/]*

Housing

Homelessness [www.huduser.org]

Nonprofit Leadership and Management

The Free Management Library [http://www.managementhelp.org/]*

Planning

Association for Community Organization and Social Administration
  [http://www.acosa.org/]*
Charting Software [www.shareware.com]
Goals and Objectives [www.myGoal.com], and [www.brookespublishing.com]
University of Kansas, Work Group on Health Promotion and Community De-velopment. Community Tool Box [http://ctb.ku.edu/]*

Poverty

Institute for Research on Poverty [www.ssc.wisc.edu/irp]
Poverty Risk Factors [www.urban.org]

Substance Abuse

Substance Abuse and Mental Health Services Administration [www.samhsa.gov]

United Way of America

United Way of America [www.unitedway.org]

REFERENCES

Aspen Publishers. [http://www.aspenpublishers.com]. Jan. 2004.

Austin, M. J. "Managing Up: Relationship Building Between Middle and Top Management." *Administration in Social Work,* 1989, *12*(4), 29–46.

Austin, M. J. "The Changing Relationship Between Nonprofit Organizations and Public Social Service Agencies in the Era of Welfare Reform." *Nonprofit and Voluntary Sector Quarterly,* 2003, *32*(1), 97–114.

Babbie, E. *The Practice of Social Research.* (9th ed.) Belmont, Calif.: Wadsworth, 2001.

Balaswamy, S., and Dabelko, H. L. "Using a Stakeholder Participatory Model in a Community-Wide Service Needs Assessment of Elderly Residents: A Case Study." *Journal of Community Practice,* 2002, *10*(1), 55–70.

Barusch, A. M., and Spaulding, M. L. "Impact of Americanization on Intergenerational Relations: An Exploratory Study of the U.S. Territory of Guam." *Journal of Sociology and Social Welfare,* 1989, *16*(3), 61–80.

Beck, A., and Katcher, A. *Between Pets and People: The Importance of Animal Companionship.* New York: Putnam, 1983.

Biegel, D. E., and Blum, A. *Innovations in Practice and Service Delivery Across the Life Span.* New York: Oxford University Press, 1999.

Boehm, A. "Managing the Life Cycle of a Community Project: A Marketing Approach." *Administration in Social Work,* 2003, *27*(2), 19–38.

Bradshaw, J. "The Concept of Social Need." In N. Gilbert and H. Specht (eds.), *Planning for Social Welfare: Issues, Models, and Tasks.* Upper Saddle River, N.J.: Prentice Hall, 1977.

Broman, C. L., Neighbors, H. W., and Taylor, R. J. "Race Differences in Seeking Help from Social Workers." *Journal of Sociology and Social Welfare,* 1989, *16*(3), 109–123.

Chaves, M., and Tsitsos, W. "Congregations and Social Services: What They Do, How They Do It, and with Whom." *Nonprofit and Voluntary Sector Quarterly,* 2001, *30*(4), 660–683.

Cleary, P. D., and Demone, H., Jr., "Health and Social Service Needs in a Northeastern Metropolitan Area: Ethnic Group Differences." *Journal of Sociology and Social Welfare*, 1988, *15*(4), 63–76.

Cohen, B. "Alternative Organizing Principles for the Design of Service Delivery Systems." *Administration in Social Work*, 2002, *26*(2), 17–38.

Cole, K. M., and Gawlinski, A. "Animal-Assisted Therapy in the Intensive Care Unit." *Nursing Clinics of North America*, 1995, *30*(3), 529–537.

Crane, J. *Social Programs That Work.* New York: Russell Sage Foundation, 1998.

Delbecq, A. L., and Van de Ven, A. H. "Problem Analysis and Program Design." In N. Gilbert and H. Specht (eds.), *Planning for Social Welfare: Issues, Models, and Tasks.* Upper Saddle River, N.J.: Prentice Hall, 1977.

Delta Society. "Animals Helping People, People Helping Animals." [www.deltasociety.org]. Oct. 2003.

Etzioni, A. "Mixed Scanning: A 'Third' Approach to Decision-Making." In N. Gilbert and H. Specht (eds.), *Planning for Social Welfare: Issues, Models, and Tasks.* Upper Saddle River, N.J.: Prentice Hall, 1977.

Fadiman, A. *The Spirit Catches You and You Fall Down: A Hmong Child, Her American Doctors, and the Collision of Two Cultures.* New York: Farrar, Straus, & Giroux, 1997.

Farnsely, A. E., II, "Can Faith Based Organizations Compete?" *Nonprofit and Voluntary Sector Quarterly*, 2001, *30*(1), 99–111.

Flynn, J. P. *Social Agency Policy: Analysis and Presentation for Community Practice.* (2nd ed.) Chicago: Nelson-Hall, 1992.

Forness, S. R., and Kavale, K. "Meta-Analysis in Intervention Research: Methods and Implications." In J. Rothman and E. Thomas (eds.), *Intervention Research: Design and Development for Human Service.* Binghamton, N.Y.: Haworth Press, 1994.

Fortune, A. "Planning Duration and Termination of Treatment." *Social Service Review*, 1985, *59*(4), 647–661.

Foundation Center. [http://www.fdncenter.org]. Jan. 2004.

Garwick, G. B., and Brintnall, J. E. *An Introduction to Goal Attainment Scaling, Catalogue-Assisted and the Ideabook: 550 Indicators for Use in Setting Goals.* Minneapolis: Technical Assistance for Program Evaluation, 1977.

Gates, B. L. *Social Program Administration: The Implementation of Social Policy.* Upper Saddle River, N.J.: Prentice Hall, 1980.

Gilmore, G. D., Campbell, M. D., and Becker, B. L. *Needs Assessment Strategies for Health Education and Health Promotion.* Indianapolis: Benchmark Press, 1989.

Grantsmanship Center. [http://www.tgci.com]. Jan. 2004.

Gray, S. T. *Evaluation with Power.* Washington, D.C.: Independent Sector, 1995.

Grønbjerg K. A. "The U.S. Nonprofit Human Service Sector: A Creeping Revolution." *Nonprofit and Voluntary Sector Quarterly*, 2001, *30*(2), 276–297.

Guttmann, D., and Sussman, M. B. *Exemplary Social Intervention Programs for Members and Their Families.* Binghamton, N.Y.: Haworth Press, 1995.

Hagedorn, H. A. *A Manual on State Mental Health Planning.* Washington, D.C.: U.S. Government Printing Office, 1977.

Harms, J. B., and Wolk, J. L. "Differential Perception and Adolescent Drinking in the United States: Preliminary Considerations." *Journal of Sociology and Social Welfare*, 1990, *17*(4), 21–42.

Hasenfeld, Y. *Human Service Organizations.* Upper Saddle River, N.J.: Prentice Hall, 1983.

Hasenfeld, Y. "Organizational Forms as Moral Practices: The Case of Welfare Departments." *Social Service Review,* 2000, *74*(3), 330–351.

Hatchett, B., and Duran, D. A. "An Approach to Community Outreach Practice in the Twenty-First Century." *Journal of Community Practice,* 2002, *10*(2), 37–52.

Hayes, R. M. "Information Science Methods for Knowledge Retrieval: Basic Approaches and Emerging Trends." In J. Rothman and E. Thomas (eds.), *Intervention Research: Design and Development for Human Service.* Binghamton, N.Y.: Haworth Press, 1994.

Hunt, M. *How Science Takes Stock: The Story of Meta-Analysis.* New York: Russell Sage Foundation, 1997.

Jansson, B. S. *Becoming an Effective Policy Advocate: From Policy Practice to Social Justice.* (3rd ed.) Pacific Grove, Calif.: Brooks/Cole, 1999.

Johnson, D., and Johnson, F. *Joining Together.* (6th ed.) Upper Saddle River, N.J.: Prentice Hall, 1997.

Kettner, P. M., Moroney, R. M., and Martin, L. L. *Designing and Managing Programs: An Effectiveness-Based Approach.* (2nd ed.) Thousand Oaks, Calif.: Sage, 1999.

Krueger, R. A. *Focus Groups: A Practical Guide for Applied Research.* (3rd ed.) Thousand Oaks, Calif.: Sage, 2000.

Kruzich, J. M., Friesen, B. J., Williams-Murphy, T., and Longley, M. J. "Voices of African American Families: Perspectives on Residential Treatment." *Social Work,* 2002, *47*(4), 461–470.

Lampkin, L., Romeo, S., and Finnin, E. "Introducing the Nonprofit Program Classification System: The Taxonomy We've Been Waiting For." *Nonprofit and Voluntary Sector Quarterly,* 2001, *30*(4), 781–793.

Lauffer, A. *Social Planning at the Community Level.* Upper Saddle River, N.J.: Prentice Hall, 1978.

Libby, M. K., and Austin, M. J. "Building a Coalition of Non-Profit Agencies to Collaborate with a County Health and Human Services Agency: The Napa County Behavioral Health Committee of the Napa Coalition of Non-Profits." *Administration in Social Work,* 2002, *26*(4), 81–99.

Lindblom, C. E. "The Science of 'Muddling Through.'" In N. Gilbert and H. Specht (eds.), *Planning for Social Welfare: Issues, Models, and Tasks.* Upper Saddle River, N.J.: Prentice Hall, 1977.

Liss, P. E. *Health Care Need.* Newcastle upon Tyne, Great Britain: Athenaeum Press, 1993.

Litwak, E., and Meyer, H. J. *School, Family, and Neighborhood: The Theory and Practice of School: Community Relations.* New York: Columbia University Press, 1974.

Maddox, D. *Budgeting for Not-for-Profit Organizations.* New York: Wiley, 1999.

Manela, R. W., and Moxley, D. P. "Best Practices as Agency-Based Knowledge in Social Welfare." *Administration in Social Work,* 2002, *26*(4), 1–24.

Martin, L. L. "Total Quality Management: The New Managerial Wave." *Administration in Social Work,* 1993, *17*(2), 1–16.

Martin, L. L., and Kettner, P. M. *Measuring the Performance of Human Service Programs.* Human Services Guide 71. Thousand Oaks, Calif.: Sage, 1996.

Mayer, R. R. *Policy and Program Planning: A Developmental Perspective.* Upper Saddle River, N.J.: Prentice Hall, 1985.

McClendon, B. W., and Catanese, A. J. *Planners on Planning: Leading Planners Offer Real-Life Lessons on What Works, What Doesn't, and Why.* San Francisco: Jossey-Bass, 1996.

Miles, M. B., and Huberman, A. M. *Qualitative Data Analysis: A Sourcebook of New Methods.* Thousand Oaks, Calif.: Sage, 1984.

Miles, M. B., and Huberman, A. M. *Qualitative Data Analysis: An Expanded Sourcebook.* Thousand Oaks, Calif.: Sage, 1994.

Ministry for Children and Families, Vancouver Ethnocultural Advisory Committee. "Cultural Competency Assessment Tool." [http://www.mcf.gov.bc.ca/publications/cultural_competency/assessment_tool/tool_index1.htm]. Jan. 2004.

Netting, F. E., Wilson, C. C., and New, J. C. "The Human-Animal Bond: Implications for Practice." *Social Work,* 1987, *32*(1), 60–64.

Ng, B., Kent, J. D., and Egbert, M. A. "A 'Total Cycle Time' Approach to Re-engineering Social Services." *Administration in Social Work,* 2000, *24*(3), 35–51.

O'Donnell, J., and Giovannoni, J. M. "Consumer Perceptions of Outreach and Marketing Strategies for Family Resource Centers." *Journal of Community Practice,* 2000, *8*(2), 71–89.

Pecora, P., and Austin, M. J. *Managing Human Services Personnel.* Thousand Oaks, Calif.: Sage, 1987.

Perlmutter, F. D. "Alternative Federated Funds: Resourcing for Change." *Administration in Social Work,* 1988, *12*(2), 95–108.

Posavac, E. J., and Carey, R. G. *Program Evaluation: Methods and Case Studies.* (6th ed.) Upper Saddle River, N.J.: Prentice Hall, 2003.

Pressman, J., and Wildavsky, A. B. *Implementation: How Great Expectations in Washington Are Dashed in Oakland.* Berkeley: University of California Press, 1974.

Public Management Institute. *Needs Assessment Handbook.* San Francisco: Public Management Institute, 1980.

Pynes, J. E. *Human Resources Management for Public and Nonprofit Organizations.* San Francisco: Jossey-Bass, 1997.

Raskoff, S. A., and Sundeen, R. A. "Cultural Diversity and High School Community Service: The Relationships Between Ethnicity and Students' Perceptions." *Nonprofit and Voluntary Sector Quarterly,* 2001, *30*(4), 720–746.

Rothman, J., Damron-Rodriguez, J., and Shenassa, E. "Systematic Research Synthesis: Conceptual Integration Methods of Meta-Analysis." In J. Rothman and E. Thomas (eds.), *Intervention Research: Design and Development for Human Service.* Binghamton, N.Y.: Haworth Press, 1994.

Royse, D., and Thyer, B. *Program Evaluation: An Introduction.* (3rd ed.) Chicago: Nelson-Hall, 2000.

Salvatore, A. "Eight Steps for Better Social Service Planning." In G. T. Horton (ed.), *Readings on Human Services Planning.* Atlanta, Ga.: Research Group, 1975.

Saulnier, C. F. "Deciding Who to See: Lesbians Discuss Their Preferences in Health and Mental Health Care Providers." *Social Work,* 2002, *47*(4), 355–365.

Schaefer, M. *Implementing Change in Service Programs.* Human Services Guide 49. Thousand Oaks, Calif.: Sage, 1987.

Schorr, L. *Within Our Reach.* New York: Doubleday, 1988.

Schorr, L. *Common Purpose: Strengthening Families and Neighborhoods to Rebuild America.* New York: Anchor Books, 1997.

Schram, B. *Creating Small Scale Social Programs: Planning, Implementation, and Evaluation.* Human Services Guide 72. Thousand Oaks, Calif.: Sage, 1997.

Shapiro, J. P. *No Pity: People with Disabilities Forging a New Civil Rights Movement.* New York: Random House, 1994.

Shilts, R. *And the Band Played On.* New York: St. Martin's Press, 1987.

Shim, J. K., and Siegel, J. G. *Financial Management for Nonprofits: The Complete Guide to Maximizing Resources and Managing Assets.* New York: McGraw-Hill, 1997.

Simon, H. A. *Administrative Behavior: A Study of Decision-Making Processes in Administrative Organization.* (3rd ed.) New York: Free Press, 1976.

Soriano, F. I. *Conducting Needs Assessments: A Multidisciplinary Approach.* Thousand Oaks, Calif.: Sage, 1995.

Sovereign, K. *Personnel Law.* (4th ed.) Upper Saddle River, N.J.: Prentice Hall, 1998.

Stone, D. "Helter Shelter" (book reviews). *The New Republic,* 1994, *210*(26), 29–34.

Stone, S. D. "Marginal Women Unite! Organizing the Disabled Women's Network in Canada." *Journal of Sociology and Social Welfare,* 1989, *16*(1), 127–145.

Suchman, E. *Evaluative Research.* New York: Russell Sage Foundation, 1967.

Thomas, E. J. *Designing Interventions for the Helping Professions.* Thousand Oaks, Calif.: Sage, 1984.

Thompson, J. D. *Organizations in Action.* New York: McGraw-Hill, 1967.

United Way of America. *UWASISII: A Taxonomy of Social Goals and Human Service Programs.* (2nd ed.) Alexandria, Va.: United Way of America, 1976.

United Way of America. *Needs Assessment: The State of the Art. A Guide for Planners, Managers, and Funders of Health and Human Care Services.* Alexandria, Va.: United Way of America, 1982.

United Way of America. "Outcome Measurement Resource Network." [www.unitedway.org]. Oct. 2003.

University of Kansas, Work Group on Health Promotion and Community Development. Community Tool Box. [http://ctb.ku.edu/]. Jan. 2004.

Urban Institute. [http://www.urban.org]. Oct. 2003.

Van Gundy, A., Jr., *Techniques of Structured Problem-Solving.* New York: Van Nostrand Reinhold, 1981.

Vinter, R. D., and Kish, R. *Budgeting for Nonprofit Organizations.* New York: Free Press, 1984.

Washington State University. "People Pet Partnership Program." [http://vetmed.wsu.edu/depts.-pppp]. Oct. 2003.

Westerfelt, A., and Dietz, T. J. *Planning and Conducting Agency-Based Research.* White Plains, N.Y.: Longman, 2001.

Witkin, B. R., and Altschuld, J. W. *Planning and Conducting Needs Assessments: A Practical Guide.* Thousand Oaks, Calif.: Sage, 1995.

Wuenschell, P. C. "Houston Homeless Street Outreach." *Journal of Community Practice,* 1997, *4*(4), 69–80.

York, R. O. *Human Service Planning: Concepts, Tools, Methods.* Chapel Hill: University of North Carolina Press, 1982.

Young, D. R. "Alternative Models of Government–Nonprofit Sector Relations: Theoretical and International Perspectives." *Nonprofit and Voluntary Sector Quarterly,* 2000, *29*(1), 149–172.

Zippay, A. "Establishing Group Housing: Community Outreach Methods." *Administration in Social Work,* 1999, *23*(2), 33–46.

Zisselman, M. H., Rovner, B. W., Shmuely, Y., and Ferrie, P. "Pet Therapy Intervention with Geriatric Psychiatry Inpatients." *American Journal of Occupational Therapy,* 1996, *50*(1), 47–51.

Index